HENRY J. FRIENDLY

FEDERAL JURISDICTION: A GENERAL VIEW $_1$ 1973.

Published for the School of Law
of Columbia University
BY COLUMBIA UNIVERSITY PRESS
New York and London

HENRY J. FRIENDLY

FEDERAL JURISDICTION: A GENERAL VIEW

COLUMBIA UNIVERSITY PRESS

New York and London   1973

Henry J. Friendly is Chief Judge
of the United States Court of
Appeals for the Second Circuit

Copyright © 1973
Columbia University Press

Printed in the United States of America

ISBN 0-231-03741-4

JAMES S. CARPENTIER LECTURES

1904–5   James Bryce, Viscount Bryce
Law in Its Relation to History

1907–8   John Chipman Gray
The Nature and Sources of the Law

1910–11 Arthur Lionel Smith
English Political Writers of the Seventeenth and Eighteenth Centuries and the Development of English Political Theory from Hobbes to Burke
David Jayne Hill
The Problem of World Organization As Affected by the Nature of the Modern State

1911–12 Sir Frederick Pollock
The Genius of the Common Law

1913–14 Sir Courtenay Ilbert
The Mechanics of Law Making

1916–17 Harold Dexter Hazeltine
English Legal History

1919–20 Willard Barbour
English History with Special Reference to the Development of Rights through Procedure

1923–24 Sir Paul Vinogradoff
Some Problems of Jurisprudence

1926–27 Sir William Searle Holdsworth
The Historians of Anglo-American Law

1927–28 Benjamin Nathan Cardozo
The Paradoxes of Legal Science

1940–41 Sir Cecil Thomas Carr
Aspects of Administrative Law

1955   Edmund Morris Morgan
Some Problems of Proof under the Anglo-American System of Litigation
Thomas Reed Powell
Vagaries and Varieties in Constitutional Interpretation

Foreword

IT IS NOT EASY to be both timely and timeless on any subject, least of all Federal Jurisdiction, but Henry Friendly has managed it in this volume. The Congress, currently considering many of the issues discussed in the pages that follow, will find Judge Friendly's analysis invaluable. But long after the Solons have put this book aside and concluded their work for this session and the next, the savants will be reading it. It is impossible to imagine a scholarly consideration of Federal Jurisdiction in the future that does not take notice of what is said here.

The main portions of this extraordinary work were originally delivered as the Columbia Carpentier Lectures in November, 1972. Judge Friendly was the 22nd Carpentier Lecturer in a series that began with Viscount James Bryce in 1904. From the very beginning, the Faculty of Law of Columbia University has sought to be faithful to the terms of the gift of General Horace Carpentier. Endowing the Lectures at Columbia in memory of his brother James, General Carpentier said: "And I hope this lectureship will be made so honorable that nobody, however great or distinguished, will willingly choose to decline your invitation." Lord Bryce was followed by John Chipman Gray and over the years the Carpentier Lecturers have included Sir Frederick Pollock, Sir William Holdsworth, Justice Benjamin Cardozo, Professor Glanville Williams, Professor Elliott Cheatham, Sir Leon Radzinowicz, Professor Adolf Berle, Judge (then Professor) Benjamin Kaplan, and Judge Friendly's most recent predecessor, Justice Hugo Black. Judge Friendly has managed a rare feat—he has brought fresh distinction to this awesome group.

That he would do so was clear to the Faculty of Law when it

invited him to give the Lectures. Judge Friendly's career has been marked by distinction from its earliest moments. He graduated from Harvard College in 1923, summa cum laude, and from Harvard Law School in 1927, summa cum laude. As an earnest academic, I note with pleasure how accurately the grading system predicted young Henry Friendly's future performance. He went on to clerk for Mr. Justice Brandeis, to mature into the most judicious of lawyers and to become the most scholarly of judges.

Throughout the years of professional distinction that culminated in his becoming Chief Judge of the Second Circuit, Judge Friendly was invited time and again by thoughtful professionals and communities of scholars to deliver their most esteemed lectures. He has delivered Harvard's Holmes Lectures, the County Lawyers' Hughes Lecture, the City Bar's Cardozo Lecture, and the lecture on the Holmes devise, given in that instance at Dartmouth. And the eastern establishment is not alone in valuing his scholarship highly. He has also given the Morrison Lecture before the State Bar of California, the Ernst Freund Lecture at the University of Chicago, the Robert S. Marks Lectures at the University of Cincinnati, and more. Even while he has been an outstanding judge, Henry Friendly has written scholarly works of such excellence that any law faculty in the land would offer him a place of honor among its members.

In 1928, Henry Friendly published a piece entitled "The Historic Basis of Diversity Jurisdiction," 41 *Harvard Law Review* 510. The article's closing paragraph observed that, "The steady expansion of the jurisdiction of the federal courts, especially since Reconstruction days, has been but a reflex of the general growth of federal political power. That growth will not abate, since it is responsive to deep social and economic causes."

Forty-five years later, at a time when many fear for the future of the federal courts, Judge Friendly returns to that theme. The subject and, as you will see, his treatment of it are worthy of him.

November 28, 1972

MICHAEL I. SOVERN
Dean of the Faculty of Law
Columbia University

Acknowledgments

ACKNOWLEDGMENT of the many people to whom I am indebted for whatever merit these lectures may possess would require many pages. In considerable measure this is done in the footnotes. But I cannot forego mention of two dear friends—Professor Felix Frankfurter, as he then was, who revealed the fascinations of federal jurisdiction to me more than forty years ago, and Professor Herbert Wechsler, today's recognized dean of the subject, who encouraged me to engage in this project.

While I am indebted to several generations of law clerks, I must single out two for special thanks—Stuart C. Stock, of the Harvard Law School class of 1971, who contributed greatly to the substance of Parts III, IV and V, and Frederick T. Davis, of the Columbia Law School class of 1972, who shouldered most of the work in preparing the lectures for publication. Mrs. Edith C. Opper cheerfully bore the burden of both the initial typescript and countless revisions. My friend Joseph L. Weiner, LL.B., Columbia, 1926, again favored me by reading a version of the manuscript midway along its course, and making helpful suggestions.

Dean Sovern has made the giving of these lectures a delight; I appreciate his generous foreword more than I can say. His staff, particularly Mr. Jess Cloud, labored mightily on the logistics and on getting the lectures swiftly into print.

H.J.F.

New York, N.Y.
December 7, 1972

To David, Joan and Ellen

Table of Contents

FREQUENTLY CITED WORKS

ALI STUDY   AMERICAN LAW INSTITUTE, STUDY OF THE DIVISION OF JURISDICTION BETWEEN STATE AND FEDERAL COURTS (1969).

A.O. ANN REP. (date)   ANNUAL REPORT OF THE DIRECTOR OF THE ADMINISTRATIVE OFFICE OF THE UNITED STATES COURTS (unless otherwise stated, all references are to "fiscal years," *i.e.,* years ending on June 30 of the calendar year cited).

FRANKFURTER & LANDIS   FRANKFURTER & LANDIS, THE BUSINESS OF THE SUPREME COURT (1928).

HART & WECHSLER   HART & WECHSLER, THE FEDERAL COURTS AND THE FEDERAL SYSTEM (1953).

SCHWARTZ & WADE   B. SCHWARTZ & H.W.R. WADE, LEGAL CONTROL OF GOVERNMENT: ADMINISTRATIVE LAW IN GREAT BRITAIN AND THE UNITED STATES (1972).

SUPREME COURT REPORT   REPORT OF THE STUDY GROUP ON THE CASELOAD OF THE SUPREME COURT (December, 1972).

PART I

Introductory Comments; and a Minimum and Maximum Model of Federal Jurisdiction

ALMOST TWO centuries ago a young man, who had attended what is now this University, addressed himself to the "propriety" of the proposed constitutional grant to Congress "of the power of constituting inferior [federal] courts."[1] He sought to dispel fears that these courts would encroach unduly on the state tribunals. Hamilton's thesis speedily received endorsement in the ratification of the Constitution and in enactment of what is quite regularly termed the "great" Judiciary Act of 1789.[2] Not even the most violent iconoclast would think it worthwhile today to raise the issue whether the decision to establish such courts should be reversed, although other federations have not chosen to follow our example.[3]

1. THE FEDERALIST No. 81, at 506 (B. Wright ed. 1961) (Hamilton). See also Nos. 80 & 82.
2. 1 Stat. 73. In what Frankfurter & Landis, at 4, characterized as "the heightened rhetoric of eloquence," the statute has been called "probably the most important and satisfactory act ever passed by Congress" Mr. Justice Henry B. Brown, The New Federal Judicial Code, 36 A.B.A. REP. 339, 345 (1913), quoted in Charles Warren, New Light on the History of the Federal Judiciary Act of 1789, 37 HARV. L. REV. 49, 52 (1923). This was far from being the universal opinion at the time the Act was adopted. See FRANKFURTER & LANDIS 5–6 n.10; Warren, supra, 37 HARV. L. REV. at 52–53.
3. See FRANKFURTER & LANDIS 4–5 & n.7; K. WHEARE, FEDERAL GOVERNMENT 66–69 (4th ed. 1963); Riesenfeld & Hazard, Federal Courts in Foreign Systems, 13 LAW & CONTEMP. PROB. 29 (1948); BOWIE & FRIEDRICH, STUDIES IN FEDERATION 106–65 (1954). In some instances, such as Germany and Switzerland, the constitution or its equivalent makes no provision for such courts. The British North America Act, 30 & 31 Vict., ch. 3, § 101 (1867), and the Commonwealth of Australia Constitution Act, 63 & 64 Vict., ch. 12, § 31 (1900), authorized the Canadian and Australian Parliaments to create inferior federal courts, but the authorization has not been used.

1

We do not need to go so far as a recent assertion that the creation of some such courts was constitutionally required.[4] It is enough that, as Judge McGowan has said:[5]

Without the judicial machinery at hand in the form of the lower federal courts, it seems most unlikely that the "one Supreme Court" of Article III could have played anything like the role it has in containing the energies of our people within the framework of a civilized and civilizing jurisprudence.

The implementation of *Brown v. Board of Education*,[6] slow though that has been, is a sufficient example. Indeed, although I am scarcely an impartial observer, I believe that in a popularity contest among our institutions of government, the inferior federal courts would rank exceedingly high. To be sure, this may be due in part to their rather low visibility, since the Supreme Court serves as the lightning rod that attracts public ire in respect of constitutional decisions for which many citizens are not yet prepared. Yet I think the impression is rather general that, with the exceptions inevitable for an institution that has endured for so many generations and been served by so many men and a few women,[7] they have largely fulfilled Hamilton's

4. Arguing from a change in the text of Article III made by the Committee on Style, Professor Julius Goebel, Jr., contends that the creation of *some* inferior courts was mandatory. GOEBEL, HISTORY OF THE SUPREME COURT OF THE UNITED STATES, VOL. I: ANTECEDENTS AND BEGINNINGS TO 1801, at 246–47 (1971). I find it hard to read Article III, Section 1, that way. Certainly many of the framers did not. *See* Warren, *supra*, 37 HARV. L. REV. at 65–66. The Supreme Court has determined the contrary. Cary v. Curtis, 44 U.S. (3 How.) 236, 245 (1845).

5. McGOWAN, THE ORGANIZATION OF JUDICIAL POWER IN THE UNITED STATES 11–12 (1969).

6. 349 U.S. 294 (1955).

7. The inferior federal courts have not been wholly free from instances of corruption. *See* J. BORKIN, THE CORRUPT JUDGE 23–186 (1962). So far as concerns policy, only two abuses have aroused widespread concern in this century. One was what was deemed an overuse of the injunction in the interest of employers against unions. See FRANKFURTER & GREENE, THE LABOR INJUNCTION (1930). When the courts, notably the Supreme Court, failed to get the message intended by § 20 of the Clayton Act, 38 Stat. 738 (1914), 29 U.S.C. § 52, Congress responded with the Norris-LaGuardia Act, 47 Stat. 70 (1932), 29 U.S.C. §§ 101–15. *See* United States v. Hutcheson, 312 U.S. 219, 229–31 (1941). The other was what was considered excessive use of

expectations that "[j]ustice through them may be administered with ease and dispatch"[8] and that, owing their "official existence to the union," they "will never be likely to feel any bias inauspicious to the principles on which it is founded."[9] At least some evidence of this is the resistance that even modest proposals for retraction of their jurisdiction have evoked.[10]

In an era when so many institutions are in disrepute, deservedly or not, why then devote lectures of so distinguished a lineage to an institution that is generally admired? You may well be tempted to class one who does that as being among the pundits who are unhappy, as has been said, unless they can find a problem for every solution. My answer is that the inferior federal courts, and indeed the Supreme Court as well, are faced with the prospect of a breakdown. The old issue of encroachment on the state tribunals is still with us, but it is only one aspect of the problem. This, as I see it, is that the inferior federal courts now have more work than they can properly do—in-

the injunction against state officials, resulting from *Ex parte* Young, 209 U.S. 123 (1908). *See, e.g.,* Frankfurter, *Distribution of Judicial Power Between United States and State Courts,* 13 CORNELL L.Q. 499, 519–20 (1928); Lilienthal, *The Federal Courts and State Regulation of Public Utilities,* 43 HARV. L. REV. 379, 381–82 (1930). These excesses were corrected by the three-judge court requirement, Act of June 18, 1910, ch. 309, § 17, 36 Stat. 557, *as amended,* 28 U.S.C. § 2281; the Johnson Act of 1934, relating to public utility rates, ch. 283, 48 Stat. 775, *now* 28 U.S.C. § 1342; and the anti-tax injunction act, Act of Aug. 21, 1937, ch. 726, 50 Stat. 738, *now* 28 U.S.C. § 1341. Ironically, *Ex parte* Young, the *bête noire* of liberals in the writer's law school days, has become "the fountainhead" of federal power to enforce the Civil Rights Act, 42 U.S.C. § 1983. *See* Dombrowski v. Pfister, 380 U.S. 479, 483–84 (1965).

8. THE FEDERALIST, *supra* note 1, No. 81, at 510.
9. *Id.* No. 80, at 502.
10. The more important of these will be considered in the discussion of diversity jurisdiction, *infra,* Part VII. An interesting sample of the degree of thought given to such proposals is the resolution of the Oregon Bar Association adopted in the fall of 1966, *see Hearings on S. 1876 Before the Subcomm. on Improvements in Judicial Machinery of the Senate Comm. on the Judiciary,* 92d Cong., 1st Sess. 270 (1972). The Bar resolved to disapprove "all of the [ALI] proposals limiting federal jurisdiction," with a single exception, and to "approve all of the proposals tending to increase federal jurisdiction, and approve the neutral proposals." When the Bar adopted the resolution, most of the approved proposals had not yet been formulated.

cluding some work they are not institutionally fitted to do. This arises in part because Congress is continually giving them more to do and, in part, because of the Supreme Court's generosity in construing the grants made by the Constitution and congressional legislation. In a paper given at a Conference on Federalism held at this University on the occasion of its bicentennial in 1954, a master of this subject, Professor Henry M. Hart, Jr., of the Harvard Law School, whose untimely death is so deeply to be deplored, said that "[t]he time has long been overdue for a full-dress re-examination by Congress of the use to which these [federal] courts are being put."[11] It is now overdue by nearly twenty years more.

Another point requiring preliminary mention is what justification there can be for further discussion of this subject only three years after publication of the Study of the Division of Jurisdiction Between State and Federal Courts prepared by the American Law Institute, in which I participated as an adviser. There are several: The Law Institute's work, although not published until 1969, began in 1961, before the tidal wave of litigation that has engulfed the federal courts; consequently its approach naturally does not reflect the proper amount of alarm. The assumption was that the level of business in the federal courts was manageable and would remain so; the desideratum was to eliminate the most indefensible portion of the diversity jurisdiction, the suit by the instate plaintiff against the outstate defendant, and replace this with a roughly equivalent volume of cases

11. Hart, *The Relations between State and Federal Law*, 54 COLUM. L. REV. 489, 541 (1954).

    Such a review would be pointless if, as held by Professor Goebel, going beyond the view indicated in note 4, *supra*, the proceedings of the Constitutional Convention support the view of Mr. Justice Story, Martin v. Hunter's Lessee, 14 U.S. (1 Wheat.) 304, 328–30 (1816), that Congress is bound to empower the inferior courts to exercise the full gamut of jurisdiction permitted by Article III. *See* GOEBEL, *supra* note 4, at 243 n.228. But the proof is far too slight to overcome the contrary evidence from the debates on the ratification of the Constitution and the text of the First Judiciary Act. *See* Warren, *supra*, 37 HARV. L. REV. at 65 *et seq.* While the power of Congress to restrict the jurisdiction of the inferior courts or not to create them at all would have been even clearer before "the events of August 27," 1787, cited by Professor Goebel, the language adopted is clear enough.

12. Wechsler, *Federal Jurisdiction and the Revision of the Judicial Code*, 13 LAW & CONTEMP. PROB. 216 (1948).

more deserving of federal cognizance. Second, the Institute avoided such areas as suits under the Federal Employers' Liability Act, automobile accident litigation, federal criminal jurisdiction, and the creation of specialized federal courts. In the third place, criticisms of the Institute's proposals and further reflection have caused me to change my views in some respects. The very fact that the Institute furnished the impetus needed to get things started argues for rather than against the project being undertaken here.

One issue that had best be confronted at the outset is this: In an examination of inferior federal court jurisdiction, how far should the lecturer feel himself limited to what is believed to be politically feasible? Surely there are *some* limits. One could argue, for example, that the states have almost totally lost their historical significance and should be replaced by regions.[13] While Rhode Island, for example, had a distinct identity in 1787 despite its minute size,[14] the spirit of Roger Williams scarcely looms large to the Pawtucket mill-hand of the 1970's, and in the era of the jet airplane it may be difficult to perceive much validity in a state that can be crossed in the time it takes to drink a cocktail. In an age of one-man one-vote it is even harder to defend the thesis that Nevada's 500,000 people should have the same voice in the Senate as California's 20,000,000. If the states were to be replaced by regions having no previous historic identity, a single judicial system might suffice. While speculation of this sort may have its utility, I do not want to range so far from the feasible; all my proposals will be well within the existing constitutional framework, and I shall eschew some others that seem totally devoid of political reality. On the other hand, I would think it a mistake to refrain from proposals for reform of the federal judicial system simply because of doubt that Congress will react favorably

13. Under a model constitution prepared under the direction of Professor Rexford Tugwell at the Center for the Study of Democratic Institutions, the nation would be divided into a maximum of twenty republics, each containing at least five percent of the total national population. Each republic would have a government with powers similar to those now vested in state government; however, the autonomy of these republics would be limited, since the national senate would have power to remove officials of the republics for ineptitude or corruption. N.Y. Times, Sept. 8, 1970, at 30, col. 3.
14. *See* McDONALD, E PLURIBUS UNUM, THE FORMATION OF THE AMERICAN REPUBLIC 1776–1790, at 119–27 (1965).

within a short span of time. For one thing, no one can be that sure. Who would have predicted, for example, that a state with such a large and politically powerful Catholic population as New York would have largely repealed an anti-abortion statute that had been on the books for a century, above all in an election year, even if there was a later backlash? Moreover, the ability of special interest groups to resist reforms declines with the need for them. It was one thing to prevent the curtailment or abolition of diversity jurisdiction when the federal courts were under no serious pressure; it may be quite another when Congress becomes truly aware that they are unable to perform existing responsibilities, much less to take on needed new tasks, without vast accretions of judge-power, supporting personnel and court-houses and, in my view, even with them. Blocs that can successfully resist reform because of a desire to preserve some trifling advantage, when nobody much cares, will have considerably less muscle when action of some sort is demanded and an informed public and concerned legislators are urging that federal courts devote themselves to the tasks that are properly theirs. Professor Wechsler suggested in 1948 that support for a radical re-examination of diversity jurisdiction "may be forthcoming at a time when there is widespread interest in the organization of the federal government and the surrender of unnecessary functions now in federal hands."[15] Perhaps he was a bit ahead of his time, but the point assuredly has validity in an era when both of our last two Presidents have stressed the need for increased delegation to the states.[16] I propose therefore to take a rather broad approach, which will include not only the division of jurisdiction between state and federal courts but also the assignment of business within the federal system and the question whether the courts—both state and federal—are not engaging in some sorts of business in which they ought not to be involved at all.

A useful method for framing the problem of these lectures can be borrowed from a well-known article in a different field of law.[17]

---

15. Wechsler, *supra*, 13 Law & Contemp. Prob. at 240.
16. For remarks of President Johnson and some of his advisers, see McGowan, *supra* note 5, at 4–7. For remarks of President Nixon, see Transcript of President's State of the Union Message, N.Y. Times, Jan. 23, 1971, at 12, col. 3–6.
17. Packer, *Two Models of the Criminal Process*, 113 U. Pa. L. Rev. 1

That is to prepare a minimum and a maximum model of lower federal court jurisdiction, although, in this instance, in contradistinction to Professor Packer's two models of the criminal process, rather than the two being antithetical, the latter will, of course, include the former. For simplicity I shall ignore in both models, and indeed throughout these lectures, a few substantively important but numerically insignificant heads of federal jurisdiction, such as "Cases affecting Ambassadors, other public Ministers and Consuls,"[18] "Controversies between two or more states,"[19] "Controversies between the United States and a State,"[20] "Actions or proceedings by a State against the citizens of another State or against aliens,"[21] "Controversies between citizens of the same state claiming lands under grants from different states,"[22] and the special provisions relating to Indians.[23]

In constructing my minimum model I shall bypass, for reasons already indicated, what might be called the zero model, namely, that all original jurisdiction, save for the two instances in which the Supreme Court was given this, should be vested entirely in the courts of the states. It is hard to realize today that this course was seriously urged by such "ardent pro-Constitutionalists" as John Rutledge of South Carolina and Roger Sherman of Connecticut.[24] Reversal of Oliver Ellsworth's "transcendent achievement," that there should be

(1964), *revised and reprinted as* chapter 8 of THE LIMITS OF THE CRIMINAL SANCTION (1968).

18. For discussion of this, and the division of jurisdiction between the Supreme Court and the district courts, 28 U.S.C. §§ 1251(a)(2), 1251(b)(1), 1351, see HART & WECHSLER 260 *et seq.*; 7B MOORE, FEDERAL PRACTICE, ch. 81, § 1251 (1970).

19. Under 28 U.S.C. § 1251(a)(1) the Supreme Court is given exclusive jurisdiction of such cases. Although this would not seem to be constitutionally required, the statute is a wise policy decision.

20. *See* 28 U.S.C. §§ 1251(b)(2), 1345.

21. *See* 28 U.S.C. § 1251(b)(3). The Court has construed this basis of original jurisdiction as not to be mandatory. Ohio v. Wyandotte Chemicals Co., 401 U.S. 493, 495–99 (1971).

22. 28 U.S.C. § 1354.

23. 28 U.S.C. §§ 1353, 1360, 1362.

24. See, for these and other examples, Warren, *supra*, 37 HARV. L. REV. at 65–66, and FRANKFURTER & LANDIS 4–5 n.6. The history has also been reviewed in McGOWAN, *supra* note 5, at 18–29, in a brief and exceedingly readable way, and by Professor Goebel, *supra* note 4, at ch. XI.

some inferior federal courts,[25] is not a subject for useful debate. The minimum model proceeds rather on the theory that the best course is to put trust in the state courts, subject to appropriate federal appellate review, save for those heads of jurisdiction, by no means insignificant in case-generating power, where everything is to be gained and nothing is to be lost by granting original jurisdiction to inferior federal courts.[26]

The first category in my minimum model consists of cases where the United States is seeking to enforce its own laws.[27] One large item under this category can be traced back to the provision of the First Judiciary Act which gave to the circuit courts "exclusive cognizance of all crimes and offences cognizable under the authority of the United States,"[28] subject to a concurrent jurisdiction of the district courts to

25. *See* FRANKFURTER & LANDIS 4. As Professor Goebel puts it, *supra* note 4, at 470. "Perhaps the most important initial decision made by the full Committee before the subcommittee was charged with preparing a draft was to inter the anti-federalist proposal that state courts should serve as inferior federal courts."

26. Professor Henry M. Hart, Jr., once sketched, without in any way approving, a model that lies somewhere between the "zero model" and my minimum model. This would involve "state trial courts for both state and federal business, with the possible exception of a few highly specialized federal courts; federal courts of appeals for the review of state court decisions turning upon federal questions; and a coordinating and largely discretionary review of decisions of the federal courts of appeals by the Supreme Court." Hart, *supra*, 54 COLUM. L. REV. at 540.

27. In view of the failure to grant general federal question jurisdiction, this must have been the meaning of Madison's defense of the Judiciary Act in the House of Representatives on the ground that the state courts "cannot be trusted with the execution of the Federal laws." 1st Cong., 1st Sess., Aug. 31, 1789, at 827, *quoted in* Warren, *supra*, 37 HARV. L. REV. at 124.

28. Ch. 20, § 11, 1 Stat. 79 (1789). The exclusivity was modified in a number of early nineteenth century statutes giving state courts jurisdiction over federal crimes. *See* Warren, *supra*, 37 HARV. L. REV. at 70 n.49. The author notes, *id.* at 70–71:
This voluntary surrender to the States by Congress of Federal judicial powers granted by the Constitution only ceased when the State Courts themselves proceeded to hold that Congress had no constitutional power to impose such jurisdiction on the State tribunals and officials; and, singularly, this action by Congress which had been advocated by State-Rights adherents as a diminution of Federal powers became regarded by the States themselves as an unwarranted arrogation of Fed-

try certain minor offenses. At the time this criminal jurisdiction did not amount to much. The only federal crimes were revenue frauds and, very shortly, interference with federal justice.[29] While we shall later want to consider the proper scope of federal criminal law, there can hardly be disagreement that, for the convincing reason stated by Ellsworth nearly two centuries ago,[30] its enforcement should lie permissibly, and now indeed solely, in the United States' own courts.

The other large item in this category consists of civil claims by the United States. "When the Constitution enabled the central government to secure ways and means for its subsistence by going directly against the individual citizen instead of depending on the largess of the states, it was inevitable that power should be written into the Constitution whereby the Federal Government could fashion its own judicial machinery for enforcing its own claims and safeguarding its agents against the obstructions and prejudices of local authorities."[31] Accordingly it is no surprise that the First Judiciary Act gave the circuit courts jurisdiction in all civil suits at law or in equity where the United States was a plaintiff, subject to their exceeding a jurisdictional amount of $500, and the district courts jurisdiction of all such suits at law where the amount was $100 or more, as well as of seizures and suits for penalties or forfeitures under the laws of the United States.[32] There is no need to make federal jurisdiction exclusive in such cases, although in practice it is almost certain to be so.[33] Although this head of jurisdiction was initially conceived in terms of claims for money or property, the underlying principle includes cases where the United States or one of its agencies seeks civil enforcement of a federal law. Removal jurisdiction to protect federal officers came early in the nineteenth century.[34]

A second category, in this instance one of exclusive jurisdiction, consists of suits against the United States. This embraces not only claims in contract and tort directly against the Government, to

---

eral power—an attempt on the part of the Congress to control the sovereignty of the States.

29. Act of April 30, 1790, ch. 9, 1 Stat. 112.

30. *See* Warren, *supra*, 37 HARV. L. REV. at 66.

31. FRANKFURTER & LANDIS 10.

32. Ch. 20, §§ 9, 11, 1 Stat. 76–78 (1789).

33. Wechsler, *supra*, 13 LAW & CONTEMP. PROB. at 217.

34. *See* FRANKFURTER & LANDIS 11 n.22; 28 U.S.C. § 1442.

such extent as it has consented to be sued,[35] but the multitude of suits to prevent federal officers or agencies from taking action claimed to be prohibited, or to require them to take action claimed to be demanded, by federal law. It is altogether fitting that the sovereign should insist that such issues be decided by its own courts. Moreover, these courts should be open to all such claims regardless of medieval forms of action or financial amount.[36]

A third category, which has attracted enthusiasm almost from the beginning, consists of "civil causes of admiralty and maritime jurisdiction."[37] There was no contradiction to Hamilton's rather strong statement in The Federalist No. 80, that "[t]he most bigoted idolizers of State authority have not thus far shown a disposition to deny the national judiciary the cognizance of maritime causes,"[38] although his reasons, that "these so generally depend on the laws of nations, and so commonly affect the rights of foreigners, that they fall within the considerations which are relative to public peace," hardly carry conviction today.[39] Even such strong anti-federalists as Richard Henry Lee of Virginia in the Senate and Tucker, also of that state, in the House favored federal jurisdiction in admiralty.[40] To my knowledge it has never been challenged.

The minimum model would also include, I should suppose, proceedings under legislation enacted pursuant to two provisions of Article I, Section 8. One of these is the power to establish "uniform Laws on the subject of Bankruptcies throughout the United States." In strict theory there is no reason why the administration of such laws, involving only private rights, could not be confided to state courts. Indeed, the leading text tells us that "the difficulty of travel to the more or less remote and unpopular federal courts" was one of the factors that led to the repeal of the short-lived Bankruptcy Act of 1800.[41] But the very mention of uniformity in the Constitution and

---

35. 28 U.S.C. §§ 1346, 1491.
36. Wechsler, *supra*, 13 Law & Contemp. Prob. at 220. See p. 70 *infra*.
37. Judiciary Act of 1789, ch. 20, § 9, 1 Stat. 77.
38. The Federalist, *supra* note 1, at 502 (Hamilton).
39. Cases involving the rights of foreigners against United States citizens could be covered under the diversity jurisdiction, even with the limitations that I advocate. *See* pp. 149–50 *infra*.
40. Warren, *supra*, 37 Harv. L. Rev. at 67, 123.
41. 1 Collier, Bankruptcy ¶ 0.04, at 8 (14th ed. 1971).

the desirability of nationwide powers suggest the contrary[42] and, whenever there has been a bankruptcy act,[43] Congress has given the federal courts exclusive jurisdiction. The other is the power "to promote the Progress of Science and useful Arts, by securing for limited Times to Authors and Inventors the exclusive Right to their Respective Writings and Discoveries." While here the case for federal jurisdiction is not quite so compelling, it is compelling enough. There is a rather obvious appropriateness in having the effect of a grant from the United States adjudicated by a federal court, and patent infringement cases often involve in fact although not in form a review of action by the Patent Office. In any event Congress has acted on this assumption and has not only created federal jurisdiction but has long made this exclusive,[44] creating a considerable array of problems thereby.[45]

Here is where the minimum model would end. Its version of federal jurisdiction would be broader than that of the First Judiciary Act, with one notable exception, the omission of diversity jurisdiction. The other striking contrast with federal jurisdiction as we know it today would be the elimination of general federal question jurisdiction. Except at the suit of the United States or an agency, vindication of federal rights other than those just specified would be left initially to the courts of the states, with review by the Supreme Court[46] or, if needed, by intermediate federal appellate courts.[47] Save for a

42. *See* THE FEDERALIST No. 42 (Madison).

43. Today it is hard to believe that for the first 109 years of the nation's existence, bankruptcy acts were in effect for only 18.

44. The Patent Act of 1793 gave concurrent jurisdiction to state courts, ch. 11, § 5, 1 Stat. 322, but this was altered seven years later, Act of April 17, 1800, ch. 25, § 3, 2 Stat. 38. The initial copyright act also allowed an action to be maintained "in any court having cognizance thereof." Act of May 31, 1790, ch. 15, § 6, 1 Stat. 125–26.

45. *See* HART & WECHSLER 754–58; Note, *The Jurisdiction of State Courts over Cases Involving Patents*, 31 COLUM. L. REV. 461 (1931); NIMMER, COPYRIGHT § 131.11 (1972).

46. The added burden on the Court might not be so staggering as would first appear since, as against the possible increase in federal question cases, petitions for certiorari in diversity cases would be eliminated. *See* Part VII *infra*.

47. The constitutionality of this has never been doubted, *see* THE FEDERALIST No. 82 (Hamilton), except perhaps if such a scheme pre-

single interval of thirteen months,[48] that was the regime that prevailed with respect to federal questions until the Civil Rights Act following the war between the states and the more comprehensive enlargement of federal jurisdiction by the Act of March 3, 1875.[49] As will be developed in Part III of these lectures, even under this minimum model the federal courts would have an abundance of work.

Now let us look at the maximum model, which would go to the full sweep of constitutional power. The argument would be that since the federal courts provide a "juster justice"[50] than the state courts, the more cases there were in the federal courts, the better. Diversity jurisdiction would be broadened in many ways. The complete diversity requirement of *Strawbridge v. Curtiss*[51] would be abolished. Jurisdictional amount would be lowered from more than $10,000 to a figure approximating that used by the states in defining the jurisdiction of small claims courts. The prohibition on removal by a citizen of the state where the action was brought[52] would be stricken. So also, if one wanted to go all the way, would be the amendments[53] of 1958 and 1964 providing that a corporation shall be deemed a citizen of the state where it has its principal place of business as well as of the state where it is incorporated and that under "direct action" statutes a liability insurer shall also be deemed a citizen of the insured's state.[54] Federal question jurisdiction would exist, irrespective of the amount in suit, not only when the complaint was grounded on a federal claim but when it anticipated a federal defense. The making

vented Supreme Court review of action of the intermediate federal appellate court, *compare* HART & WECHSLER 312–13.

48. Act of Feb. 13, 1801, ch. 4, § 11, 2 Stat. 89, 92, *repealed by* Act of March 8, 1802, ch. 8, § 1, 2 Stat. 132.

49. Ch. 137, 18 Stat. 470. Today it seems incredible that so distinguished a scholar as Charles Warren thought that, whatever the justification in 1875, this was a mistake under conditions prevailing in 1927. See Warren, *supra*, 37 HARV. L. REV. at 69–70, 131–32.

50. This oft used phrase is Professor Hart's, *supra*, 54 COLUM. L. REV. at 513.

51. 7 U.S. (3 Cranch) 267 (1806).

52. 28 U.S.C. § 1441(b).

53. Act of July 25, 1958, 72 Stat. 415; Act of Aug. 14, 1964, 78 Stat. 445, 28 U.S.C. § 1332(c).

54. Professor Moore comes very close to this maximum model. See Moore & Weckstein, *Diversity Jurisdiction: Past, Present, and Future*, 43 TEXAS L. REV. 1, 27–36 (1964).

of a federal defense or counterclaim, again irrespective of amount, would allow removal by either side. Criminal prosecutions would be removable whenever a defendant asserted that he would rely on a right protected by the Constitution or a law or treaty of the United States. Indeed, removal would be allowed even after trial commenced if unanticipated developments required the presentation of such a defense. Finally, for good measure, whenever original federal jurisdiction existed, it would be exclusive save in diversity cases,[55] at least if the point was seasonably taken in a state court suit.

I assume, as Professor Packer did with his two models of the criminal process,[56] that no one in his senses would advocate either the minimum model, with its drastic retraction of federal judicial powers, or the maximum model, with its enormous expansion of them. They are useful only in showing how wide an area is open to choice between two extremes, both principled but unwise. Before we can make an intelligent choice, we must survey the present and probable future conditions of the federal courts with respect to workload and judge-power. Since, if I may anticipate, such a survey will show that, without enormous expansion, the general federal courts cannot do all they are now doing and will have to do under inevitable congressional legislation, we must also consider whether such an expansion is practicable and desirable. If the answer is negative, as I believe it to be, we must then consider from what tasks the general federal courts can be relieved, by removing some cases altogether from the judicial area, by withdrawing others from federal jurisdiction, or by vesting still others in specialized courts. My thesis will be that the general federal courts can best serve the country if their jurisdiction is limited to tasks which are appropriate to courts, which are best handled by courts of general rather than specialized jurisdiction, and

55. "The power of Congress to make exclusive any valid grant of jurisdiction has hardly been in issue," HART & WECHSLER 373; The Moses Taylor, 71 U.S. (4 Wall.) 411 (1867). Despite Hamilton's doubts, THE FEDERALIST No. 82, I should suppose Congress could make diversity jurisdiction exclusive if it so willed. But even a maximalist would be hard put to find a reason for requiring a plaintiff in such a case to resort to the federal courts, and the defendant is sufficiently protected by removal.

56. *Supra*, 113 U. PA. L. REV. at 6; THE LIMITS OF THE CRIMINAL SANCTION, *supra* note 17, at 154.

where the knowledge, tenure and other qualities of federal judges can make a distinctive contribution. Presumably there will be little disagreement with so general a statement; the troubles will come in its application.

PART II

The Explosion of Federal Court Litigation and the Consequent Problems of the District Courts, the Courts of Appeals and the Supreme Court

THOMAS REED POWELL, long a teacher at this law school, used to speak with disdain of the kind of social study where "counters don't think, and thinkers don't count." I have seen many samples of what he had in mind; I recall, for example, a thesis establishing, with elaborate statistical detail, that there was a closer correlation between the marriage rate and the birth rate than between either and the business cycle—a conclusion which most could have reached without aid from the computer. But figures do not have to be dull. In any event I see no way to examine the present situation and future prospects of the federal courts without them, although I will also try to get behind the figures and identify the causes. If your verdict should accord with Reed Powell's, I shall simply have to bear it. The three layers of federal courts must be treated separately, since each has its special problems and—what has not been sufficiently realized—the problems are more intractable at the appellate than at the trial level.

The observer looking broadly at the loads of the district courts at the end of fiscal 1968, and I shall use fiscal year figures as regards the federal courts save when otherwise stated, would not have found much cause for concern. Civil filings,[1] which by 1961 had declined rather drastically to a level of around 58,000 as a result of the 1958 legislation[2] that raised to $10,000 the jurisdictional amount in diversity and general federal question cases and broadened the definition of corporate citizenship to include the state of the corporation's principal place of business—with the addition, in 1964, of a provision that in direct actions against liability insurers the latter should be

1. Bankruptcy proceedings are not included in the figures of filings.
2. 72 Stat. 415, *amending* 28 U.S.C. §§ 1331, 1332.

deemed to have also the citizenship of the true defendant[3]—had climbed to 71,449,[4] a sizeable increase but still only 23% over seven years. The picture on the criminal side seemed even more comforting. Criminal filings had risen only imperceptibly; 30,714 cases in 1968 as against 28,897 a decade before.[5] With district judgeships having increased from 245 in 1960 to 342 in 1968, the situation seemed well under control—at least for the country as a whole.

The observer would have been badly mistaken in his optimism. Civil filings jumped from 71,449 in 1968 to 87,321 in 1970,[6] approximately the same increase in two years as in the preceding seven. They grew further to 93,396 in 1971[7] and 96,173 in 1972.[8] The change on the criminal side has been even more dramatic. After the almost static picture of the previous decade, these bounded from 30,714 in 1968 to 38,102 in 1970,[9] 41,290 in 1971,[10] and 47,043 in 1972.[11] The total filings in the district courts have thus increased from the 1961 low of 86,753 or the not uncomfortable 1968 figure of 102,163 to 143,216 in 1972—roughly 10,000 added cases a year.

This, however, is by no means the whole story. Unlike the expansions of earlier years, what has recently been experienced is not simply the gradual increase that could be expected as a result of population growth but is concentrated in areas that have increased and will increase at a far greater rate. Here I shall mention just two examples: Between 1961 and 1970, civil rights actions grew from 296[12] to 3,985,[13] or 1346%. In the same period state prisoner petitions, including both those seeking release and those complaining of maltreatment, increased from 1,020 to 11,812,[14] or 1158%. In 1972 there were 6,133 civil rights actions,[15] and 12,088 state prisoner peti-

3. 78 Stat. 445, *amending* 28 U.S.C. § 1332(c).
4. A.O. ANN. REP. 105–07 (1968).
5. *Id.* at 117.
6. A.O. ANN. REP., Table C2, at 231 (1970).
7. A.O. ANN. REP., Table C2, at 262 (1971).
8. A.O. ANN. REP., Table C2 (1972).
9. A.O. ANN. REP., Table D1, at 264 (1970).
10. A.O. ANN. REP., Table D1, at 317 (1971).
11. A.O. ANN. REP., Table D1 (1972).
12. A.O. ANN. REP., Table C2, at 238 (1961).
13. A.O. ANN. REP., Table C2, at 232 (1970).
14. *Id.* Table 16, at 121.
15. A.O. ANN. REP., Table C2 (1972).

FILINGS IN UNITED STATES DISTRICT COURTS

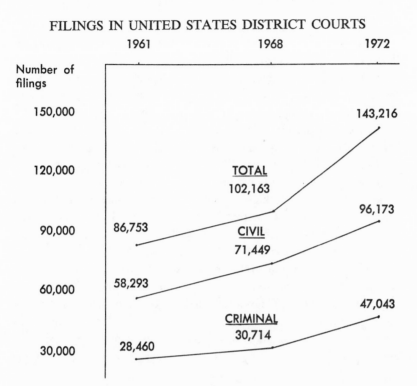

tions.[16] Civil rights actions and state and federal prisoner petitions constituted 22% of the civil actions filed in the district courts in 1972 as against some 5% in 1961.

Before we can intelligently determine what courses may be appropriate with respect to the jurisdiction of the lower federal courts, we must attempt to identify the causes underlying these increases in workload. At least three distinct, yet interrelated, forces can be perceived—decisions of the federal courts themselves, the attitude of litigants, and the work of Congress.

Although Congress in the first instance prescribes the framework of jurisdiction of the federal courts, both procedural and substantive decisions by these courts, and notably by the Supreme Court, have an important effect upon its content. While it is an impossible task to ascertain the quantitative impact of any single decision, one can readily discern certain areas where judicially effected doctrinal development has had substantial consequences upon the business of

16. *Id.* Table 17.

the federal courts. At this point I shall simply attempt to identify these areas; the issues whether legislative response is appropriate and, if so, what, will be considered later.

One such development has been the selective incorporation[17] of the Bill of Rights into the due process clause of the Fourteenth Amendment.[18] This process, in combination with the Supreme Court's landmark habeas corpus decision, *Brown v. Allen*,[19] has required the lower federal courts to assume an extremely heavy supervisory role with respect to state systems of criminal justice. Although, as I shall later develop, the last few years have seen some decrease in state prisoner petitions attacking convictions, this is more than offset by the dramatic growth in petitions challenging the length and conditions of confinement, also on the basis of selective incorporation, primarily of the First and Eighth Amendments.

Judicial expansion of federal substantive law has been important on the civil side as well. Here the greatest single development has been the Supreme Court's revitalization of the Fourteenth Amendment guarantee of "equal protection of the laws." The implementation of *Brown v. Board of Education*[20] has demanded Herculean effort, in no way reflected by the mere number of case filings. A single

17. At this point in history it is far easier to catalogue those provisions of the first eight amendments which have *not* been incorporated into the due process clause by the Supreme Court than those that have. Those in the former category are: the Second Amendment guarantee of the right to bear arms; the Third Amendment guarantee regarding the quartering of soldiers; the grand jury requirement of the Fifth Amendment; the Seventh Amendment guarantee of jury trial in suits at law where the value in controversy exceeds $20; and finally the Eighth Amendment guarantee that "[e]xcessive bail shall not be required, nor excessive fines imposed . . . ." One can hardly doubt that the last will be incorporated. *See* Schilb v. Kuebel, 404 U.S. 357, 365 (1971), and U.S. ex rel. Goodman v. Kehl, 456 F.2d 863 (2d Cir. 1972).

18. This is the foremost instance in which legislative retrenching on the substantive side is not possible; nor for that matter would I expect much judicial back-tracking in this area. *See* Friendly, *Mr. Justice Harlan, As Seen by a Friend and Judge of an Inferior Court*, 85 HARV. L. REV. 382, 385–86 (1971). Action on the procedural side, including judicial or legislative modification or even the overruling of Fay v. Noia, 372 U.S. 391 (1963), is another matter.

19. 344 U.S. 443 (1953).

20. 347 U.S. 483 (1954), 349 U.S. 294 (1955).

school desegregation action may require a half dozen long hearings and decisions by a district judge. While we may be nearing the end of this problem in the South, we may be only at the beginning of it in the North and West. As revealed in a recent scholarly article,[21] the complexities of the problem of de facto segregation are such that it is impossible that a single Supreme Court decision can make these disappear. Reapportionment has likewise imposed a burden, altogether beyond that reflected by case filings, of which we have not seen the end. Two types of claims of discrimination, those based on age and on sex, which had not figured very prominently in the dockets of the past, now bulk large, and the latter will bulk still larger if a constitutional amendment addressed specifically to sex discrimination should be adopted.[22] Still more important are some decisions indicating that a statute which on its face is as equal as can be may be held invalid because it bears more heavily on the poor. Whatever the ultimate stance may be,[23] and the attack on the historic method for financing public education will be a testing case, the Court has already done and said enough to provide a flow of litigation through the lower courts on this subject that could not have been anticipated as recently as 1968.

The prime vehicle for equal protection litigation, as well as for state prisoner applications attacking the length or conditions of custody, has been the Civil Rights Act of 1871,[24] 42 U.S.C. section 1983, and its jurisdictional implementation, 28 U.S.C. section 1343(3), which are peculiarly attractive because of the appropriate absence of any amount in controversy requirement. However, civil rights litigation has not been limited to actions brought under section 1983, with its requirement of state action. The Supreme Court has

21. Goodman, *De Facto School Segregation: A Constitutional and Empirical Analysis*, 69 CALIF. L. REV. 275 (1972).
22. Consider such an unexpected example as Wark v. Robbins, 458 F.2d 1295 (1st Cir. 1972), where a male convicted of escaping from a Maine prison complained that the punishment was more severe than that of a female escaping from a reformatory.
23. *See* Friendly, *supra*, 85 HARV. L. REV. at 387–88, and cases there cited; Michelman, *The Supreme Court, 1968 Term, Foreword: On Protecting the Poor Through the Fourteenth Amendment*, 83 HARV. L. REV. 7 (1969).
24. Act of April 20, 1871, ch. 22, § 1, 17 Stat. 13.

displayed a penchant for breathing new life into old civil rights statutes just at the time when the enactment of new ones has largely removed the need for this. The textbook example is the discovery, in *Jones v. Alfred H. Mayer Co.,*[25] to which I will return in Part IV, of a theretofore unsuspected meaning in 42 U.S.C. section 1982. A ruling having equal or greater potential for new litigation is the decision in *Griffin v. Breckenridge*[26] eliminating, in certain types of cases, any state action requirement for application of the civil rights conspiracy statute.[27] It is too early to determine what effect *Griffin* will have upon federal court dockets, since, among other reasons, it leaves a number of important questions unanswered.[28] But it is impossible to doubt that these two decisions will cause a further increase in civil rights actions. We have yet to see what will be the impact of the Court's holding that, at least in the field protected by the Fourth Amendment, a federal remedy can be implied from the Constitution itself.[29] In a quite different area, the Supreme Court's announcement of a federal common law of nuisance[30] will give rise to many complicated cases when an industry in one state affects the environment of another.

Turning from essentially substantive developments, we are confronted with a wealth of decisional law that has increased the accessibility of a federal forum for private litigants. Thus, the Supreme Court has liberalized the requirements for standing to initiate federal judicial proceedings,[31] and has contracted the concept of what con-

25. 397 U.S. 409 (1968). *See also* Sullivan v. Little Hunting Park, Inc., 396 U.S. 229 (1969).
26. 403 U.S. 88 (1971).
27. 42 U.S.C. § 1985(3).
28. *See The Supreme Court, 1970 Term*, 85 HARV. L. REV. 3, 95–104 (1971). If Action v. Gannon, 450 F.2d 1227 (8th Cir. 1971), was correctly decided, *Griffin* goes far beyond conspiracies to thwart the civil rights of blacks and of those traveling to aid them. *See also* Dombroski v. Dowling, 459 F.2d 190 (7th Cir. 1972).
29. Bivens v. Six Unknown Named Agents of the Fed. Bureau of Narcotics, 403 U.S. 388 (1971). It has been suggested that, in light of this decision, the Civil Rights Act may have been unnecessary. See the interesting article, Dellinger, *Of Rights and Remedies: The Constitution as a Sword*, 85 HARV. L. REV. 1532, 1559 (1972).
30. Illinois v. City of Milwaukee, 406 U.S. 91 (1972).
31. *Compare* Flast v. Cohen, 392 U.S. 83 (1968), *with* Frothingham v. Mellon, 262 U.S. 447 (1923).

stitutes a political question and is therefore immune from judicial consideration.[32] Even more important is that in an era when the federal government has assumed heretofore unprecedented regulatory and supervisory functions with respect to almost every aspect of our society, the courts have taken an increasingly generous view of the ability of private parties to seek judicial review of administrative action.[33] A further development is the successful effort by litigants to establish implied private actions in the context of various federal regulatory statutes which on their face provide only for administrative enforcement. While the importance of implied private actions has been most dramatically seen with respect to the federal securities laws, efforts have been and will continue to be made to imply such actions in other contexts. Along with these developments and others I am about to mention, note should be taken of the growth of the class action as a result of the 1966 revision of Rule 23 of Federal Civil Procedure. The vast increase in the size of a recovery made possible by class action designation affords a powerful incentive for the bringing of litigation by lawyers who otherwise might not find the financial prospects attractive. Admittedly, this often has its good side; for the present I merely note it as an important business enhancing factor.[34] I would add that the importance of this increase cannot be measured by the number of suits; the administration of a class action, even the disbursement of a settlement, imposes burdens on federal judges altogether beyond those reflected in the statistics.

These developments have been both a consequence of and a stimulus for the attitude of litigants. The impression is abroad that if a problem cannot be remedied elsewhere, a solution must exist in the federal courts. There are a number of causes for this: One is the lack of adequate machinery within the executive branch for the cor-

---

32. Baker v. Carr, 369 U.S. 186 (1962). *See also* Powell v. McCormack, 395 U.S. 486 (1969).

33. *See, e.g.,* Association of Data Processing Serv. Organizations, Inc. v. Camp, 397 U.S. 150 (1970); Barlow v. Collins, 397 U.S. 159 (1970); Investment Co. Institute v. Camp, 401 U.S. 617 (1971). This subject is further discussed at pp. 113–16 *infra*.

34. One must be grateful for the Supreme Court's refusal to endorse what would have been another large source of business—suits by a state as *parens patriae*, Hawaii v. Standard Oil Co. of California, 405 U.S. 251 (1972).

rection of "maladministration" by lower officials; although we have talked of ombudsmen for a decade, we have done almost nothing to provide them.[35] Another has been the slowness of our legislatures, due partly to the power of lobbies and partly to sheer inertia, to respond to demonstrated needs.[36] Beyond that is the availability of the Constitution in providing the courts with a norm to which executive or legislative action must be required to conform. De Tocqueville's time-worn statement, "scarcely any political question arises in the United States that is not resolved sooner or later into a judicial question,"[37] has come to have an application far wider than he could have foreseen. As has been well said, "Americans have become a people of constitutionalists, who substitute litigation for legislation and see constitutional questions lurking in every case."[38] To quote the same authors: "No observer of the American scene is likely to doubt that the courts, under the vigorous leadership of the Supreme Court, have recently come to regard themselves as an agency for supplying legal reforms which are demanded by public opinion but not effected by Congress."[39]

Moreover, Congress has been far from idle in creating new federal statutory rights during the last decade. I shall be able to mention only a few of the categories in which Congress has been active.

A considerable portion of the increase in civil rights cases is attributable to such important pieces of federal legislation as the Civil Rights Act of 1964,[40] the Voting Rights Act of 1965,[41] the Age Discrimination in Employment Act of 1967,[42] and the Civil Rights

35. *See* SCHWARTZ & WADE 207.

36. *See* Friendly, *The Gap in Lawmaking—Judges Who Can't and Legislators Who Won't*, 63 COLUM. L. REV. 787 (1963), *reprinted in* BENCHMARKS 41 (1967); THE FEDERAL ADMINISTRATIVE AGENCIES 166–68 (1962).

37. 1 DEMOCRACY IN AMERICA 290 (Bradley ed. 1954).

38. SCHWARTZ & WADE 6 (footnote omitted).

39. *Id.* 15–16.

40. 78 Stat. 241, *as amended*, 42 U.S.C. §§ 1971, 1975a–d, 2000a to 2000h–6.

41. 79 Stat. 437, *as amended*, 42 U.S.C. §§ 1971, 1973, 1973a to 1973bb–4.

42. 81 Stat. 602, 29 U.S.C. §§ 621–34.

Act of 1968.[43] Clearly these are not the last major statutes that Congress will enact in an effort to outlaw unwarranted discrimination; at least they ought not to be. Recent Congresses have also passed many important but as yet relatively unknown statutes dealing with a host of problems ranging from brokers to polluters. Some of these are enforceable in the district courts; others create new tasks for the courts of appeals; and still others involve both direct enforcement in the district courts and review of agency actions in the courts of appeals.

Probably the most important single group are statutes relating to problems of the environment. The head and front of this is the National Environmental Policy Act of 1969.[44] Perhaps the framers did not think this would impose a burden on the courts; the agencies would simply comply with the obligations placed upon them. This failed to take account of two factors—agency stubbornness and the desire of conservationist groups to test in court not only agency procedures but the merits of agency action. Along with this are more specific statutes concerned with air and water quality which will give rise to public and, in some cases, private actions.[45] Clearly we are at the beginning of this development, not the end. If the present pace continues, both statutory and non-statutory environmental actions may become as large a head of federal jurisdiction, at least in terms of burden, as actions under the Civil Rights Acts.

In still other fields Congress has given the district courts new tasks varied in both procedural and substantive complexity. For example, under the Securities Investor Protection Act,[46] district courts

43. 82 Stat. 81–90, 42 U.S.C. §§ 3601–19, 3631.
44. 83 Stat. 852, 42 U.S.C. §§ 4321–47.
45. *See* Clean Air Amendments of 1970, §§ 4(a), 12(a), 84 Stat. 1676, 42 U.S.C. §§ 1857d(g), 1857h–2 (permitting actions by the Attorney General on behalf of the Administrator of the Environmental Protection Agency and, on certain conditions, by any person to enjoin violations of the Act); Water Quality Improvement Act of 1970, § 102, 84 Stat. 100, 33 U.S.C. § 1163(i) (authorizing actions by the United States to enjoin violations of the Act); Ports and Waterways Safety Act of 1972, 86 Stat. 424 (1972) (permitting actions by the United States to collect fines); Noise Control Act of 1972, § 11, 86 Stat. 1234 (1972) (authorizing actions by the United States to restrain violations of the Act).
46. 84 Stat. 1636 (1970), 15 U.S.C. §§ 78aaa–*lll*.

have been given jurisdiction analogous to, but independent of, a Chapter X bankruptcy proceeding. The Act provides for applications in the district courts by the Securities Investor Protection Corporation (SIPC) for a decree "adjudicating that customers of such member [broker] are in need of the protection provided by this chapter."[47] If the decree issues, the district court then appoints a trustee,[48] and presides over a highly complex "liquidation proceeding."[49] The Act further provides that the SEC may, if necessary, seek an order from the district court wherein SIPC maintains its principal office, requiring SIPC to discharge its obligations under the Act.[50]

An example in a quite different area is the Federal Railroad Safety and Hazardous Materials Transportation Act of 1970.[51] This authorizes the Secretary of Transportation to promulgate regulations and standards on all aspects of railway safety. Both the Secretary and state regulatory agencies are entrusted with the investigation of violations of these regulations. The Secretary and, in certain instances, the state agencies, may, with the assistance of the Attorney General, institute proceedings in the district courts to enjoin violations and recover civil penalties.[52] A variety of other recent enactments placing new responsibilities on the district courts for the enforcement of federal regulatory programs are listed in a footnote.[53] The last Con-

47. § 5(a)(2), 15 U.S.C. § 78eee(a)(2). For a decision arising under this act see SEC v. Allen Hughes, Inc., 461 F.2d 974 (2d Cir. 1972).
48. § 5(b)(3), 15 U.S.C. § 78eee(b)(3).
49. § 6, 15 U.S.C. § 78fff.
50. § 7(b), 15 U.S.C. § 78ggg(b).
51. 84 Stat. 971, 45 U.S.C. §§ 421–41, 49 U.S.C. §§ 1761–62.
52. §§ 207, 209, 210, 45 U.S.C. §§ 436, 438, 439.
53. The statutes below are a representative but by no means a complete sampling of recent legislation authorizing actions in the district courts to enforce federal regulatory schemes: Investment Company Act Amendments of 1970, § 20, 84 Stat. 1428, 15 U.S.C. § 80a–35 (permitting actions by the SEC and private parties for certain violations of the Act); Egg Products Inspection Act, §§ 20, 21, 84 Stat. 1631–32 (1970), 21 U.S.C. §§ 1049, 1050 (authorizing actions by the United States for the seizure of products which are to be sold in violation of the Act); Fair Credit Reporting Act, § 601, 84 Stat. 1134 (1970), 15 U.S.C. § 1681p (actions by private parties to recover penalties specified in the Act); Public Health Cigarette Smoking Act of 1969, § 2, 84 Stat. 89, 15 U.S.C. § 1339 (authorizing actions by the Attorney General to enjoin violations of the Act); Federal Coal Mine

gress adopted a Consumer Product Safety Act, and the prospect of legislation greatly expanding consumers' suits is very real.[54]

Another quite different category consists of legislation adopted under the "spending power." Congress has increasingly engaged in grants-in-aid to the states conditioned on their conforming to federal standards. Although the Aid to Families with Dependent Children program goes back to the Social Security Act of 1935,[55] it has been only in recent years that many suits involving the conformance of state programs to federal standards have been reaching the courts.[56] Now this legislative example has been followed in the field of medical care,[57] and this also has given rise to abundant and difficult litigation.[58] There have been similar developments with respect to hous-

Health and Safety Act of 1969, § 108, 83 Stat. 756, 30 U.S.C. § 818 (authorizing actions by the Secretary of the Interior to enjoin violations of the Act); Consumer Credit Protection Act, § 130, 82 Stat. 157 (1968), 15 U.S.C. § 1640 (suits by private parties to recover statutory penalties); Interstate Land Sales Full Disclosure Act, 82 Stat. 595 (1968), 15 U.S.C. § 1710 (suits for untrue statement or omission to state material fact, or for prohibited sale or lease); Wholesome Meat Act, § 16, 81 Stat. 597–99 (1967), 21 U.S.C. §§ 671–74 (actions by private parties to challenge certain determinations of the Secretary of Agriculture and actions by the Secretary to enjoin violations of the Act); National Traffic and Motor Vehicle Safety Act of 1966, § 110, 80 Stat. 723, 15 U.S.C. § 1399 (authorizing actions by the Attorney General to enjoin violations of the Act); 1971 Economic Stabilization Act Amendments, 85 Stat. 743 (suits in respect of prices exceeding those permitted by Price Commission); Federal Water Pollution Control Act Amendments of 1972, § 309(b), 86 Stat. 815 (suits by Administrator to enjoin violation of the Act).

54. 86 Stat. 1207 (1972); *see also* the article by Representative John E. Moss, *Consumer Legislation in Congress,* 58 A.B.A.J. 632 (1972).

55. Ch. 531, 49 Stat. 627, *as amended,* 42 U.S.C. §§ 601–10.

56. The first significant Supreme Court decision was King v. Smith, 392 U.S. 309 (1968).

57. *See* the Medicare Act and the Grants to States for Medical Assistance Programs Act, 79 Stat. 290–343, 343–53 (1965), (codified in scattered sections of 26, 42, 45 U.S.C.), and the Social Security Amendments of 1967, 81 Stat. 821, 42 U.S.C. §§ 301, 415, providing, among other things, for the expansion and improvement of Medicare, 81 Stat. 845–59, of Medical Assistance Programs, 81 Stat. 898–911, and of AFDC, 81 Stat. 877–98.

58. *See, e.g.,* Catholic Medical Center of Brooklyn & Queens, Inc. v. Rockefeller, 305 F. Supp. 1256, 1268 (E.D.N.Y. 1969) (three-

ing;[59] this too has led to important litigation.[60] In a different area, a retail store or wholesale concern disqualified from participation in the food stamp program is entitled not merely to judicial review but to trial *de novo* in a district court.[61] The full impact of this extensive legislative output under the spending power has not yet been felt in district court dockets.[62] Experience shows that some time is required before such statutes make themselves felt in the courts. Moreover, potential litigation under all these statutes has been greatly increased by two developments already mentioned—the liberalization of the requirement of standing and the growth of the class action. Here again we are by no means at the end of the road. A single recent issue of *The New York Times* reported two developments that could add significantly to the flow of federal litigation in this area—attempts by poverty groups, probably to be joined by the Department of Health, Education and Welfare, to enforce the neglected provision of the Hill-Burton Act requiring hospitals that had received federal funds for construction to furnish a reasonable amount of free care,[63] and likely enactment of a bill that would withhold certain federal grants from states that did not seasonably enact and enforce proper land development codes.

Taking all these developments into account, it is not surprising that on June 30, 1972, the backlog of civil cases pending in the district courts reached an all-time high of 101,032 an increase of 8.4% over 1970.[64]

judge court), *vacated and remanded,* 397 U.S. 820, *aff'd,* 430 F.2d 1297 (2d Cir.), *appeal dismissed,* 400 U.S. 931 (1970); Maxwell v. Wyman, 458 F.2d 1146 (2d Cir. 1972).

59. *See* 42 U.S.C. ch. 8 (Low Rent Housing); *id.* ch. 8A (Slum Clearance, Urban Renewal and Farm Housing).

60. *See, e.g.,* Thorpe v. Housing Authority, 393 U.S. 268 (1969); Langevin v. Chenango Court, Inc., 447 F.2d 296 (2d Cir. 1971); English v. Town of Huntington, 448 F.2d 319 (2d Cir. 1971).

61. 7 U.S.C. § 2022. *See* Martin v. United States, 459 F.2d 300 (6th Cir. 1972).

62. Much of the legislation may only be implemented after the designated agency has promulgated appropriate standards, and there is thus a built-in time lag before any attempts are made to enjoin violators.

63. 60 Stat. 1043 (1946), *now* 42 U.S.C. §§ 291, *et seq. See* Euresti v. Stenner, 458 F.2d 1115 (10th Cir. 1972).

64. A.O. ANN. REP., Table C3a (1972).

Beyond all this is what may have constituted the greatest single source of new business in the last year or so, additions to the more conventional federal catalogue of crimes, coupled with intensified prosecutorial activity. In the next section I shall have more to say about the philosophy of some of these new statutes. It will suffice here to mention the criminal sanctions against loan sharking,[65] the restructuring of the federal criminal statutes concerning harmful drugs[66] and the updating of the provisions regulating firearms,[67] the last of which, one may hope, will be expanded. All this has been accompanied by rapid growth in prosecutorial staffs and the creation of strike forces. Such expenditures must justify themselves by statistics, the statistics then generate new expenditures, and so on.

There are only two areas of district court litigation where, in the absence of limiting legislation, significant decreases can be expected. One is selective service cases. These are not insubstantial. Criminal prosecutions under the draft laws more than doubled from 1,826 in 1968 to 4,539 in 1971 and 5,142 in 1972;[68] there have also been a significant number of suits for pre-induction review or post-induction release. The other, due to a very recent statute later discussed, is personal injury suits by harbor workers. Making due allowance for drastic reduction in such cases, we must contemplate a continuation and, indeed, an intensification of the sharp upward trend in district court litigation that first became manifest in 1969. This would be further accentuated if Congress should adopt legislation affording judicial review to prisoners or parolees adversely affected by actions of the Federal Parole Board.[69] Continued increases of 10,000 cases per year are altogether expectable; indeed this estimate is rather on the low side. On that basis, the district courts would have twice as many cases in 1978 as they did in 1968.

---

65. This was enacted as part of the Consumer Credit Protection Act, tit. II, §§ 201–03, 82 Stat. 159–62, *as amended*, 18 U.S.C. §§ 891–94, 896.
66. Comprehensive Drug Abuse Prevention and Control Act of 1970, tit. II, §§ 401–11, 84 Stat. 1260–69, 21 U.S.C. §§ 841–51.
67. Gun Control Act of 1968, tit. I, § 102, 82 Stat. 1214–26, *amending* 18 U.S.C. §§ 921–28.
68. A.O. ANN. REP., Table D2 (1972).
69. *See* H.R. 16,276, 92d Cong., 2d Sess. § 4221 (1972); S. 3979, 92d Cong., 2d Sess. (1972).

Many people answer this with a simple "So what?" The numbers are still small compared with the caseloads of the state courts. As against 8,800 civil cases filed in the four federal districts of New York in 1971,[70] some 86,000 were filed in the civil terms of the New York Supreme Court.[71] On the criminal side, the disproportion is greater still. As against some 2,900 prosecutions begun in the four New York federal district courts,[72] dispositions by the criminal terms of the New York Supreme Court within New York City alone were nearly 16,000[73]—not to speak of the caseloads of the Supreme and County Courts outside New York City[74] and of the Criminal Court of New York City, whose business is primarily with misdemeanors. The Superior Court of California has about the same number of judges[75] as the federal district courts throughout the land. If one state can manage over 400 judges in its lowest court of general jurisdiction, what would be wrong with having 800 federal district judgeships instead of 401? Judge J. Skelly Wright has posed this question in vigorous terms. Resisting the proposals of the American Law Institute for some retraction of diversity jurisdiction, he thinks it "a scandal" that we resort "so haltingly" to "appointing a few additional judges."[76] Whether Judge Wright would consider another 400 district judges to be only "a few" is a point to which I cannot speak.

Strong voices have been raised against unrestrained expansion of the federal trial bench. A notable one was Professor Frankfurter's. Speaking at Cornell in 1928, he said:[77]

A powerful judiciary implies a relatively small number of judges. Honorific motives of distinction have drawn even to the lower federal

---

70. A.O. ANN. REP., Table C3, at 266 (1971).
71. SEVENTEENTH ANNUAL REPORT OF THE ADMINISTRATIVE BOARD OF THE JUDICIAL CONFERENCE OF THE STATE OF NEW YORK, Table 7, at A70 (1972).
72. A.O. ANN. REP., Table D3, at 322 (1971).
73. SEVENTEENTH ANNUAL REPORT, *supra* note 71, Table 30, at A108.
74. In 1971, the Supreme and County Courts outside the City of New York disposed of some 11,000 criminal cases. *Id.*
75. For 1969–70, 416 judgeships were authorized for the California Superior Court. *See* THE JUDICIAL COUNCIL OF CALIFORNIA ANNUAL REPORT 105 (1971).
76. Wright, *The Federal Courts and the Nature and Quality of State Law*, 13 WAYNE L. REV. 317, 319 (1967).
77. Frankfurter, *Distribution of Judicial Power Between United States and State Courts*, 13 CORNELL L.Q. 499, 515–16 (1928).

bench lawyers of the highest quality and thereby built up a public confidence comparable to the feelings of Englishmen for their judges. . . . Subtle considerations of psychology and prestige play havoc with the mechanical notion that increase in the business of the federal courts can be met by increasing the number of judges.

A quarter of a century later he wrote these views into the United States Reports. Arguing that the time to abolish diversity jurisdiction had arrived, he asserted:[78]

The business of courts, particularly of the federal courts, is drastically unlike the business of factories. The function and role of the federal courts and the nature of their judicial process involve impalpable factors, subtle but far-reaching, which cannot be satisfied by enlarging the judicial plant. . . . In the farthest reaches of the problem a steady increase in judges does not alleviate; in my judgment, it is bound to depreciate the quality of the federal judiciary and thereby adversely affect the whole system.

[I]nflation of the number of the district judges . . . will result, by its own Gresham's law, in a depreciation of the judicial currency and the consequent impairment of the prestige and of the efficacy of the federal courts.

While my own view generally accords with Justice Frankfurter's, as it so often has, I recognize that, at the district court level, his thesis cannot be established with certainty. Indeed, one could point to some evidence against it. When I look at the names of the six judges of the Southern District of New York in the year Professor Frankfurter spoke at Cornell, I find only one, perhaps two, of real distinction, although two more were in the offing; the present court has at least a half dozen who would deserve that description and the average is decidedly better. With the number of judges in the Eastern District of New York trebled since 1924, from three to nine, the overall quality has markedly improved. How far that same happy situation prevails elsewhere I cannot say; certainly the reports disclose that many districts have judges of high ability.

Nevertheless, as it seems to me, there must come a point when

---

78. Lumbermen's Mut. Cas. Co. v. Elbert, 348 U.S. 48, 59 (1954) (concurring opinion). While disagreeing with this statement, Professor Moore concedes that a federal judge "should not be reduced to a factory robot clearing a certain number of statistics daily from his docket." Moore & Weckstein, *Diversity Jurisdiction: Past, Present, and Future*, 43 TEXAS L. REV. 1, 26 (1964). Many district judges would regard this as a fair description of their present plight.

an increase in the number of judges makes judging, even at the trial level, less prestigious and less attractive. Prestige is a very important factor in attracting highly qualified men to the federal bench from much more lucrative pursuits. Yet the largest district courts will be in the very metropolitan areas where the discrepancy between uniform federal salaries[79] and the financial rewards of private practice is the greatest, and the difficulty of maintaining an accustomed standard of living on the federal salary the most acute. There is real danger that in such areas, once the prestige factor was removed, lawyers with successful practices, particularly young men, would not be willing to make the sacrifice. Further, as district courts grow in size, there is a more than corresponding increase in the amount of administrative work. Either an increased amount of time of each judge must be spent on administration or, more likely, this function must be delegated to an administrative judge or board. This will impair the kingship of the judge in his own courtroom, subject only to appellate review, which has been one of the attractions of the district bench. Whether because of increased time spent on administration or for some other reason, increases in the number of district judges have not produced corresponding augmentation of output.[80] Moreover, there are many functions which a district court must or should perform as a court, rather than as individual judges. In addition to the preparation of local rules, Congress has given the district courts responsibility for devising plans for the administration of the Criminal Justice Act[81] and the Jury Selection Act,[82] and the Rules of Criminal Procedure now require each district court to adopt a plan for the speedy trial of criminal cases.[83] There are other subjects where a district court could act collegially to adopt uniform standards. Instances are the rules for the conduct of the trials of unruly criminal defendants adopted by the

79. While nothing in the nature of things requires such uniformity, I suspect the chances of Congress' authorizing geographical differentials in judicial salaries, even based on such objective standards as living costs, are negligible.

80. *See* Note, Ross v. Bernhard: *The Uncertain Future of the Seventh Amendment*, 81 YALE L.J. 112, 125 n.74 (1971).

81. 18 U.S.C. § 3006A(a).

82. 28 U.S.C. § 1865(a).

83. F.R. CRIM. P. 50(b).

Northern District of Illinois,[84] and the General Order on Judicial Standards of Procedure and Substance in Review of Student Discipline in Tax Supported Institutions of Higher Education adopted by the Western District of Missouri.[85] Sentencing is another area where conferences among the district judges could do much to answer the complaints about lack of uniformity. None of these things can be done effectively in a 40-man district court.

Any deterioration in the quality of the district judges individually or of their performance collectively would destroy the very values the federal court system is meant to attain. Once such a deterioration began, it would get steadily worse. However, I can afford to leave the question how far we can safely multiply the number of district judges undetermined. For even if we could assume that the number of judges at the district court level could be doubled without adverse consequences to those courts,[86] any such increase would prove utterly destructive to the courts of appeals and to the Supreme Court.

The courts of appeals are already in a state of crisis. In 1960, when 87,421 cases were filed in the district courts, there were 3,899 in the courts of appeals.[87] By 1968 district court filings had grown modestly to 102,163, but filings in the courts of appeals had more than doubled, to 9,116.[88] A study made for the Administrative Office of the Courts in 1967[89] projected 1972 filings of 9,197. As noted, that figure was approached before the ink on the survey was dry. In 1972 when district court filings had grown to 143,216, filings in the courts of appeals increased to 14,535, not only an all-time high, but the biggest jump over the previous year yet experienced.[90]

Why, with a 64% increase in district court filings between 1960 and 1972, was there an increase of 273% in the workload of the

---

84. *See In re* Trials of Pending and Future Criminal Cases, 306 F. Supp. 333 (1969).
85. 45 F.R.D. 133 (1968).
86. One factor that might hold down the rate of increase in district judgeships otherwise required is the availability of United States magistrates, 28 U.S.C. § 636, to perform many pre-trial functions.
87. A.O. ANN. REP., Table B1, at 210 (1960).
88. A.O. ANN. REP., Table B1, at 174 (1968).
89. Shafroth, *Survey of the United States Courts of Appeals*, 42 F.R.D. 243, 261.
90. A.O. ANN. REP., Table B1 (1972).

FILINGS IN UNITED STATES COURTS OF APPEALS

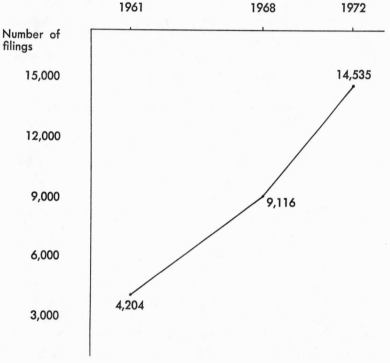

1961   1968   1972

Number of filings

15,000   14,535

12,000

9,000   9,116

6,000

3,000   4,204

courts of appeals?[91] Not surprisingly, criminal appeals more than quadrupled; with the Government providing a free lawyer and a free transcript for an indigent defendant, more liberal bail procedures, and, except in most unusual cases, an assurance against a heavier sentence on retrial,[92] it is hard to see why almost every convicted defendant should not appeal. However, there was also a trebling of what are characterized as "private civil appeals," although these include petitions by state and federal prisoners which are not "civil" in the usual

91. The two figures are not entirely comparable since about 12% of the workload of the courts of appeals in 1972 came from administrative agencies and the Tax Court. *See* A.O. ANN. REP., Table B3 (1972). However, since these only doubled during the decade, the disproportion between the growth of district court filings and of appeals from district court decisions was even greater.

92. North Carolina v. Pearce, 395 U.S. 711, 719–26 (1969). The grant of certiorari in *Michigan v. Payne*, — U.S. —, 41 U.S.L.W. 3207 (Oct. 17, 1972) (No. 71-1005), may presage some reconsideration of this decision.

sense. Almost all of these cases involve questions of principle and not merely of money, where a successful plaintiff's offer to accept a small reduction or a successful defendant's willingness to waive costs has prevented many an appeal.

There is no reason to suppose that the high percentage of appeals to dispositions experienced in the last few years will not continue. Indeed, as suggested, one wonders why the criminal appeal rate should not ultimately approach 100%. But there are added factors that are certain to aggravate the problems of the courts of appeals. Sometime Congress will get around to abolishing the anomalous procedure for review of Interstate Commerce Commission cases by three-judge district courts.[93] While only 52 of these were heard in 1972,[94] they are considerably more burdensome than the usual appeal. Hopefully the three-judge court is on its way out in most other cases as well, as a result of the proposal of the American Law Institute[95] or the more radical and better ones of the Judicial Conference[96] and Senator Burdick,[97] now strongly endorsed by the Chief Justice.[98] Since almost all such cases would be appealed, this would add still another 258 cases[99] of more than usual difficulty, although there would be some compensation in eliminating appeals on the issue whether a single judge had erred in refusing to ask that a court of three be convoked and the service of at least one circuit judge on the three-judge court. Congress will ultimately heed the Supreme Court's requests to be relieved of direct review in government civil antitrust cases;[100] while the filings that such a reform would

93. *See* ICC v. Atlantic Coast Line R.R., 383 U.S. 576, 586 n.4 (1966).

94. A.O. ANN. REP., Table 47b (1972). Three-judge court hearings in other than ICC cases grew from 62 in 1963 to 258 in 1972. A.O. ANN. REP., Table 47b (1972).

95. *See* S. 1876, 92d Cong., 1st Sess. § 1374 (1971).

96. *See* REPORTS OF THE PROCEEDINGS OF THE JUDICIAL CONFERENCE OF THE UNITED STATES 78–79 (1970), introduced by Representative Celler as H.R. 3805, 92d Cong., 1st Sess. (1971).

97. S. 3653, 92d Cong., 2d Sess. (1972).

98. Burger, *The State of the Federal Judiciary—1972*, 58 A.B.A.J. 1049, 1053 (1972).

99. A.O. ANN. REP., Table 47b (1972).

100. United States v. Singer Mfg. Co., 374 U.S. 174, 175 n.1 (1963); *id.* at 202 (Harlan, J., dissenting); Tidewater Oil Co. v. United States, — U.S. —, 41 U.S.L.W. 4053 (Dec. 6, 1972). Mr. Justice Douglas dissociated himself from this expression.

add to the dockets of the courts of appeals would not be significant, numbers do not afford a fair indication of the burden these cases impose.

More important than any of the above factors is the host of recent but as yet relatively little known statutes providing for direct review by the courts of appeals of determinations of administrators under specialized administrative schemes. To take just one example, the Occupational Health and Safety Act of 1970[101] authorizes the Secretary of Labor to propose health and safety standards which, upon objections by interested persons, are to be reviewed in a public hearing.[102] Final promulgations of standards by the Secretary may then be challenged in the court of appeals by "any person who may be adversely affected."[103] The Act further provides for the inspection of any working establishment by the Secretary,[104] and the citation of employers failing to comply with promulgated standards.[105] The Secretary also has the power to assess civil penalties.[106] Citations for failure to comply, as well as assessments of civil penalties, are appealable to the Occupational Health and Safety Commission and, thereafter, to the court of appeals.[107]

This is but one of many pieces of new legislation placing additional responsibilities on the courts of appeals in reviewing agency action.[108] The old idea that administrative appeals concern mainly the

101. 84 Stat. 1590, 29 U.S.C. §§ 651–78.
102. § 6, 29 U.S.C. § 655.
103. § 6(f), 29 U.S.C. § 655(f).
104. § 8, 29 U.S.C. § 657.
105. § 9, 29 U.S.C. § 658.
106. § 17, 29 U.S.C. § 666.
107. § 11, 29 U.S.C. § 660. Under this section, the Secretary may also proceed in the court of appeals to procure enforcement of orders issued by him under the Act.
108. The statutes below are a representative sample of recent legislation authorizing proceedings in the courts of appeals to review agency action and to procure enforcement of agency orders: Education Amendments of 1972, 86 Stat. 235, § 415D(b) (authorizing action by state in court of appeals to challenge disapproval of student incentive grant plan by Commissioner of Education); § 708(b) (authorizing review in court of appeals of Commissioner's disposition of state financing plans as to construction of undergraduate academic facilities); § 1058(b)(2) (authorizing state administrative agency to challenge in court of appeals Commissioner's action as to occupational education financing plans); The Older Americans Act Amend-

independent agencies—the NLRB, FCC, FTC, CAB, FPC, SEC, FMC, and AEC—has gone by the board, although we are not yet fully aware of it. It is not going too far to predict that by the end of the decade appeals to courts of appeals from agencies within the executive branch will be as numerous as those now coming from all independent commissions other than the NLRB.[109]

ments of 1972, 86 Stat. 93 (providing for review of Secretary's final action with respect to approval of a state plan on petition of dissatisfied state); Comprehensive Drug Abuse Prevention and Control Act of 1970, § 507, 84 Stat. 1273, 21 U.S.C. § 877 (review by "persons aggrieved" of "[a]ll final determinations, findings, and conclusions" of the Attorney General under the Act); Egg Products Inspection Act, § 7, 84 Stat. 1625 (1970), 21 U.S.C. § 1036 (review by persons "adversely affected" of the Secretary of Health, Education and Welfare's pasteurizing and labeling requirements); Child Protection and Toy Safety Act of 1969, § 2(b), 83 Stat. 187, 15 U.S.C. § 1262(e) (review by "any person who will be adversely affected" of determinations of the Secretary of Health, Education and Welfare); Federal Coal Mine Health and Safety Act of 1969, § 106, 83 Stat. 754, 30 U.S.C. § 816 (review by "any person aggrieved" of determinations by the Secretary of the Interior); Animal Drug Amendments of 1968, § 101(b), 82 Stat. 343, 21 U.S.C. § 360b(h) (review by applicants of the refusal or withdrawal of approval of certain drugs by the Secretary of Health, Education and Welfare); Natural Gas Pipeline Safety Act of 1968, § 6, 82 Stat. 724, 49 U.S.C. § 1675 (review by "any person who is or will be adversely affected or aggrieved" of orders by the Secretary of Transportation under the Act); Wholesome Poultry Products Act, §§ 8(c), 16(c), 82 Stat. 799, 805 (1968), 21 U.S.C. §§ 457(c), 467(c) (review by any person "adversely affected" of determinations by the Secretary of Agriculture under the Act); Radiation Control for Health and Safety Act of 1968, § 2(3), 82 Stat. 1177, 42 U.S.C. § 263f(d) (review by any person who will be adversely affected of the validity of regulations issued by the Secretary of Health, Education and Welfare); Flammable Products Act Amendments, § 3(e), 81 Stat. 569 (1967), 15 U.S.C. § 1193(e) (review by persons adversely affected of standards and regulations of the Secretary of Commerce); Wholesome Meat Act, § 6(c), 81 Stat. 588 (1967), 21 U.S.C. § 607(e) (review by persons affected by determinations on markings and labelings by the Secretary of Agriculture); National Traffic and Motor Vehicle Safety Act of 1966, § 105, 80 Stat. 720, 15 U.S.C. § 1394 (review by persons affected of orders of the Secretary of Transportation); Federal Metal and Nonmetallic Mine Safety Act, §§ 6, 12, 80 Stat. 774, 781 (1966), 30 U.S.C. §§ 725, 731 (review by persons aggrieved of standards and other determinations of the Secretary of the Interior).

109. Since the orders or regulations here considered generally become effective immediately or within a short interval, applications for

I have not yet mentioned the worst spectre of all—appellate review of sentences. I do not call it a spectre because of lack of sentiment for it.[110] But I would hope there will be enough good judgment in Congress to realize that adoption of such a measure would administer the *coup de grâce* to the courts of appeals as we know them. The problem of volume is not so much with the cases where a sentence is imposed after a trial, since most of these will be appealed anyway[111] and the sentence would be just one more point to be considered, although sometimes an important and difficult one, but with the great mass of convictions, nearly 90% of the total, obtained on pleas of guilty or *nolo contendere*.[112] If the sentences in only half these were appealed, and that seems a conservative figure since most proponents of appellate review of sentences reject out of hand the main device, a possible increase of sentence on an appeal by the defendant,[113] that might have a limiting effect,[114] the caseload of the

> stays will usually accompany such appeals. These represent a considerable added burden. The court must either spend a substantial amount of time considering the merits in deciding whether or not to grant a stay or grant one rather routinely in any case having some apparent merit conditioned on an expedited hearing of the appeal. This latter course often creates pressure for very speedy decision, on briefs that are likely to be inadequate because of the short time available for preparation.

110. *See, e.g.,* REPORTS OF THE PROCEEDINGS OF THE JUDICIAL CONFERENCE OF THE UNITED STATES 94–95 (1964); ABA STANDARDS RELATING TO APPELLATE REVIEW OF SENTENCES (1968); FINAL REPORT OF THE NATIONAL COMMISSION ON REFORM OF FEDERAL CRIMINAL LAWS 317 (1971); S. 1540, 90th Cong., 1st Sess. (passed by the Senate); S. 2228, 92d Cong., 1st Sess.; Frankel, *Lawlessness in Sentencing*, 41 U. CINN. L. REV. 1, 23–28 (1972).

111. In 1972, 3,980 criminal appeals were filed in the courts of appeals as compared with 5,506 convictions after trial. A.O. ANN. REP., Tables B1, D4 (1972).

112. These amounted to 31,714 in 1972. *Id.* Table D4 (1972). Although the ABA STANDARDS, *supra* note 110, propose a so-called "streamlined" procedure for guilty plea cases, at 35–37, 39–41, I do not perceive that this will materially lighten the tasks of the reviewing court.

113. *See* ABA STANDARDS, *supra* note 110, § 3.4 at 54–55, & accompanying commentary, 55–63. The ABA STANDARDS also reject a procedure requiring leave to appeal from sentence. *Id.* at 37–38.

114. The only other factor that might have a limiting effect would be if all or substantially all guilty pleas included a sentence approved in

courts of appeals would be doubled by this means alone. While there would not be an equivalent increase in burden, Professor Carrington is right in saying that if even a small percentage of those convicted on pleas of guilty should appeal their sentence, "the courts would be swamped."[115]

I do not mean by this to minimize the problem of disparate or excessive sentences, but rather to indicate that the solution does not lie in imposing still another burden on the courts of appeals. Appellate judges are ill equipped for the task, and there would be almost as much danger of disparity among panels of a court of appeals as there is among district judges. A far better solution is the creation in each circuit of a standing sentence review panel of district judges chosen because of their special interest in sentencing and with ready recourse to penologists, psychiatrists and sociologists who could aid them in their work. This would achieve a circuit-wide uniformity, at least at any one time, which shifting panels of circuit judges would not.[116] Such a system would have the further advantage of divorcing the sentencing problem from review on the merits, with the attendant danger of trade-offs.[117] In any event, whatever the desiderata may be, the courts of appeals simply cannot take on this added task.

There are a few reforms, relating specifically to court of appeals

advance by the judge, *compare* ABA STANDARDS RELATING TO PLEAS OF GUILTY § 3.3, at 71–72 (1968), since there would be almost no chance of reversal in that event. But that is not the present situation.

115. Carrington, *Crowded Dockets and the Courts of Appeals: The Threat to the Function of Review and the National Law*, 82 HARV. L. REV. 542, 578 (1969).

116. *See Hearings on H.R. 7378 Before Subcomm. No. 5 of the House Comm. on the Judiciary*, 92d Cong., 1st Sess. 25 (1972) (testimony of Judge Lumbard). The principal objection voiced to this system is that the panel could not achieve objectivity since it would sometimes have to pass on sentences of members or colleagues. *See* ABA STANDARDS, *supra* note 110, at 121–22. This could be mitigated by having the panel composed of judges who would be temporarily relieved from criminal work. If the objection is deemed truly serious, consideration could be given to following the English model of a separate court for review of sentences, perhaps on a national basis.

117. Judge Frankel has forcefully argued that this danger is less than feared—indeed that, to some extent, a court reviewing the merits should or, at any rate, does have the severity of sentence in mind. Frankel, *supra*, 41 U. CINN. L. REV. at 24–26. Still the danger seems existent in some degree.

jurisdiction rather than federal jurisdiction generally, that might help in a small degree. Two minor ones with respect to the review of administrative orders, to be later discussed,[118] would, after taking account of the increase from court of appeals review of ICC orders, effect a net diminution of five or six hundred such cases a year. The power of a district judge or of a single judge of the court of appeals to issue a certificate of probable cause in state prisoner habeas corpus cases[119] should be eliminated and placed solely in the court of appeals.[120] The same procedure should be applied to appeals from the denials of motions by federal prisoners under 28 U.S.C. section 2255 for vacation of judgment or reduction or correction of sentence. In all these instances the case has already gone through, or had an opportunity to go through, the judicial hierarchy at least once, and has now been considered by a district judge again; before further time of an appellate court is taken, the court should be convinced there is some merit in the appeal. On the same theory, that one review of right is enough, an argument could be made for a certiorari type jurisdiction when a district judge has reviewed the decision of a referee in bankruptcy, at least when such a review has resulted in an affirmance. There are further possibilities along these lines which I will explore when I come to review of administrative orders.[121] There could be wider provisions, or wider use of existing provisions such as FRAP 38, for the award of more substantial costs, but, apart from other difficulties, these would be of little avail in the most rapidly growing heads of appeals—criminal appeals, post-conviction attacks by indigents, and civil rights litigation.

The very best one could hope from such reforms, and I believe this to be overly optimistic, is that the volume in the courts of appeals might be held at not greatly in excess of present levels[122] *if there were*

---

118. *See* pp. 173–90 *infra.*

119. 28 U.S.C. § 2253; *see* Friendly, *Is Innocence Irrelevant? Collateral Attack on Criminal Judgments*, 38 U. Chi. L. Rev. 142, 144 n.9 (1970).

120. Experience has shown that the reversal rate in these cases, small as it is in total, is even smaller when the certificate has been granted by the district judge.

121. *See* pp. 173–90 *infra.*

122. This assumes, of course, that the courts of appeals will not be required to review sentences.

no significant increase in district court litigation. But if I am anywhere near right in thinking that under the present jurisdictional framework district court litigation in 1978 will be twice the 1968 volume, the filings in the courts of appeals will be more than double the 9,116 in 1968 when the complement of circuit judges was raised to 97. Indeed, if the recent experience whereby each 1% increase in district court filings translates itself into a 4% increase in appeals should continue, they would far exceed that; a figure as high as 25,000 is by no means unrealistic.

There are some other expedients that should be mentioned before considering whether a way to handle such volume can be found in Judge Wright's "few more judges." The two circuits which for years have had a wholly disproportionate number of filings and have thus had to go beyond the traditional maximum of nine judges—the Fifth and the Ninth—could be subjected to the same surgery as the Eighth Circuit experienced, without ill effect, when the Tenth was carved out of it some forty years ago.[123] The Act of 1891 creating the courts of appeals[124] simply adopted the circuit boundaries as these had gradually evolved from the three circuits established by the First Judiciary Act.[125] Even if one were to assume that more thought was given the matter than seems to have been the case,[126] eighty years have wrought changes of sufficient significance to be taken into account. In 1891 the Deep South was only twenty-six years from the disastrous war between the states and fifteen years from the end of Reconstruction; the character of the region has entirely changed, although its federal courts remain especially burdened with the unhappy heritage of the past. In 1891 the seven states allotted to the Ninth Circuit accounted for 3.6% of the country's population; today these same states, along with Alaska, Hawaii and Guam, account for 14.9%, including the nation's most populous state, California. While I am no mathematician, I know the claims that the addition of two more circuits will produce an equivalent increase in conflicts of decision must be statistically wrong, and I do not see that the prestige of

123. Act of Feb. 28, 1929, ch. 363, 45 Stat. 1346.
124. Act of March 3, 1891, ch. 517, 26 Stat. 826.
125. Ch. 20, § 4, 1 Stat. 74 (1789).
126. *See* Frankfurter & Landis 100 n.200; Carrington, *supra*, 82 Harv. L. Rev. at 586 n.197.

the courts of appeals would be much affected if the number of circuits grew from 11 to 13. On the other hand, I think it would seriously decline if the increase were to say 20. To alter slighty the words of Professor Geoffrey Hazard, "what were once authoritative appellate tribunals, subject to occasional review by the Supreme Court . . . would have been converted into a judicial Tower of Babel. The proliferation of utterances could divest any one of these courts of significant authority."[127]

While Congress has now provided for a commission to study a revision of the circuits,[128] I see no likelihood that, aside from the splitting of the Fifth and Ninth Circuits,[129] this carries real promise of relief[130] unless we are prepared for a vast increase in the number of circuits, a course I would deprecate for the reasons stated. Even

127. Hazard, *After the Trial Court—The Realities of Appellate Review*, in THE COURTS, THE PUBLIC, AND THE LAW EXPLOSION 60, 81 (H. Jones, ed. 1965).

128. Pub. L. No. 92-489, 86 Stat. 807 (1972). The Commission is also authorized to study and make recommendations with respect to "the structure and internal procedures of the Federal courts of appeals." The Conference Report makes clear that this does not include the jurisdiction of the district courts. Whether the Commission can study and make recommendations with respect to the jurisdiction of the courts of appeals is unclear; I rather doubt this.

129. It has been argued that splitting these unwieldy circuits would accomplish nothing since judge-power would not be increased and indeed might be applied less efficiently than now. See statements of Chief Judge Brown of the Fifth and Chief Judge Chambers of the Ninth Circuit in *Revision of Appellate Courts, Hearing on S.J. Res. 122 Before the Subcomm. on Improvements in Judicial Machinery of the Senate Comm. on the Judiciary*, 92d Cong., 2d Sess. 49–50, 107–08, 155 (1972). But there is no reason why states producing large amounts of business need be left with the existing number of judges; in a split circuit Texas might well have more than four and Florida more than three judges. New York has had six since 1961.

It is true that splitting the Ninth Circuit affords less promise of relief than dividing the Fifth along the line of the Mississippi River because of the high proportion of the work of the Ninth Circuit, approximately 60%, furnished by California. Still the creation of a northwestern circuit would provide appreciable relief and also save substantial travel and communication costs for litigants and the Government.

130. Shifting a state from one circuit to another would also create a serious problem whether the governing precedents were decisions of the old circuit or the new.

that would not be of much help to the Second Circuit, long the most heavily beleaguered save for the Fifth and Ninth, since 90% of its business comes from New York. Whatever the objections to a circuit of only a single state, and these may have been exaggerated,[131] we surely do not want a state to have more than one circuit.

There has recently been a flurry of proposals to get more work out of each circuit judge. Congress has authorized an executive for each circuit.[132] This will ultimately prove a help, although most of the items proposed for the agenda of this office relate primarily to the district courts. Partly because of this, at the moment I can only echo the Chief Justice's comment:[133]

The function of a court executive is something none of us really knows very much about.

The Fifth Circuit has developed an elaborate procedure for screening out frivolous appeals and others determined not to warrant oral argument;[134] the judges of that court are enthusiastic about the practice;[135] and it has now been followed closely by the Sixth[136] and Eighth Circuits[137] and in slightly different forms by the First,[138] Fourth,[139] and Tenth.[140] The procedure is doubtless valuable in curtailing the number of arguments in those circuits where distance is

---

131. While it is important that a court of appeals contain judges from different kinds of communities, I am not altogether clear why this could not be furnished by judges living outside the large metropolitan areas in the same state as well as by judges from outside the state. Perhaps the chief virtue of preserving the multi-state circuit is in mitigating against the chances of one political party control of a court of appeals that would exist if the same party retained the presidency and had the senatorships from a single state for a long period.

132. 84 Stat. 1907 (1971), 28 U.S.C. § 332(e), (f).

133. Burger, *Deferred Maintenance*, 57 A.B.A.J. 425, 428 (1971).

134. 5TH CIR. RULES 17, 18, 20.

135. *See* Murphy v. Houma Well Serv., 409 F.2d 804, 805–08 (5th Cir. 1969); Huth v. Southern Pacific Co., 417 F.2d 526, 527–30 (5th Cir. 1969); Isbell Enterprises, Inc. v. Citizens Cas. Co., 431 F.2d 409, 410–14 (5th Cir. 1970).

136. 6TH CIR. RULES 3(e), 7(e), 8, 9.

137. 8TH CIR. RULES 6, 8, 9.

138. 1ST CIR. RULE 6.

139. 4TH CIR. RULE 7(a)–(b).

140. 10TH CIR. RULES 8, 9.

a source of inconvenience and expense to judges and counsel; whether the procedure, which necessarily involves a large amount of paper shuffling among the judges, effects a net saving of judicial time as against those followed by other circuits, smaller in geographical size, in limiting the time for argument[141] and often summarily affirming from the bench has not been established.[142] Other appellate courts have adopted still different procedures to get more work done.[143] The proportion of cases in which opinions are written has been reduced and could be further diminished. Counsel in criminal appeals should make greater use of the procedure, sanctioned in *Anders v. California*,[144] of filing a brief demonstrating that he has considered all possible appealable issues and has found that none exists, rather than blindly following the safe course of seeking a reversal to which he knows his client is not entitled; the courts should not hesitate to refuse or reduce compensation under the Criminal Justice Act in cases of flagrant abuse. Yet, when full account is taken of all these possibilities, most of which are already reflected in the rate of disposition, it is still true that, under our present notions with respect to what an appeal should be, courts of nine judges in active service, a figure already equalled, approached or exceeded in ten of the eleven circuits, will not be able to handle the caseloads of most of the circuits in the 1980's unless the rate of increased intake at the district court level is materially slackened.

In contrast to techniques directed at making the assembly line move at increased speed, an imaginative proposal of a different sort was made by Judge Shirley Hufstedler in her Charles Evans Hughes lecture of 1971.[145] The gist of this is as follows: Appellate courts perform two different kinds of functions—review for error in

141. *See* 2D CIR. RULE 34(d); 7TH CIR. RULE 11. Rules of the Third, Ninth, and District of Columbia Circuits provide for dispensing with oral argument altogether, as well as for limiting it. 3D CIR. RULE 12(6); 9TH CIR. RULE 3(a); D.C. CIR. RULES 11(d)–(e), 12(b).

142. Alternatives are affirmance "on" or "for substantially the reasons stated in" the district court's opinion.

143. *See Panel Discussion, Improving Procedures in the Decisional Process*, 52 F.R.D. 51 (1971).

144. 386 U.S. 738 (1967).

145. Hufstedler, *New Blocks for Old Pyramids: Reshaping the Judicial System*, 44 S. CAL. L. REV. 901 (1971).

the trial of the particular case (the "corrective function") and review for the determination or redetermination of principles of law (the "institutional function"). She would confide the corrective function, including the disposition of post-trial motions now handled by the trial judge, to a court of review composed of the trial judge and two appellate judges. It would meet shortly after the judgment or sentence, and its procedures would be most informal, generally without a trial transcript unless one happened to be available. It would render an oral opinion or a written memorandum, which would not be citeable as precedent. Review by the next tier of courts, the court of appeals in the federal system, would be discretionary and limited to cases where some important principle was at stake.

Perhaps because of the author's felicity of expression and, if one may still dare to say so in these days of women's liberation, her personal charm, perhaps also because of sheer desperation, this proposal has been received with more interest than it seems to me to deserve. One regards with horror what might be considered still another tier of courts, with the attendant delay and expense.[146] One is even more bothered over the trial judge sitting in judgment of himself. Judge Hufstedler's attempted vindication on the basis of the old circuit system[147] is not convincing. The presence of the district judge in these courts was one of the causes for dissatisfaction that led to the creation of the courts of appeals; it was said that:[148]

Such an appeal is not from Philip drunk to Philip sober, but from Philip sober to Philip intoxicated with the vanity of a matured opinion and doubtless also a published decision.

I know a few trial judges who could be trusted to view their own decisions with appropriate neutrality—but only a few. Would the two appellate judges feel as free to criticize a trial judge sitting with them as below them? Would both of them? Could they properly perform

146. *See* Hazard, *supra* note 127, at 82.
147. Hufstedler, *supra*, 44 S. CAL. L. REV. at 912.
148. W.B. Hill, *The Federal Judicial System*, 12 A.B.A. REP. 289, 307 (1889), *quoted in* FRANKFURTER & LANDIS 87. It has been said of the earlier practice of having Supreme Court Justices pass on their own decisions at circuit, that this "gave the judges a vested interest in error . . . ." G. DUNNE, JUSTICE JOSEPH STORY AND THE RISE OF THE SUPREME COURT 97 (1970).

the corrective function, particularly on questions of the admissibility of evidence, if they had no transcript and were largely dependent on the notes of the trial judge? Is the distinction between the "corrective" and the "institutional" function viable?[149] What would the court of review do when there was a question as to the proper rule of law? In good conscience it would feel compelled to study this with some care, just as a court of appeals does on a novel and important issue of constitutional law even though it knows its decision will be reviewed and will have no precedential effect. When the court of appeals had denied review, could certiorari be sought from the Supreme Court? Judge Hufstedler has answers to many of these criticisms; I shall not attempt to make them for her.[150] The very most I would favor with respect to this proposal would be to see the experiment tried out in some state or, still better, in part of one. In advance of such a trial we surely cannot rely on it as a panacea for country-wide application in the federal judicial system.

We thus reach the question whether there is any sufficient objection to increasing the number of judges in a court of appeals above nine. While I confessed that the case for not increasing the number of district judges in any large measure was not one that could be proved, I have no such doubt with respect to the courts of appeals. The essential difference is that the latter are collegial. Under the Act of 1891 they had only three judges each, so the same judges always sat together. As the business increased, more judges were added and the three-judge panel system developed. There was no great trouble in maintaining this effectively so long as there were no more than five judges in any court of appeals. According to my rudimentary mathematics, with five judges there would be ten possible panels and every one would have at least one member who had been on any

149. A good example of the difficulty in drawing this distinction is furnished by Cortright v. Resor, 447 F.2d 245 (2d Cir. 1971), *cert. denied*, 405 U.S. 965 (1972). The district judge and the three judges of the court of appeals agreed on the applicable "principles"—that a serviceman did not give up his First Amendment rights but that the interest of maintaining discipline justified curtailments that would not have been permissible for the ordinary citizen. They disagreed whether the disciplinary measure taken by the Army was justified by the conduct at issue. Is this "error" or "policy?"

150. *See* Hufstedler, *supra*, 44 S. Cal. L. Rev. at 912–15.

previous panel. The possibility of one panel's proceeding in ignorance of what another was doing thus did not exist. Even with the six judges of "Learned Hand's Court"[151] the chances of this were small. With nine they are much greater, and with eleven, thirteen or fifteen, greater still. There is a method for dealing with this problem, namely, the circulation of all proposed opinions to each judge, as is done to a considerable extent in the Third, Fourth and District of Columbia Circuits, but this means more work[152] and certainly more delay, particularly in view of the present condition of the mails. An increase in the number of judges would increase the number of requests for votes upon en banc consideration, although not in direct proportion, and would greatly enhance the difficulty of handling those that were granted. And the suggestion that en banc proceedings be limited to a "reviewing division," presumably of the active judges ranking highest in precedence although with an age limitation,[153] would inevitably breed justifiable dissension.

151. *See* SCHICK, LEARNED HAND'S COURT (1970).
152. If it be said the procedure would not involve more work since, presumably, all the judges read all the opinions *after* they appear, I would strongly disagree. The responsibility I would feel with respect to a proposed opinion is quite different from that concerning one that has already appeared. In the latter case, I am concerned only with two situations: One is where the result seems so wrong on a point within the ambit of F.R.A.P. 35(a)—a situation usually flagged by a dissent—that I should make or support a request for reconsideration en banc. The other is where some remark, very likely not affecting the result, is in conflict with a previous decision of our court or the Supreme Court or otherwise contains serious seeds of future trouble, so that I should ask the opinion writer to consider a modification. If I saw the opinion prior to its filing and thought the result wrong, could I in good conscience refrain from saying so, even though I would not regard the precedent as sufficiently important that I would support reconsideration en banc? Would I not feel an obligation to suggest changes where I thought the language murky or the reasoning illogical, even though I agreed with the result? In short, does not the practice result either in largely defeating the very objective of the panel system or in a judge sitting by and saying nothing about what he regards as mistakes? To me neither result is attractive.
153. *See* testimony of Judge J. Skelly Wright in *Revision of Appellate Courts, Hearing on S.J. Res. 122 Before the Subcomm. on Improvements in Judicial Machinery of the Senate Comm. on the Judiciary,* 92d Cong., 2d Sess. 21–22 (1972). The asserted analogy to the

Again, the judges of the circuit "in regular active service" constitute the judicial council for the circuit, which is directed to "make all necessary orders for the effective and expeditious administration of the business of the courts within its circuit."[154] Since an increased number of judges would interfere with this function, it has been proposed that only the senior five, or seven, or what-have-you, should participate. I do not like the idea of second-class judges. Moreover, I am not confident that the oldest judges can make the greatest contribution to some of the council's work; yet they would rightly resent being ruled by their juniors, especially with respect to the management of their own court.

Beyond all this is the desirability of judges of a collegial court really knowing each other, by talking together, lunching together even—perhaps particularly—drinking together. This promotes understanding, prevents unnecessary disagreements, and avoids the introduction of personal animosity into those differences of opinion that properly occur. I believe that close personal relationships have been one of the sources of strength of the Supreme Court; when these have degenerated, so has the Court's performance. I thus agree again with Professor Geoffrey Hazard that "[i]t will therefore be simply impossible, in the foreseeable future, to solve the problem of 'too many appeals' by increasing the number of judges."[155]

Appellate Divisions of the Supreme Court of New York is inapposite. While called a division of the Supreme Court, the Appellate Divisions are in fact intermediate courts of appeals.
154. 28 U.S.C. § 332.
155. Hazard, *supra* note 127, at 82. *See also* FRANKFURTER & LANDIS 187, and the views of Judge Lumbard, *supra* note 116, at 21–22.

Professor Carrington has proposed an elaborate plan for endeavoring to meet the problem by separating courts of appeals of many members into subject-matter divisions through which the various judges will rotate and which will be the ultimate authority, subject only to Supreme Court review, in the type of cases confided to them. *See* Carrington, *supra*, 82 HARV. L. REV. at 587–96. Many of the difficulties in this scheme are recognized by the author but, to my mind, are not answered. A complete analysis of my grounds for disagreement would be too space-consuming. Some have been suggested in the preceding text. Another is that appeals do not neatly divide by subject-matter. For example, a criminal case may turn on the construction of a labor statute, a tax statute, or a

The final reason why we must limit the volume of cases decided by the courts of appeals and, in order to achieve this, the number of filings in the district courts, is the effect of an increase on the volume of petitions for certiorari to the Supreme Court.[156] In sharp contrast to decisions of state courts, every decision of a court of appeals is a potential for the Supreme Court's docket. There is no requirement that such a decision involve a federal question or even that it be a final judgment. Requests by the Court to the bar for restraint in the filings of such petitions have fallen on deaf ears. As said by Mr. Justice Frankfurter:[157]

The litigious tendency of our people and the unwillingness of litigants to rest content with adverse decisions after their cause has been litigated in two and often in three courts, lead to attempts to get a final review by the Supreme Court in literally thousands of cases which should never reach the highest Court of the land.

Filings in the Supreme Court grew from 1,940 for the 1960 Term to 3,643 for the 1971 Term.[158] The widespread notion that this increase results primarily from *in forma pauperis* cases is a grave error. While these cases did increase from 1,098 in the 1960 Term to 1,942 in the 1969 Term, there was almost the same propor-

securities statute. A tax claim can turn up in bankruptcy. Questions under the Administrative Procedure Act may arise in almost any litigation against government officers or agencies; issues under the Federal Rules of Civil Procedure may crop up in every piece of civil litigation. Evidence questions can arise anywhere. Furthermore, a judge of the court of appeals should not be required to sit by and allow a decision of his colleagues on an important matter with which he disagrees to become "the law of the circuit" and remain so unless and until other judges constituting that "division" choose to reconsider. While Professor Carrington is to be applauded for trying, his proposal would introduce more problems than it solves.

156. Neither more work out of judges, more circuits, more judges, nor Professor Carrington's proposal offers any help on this score.

157. Dick v. New York Life Ins. Co., 359 U.S. 437, 459 (1959) (dissenting opinion).

158. SUPREME COURT REPORT, Table II, at A2. Filings in the Supreme Court, of course, are not directly comparable with those in the courts of appeals since the Supreme Court disposes of only some 12% of its filings on the merits; in the others its task is simply to decide whether to decide.

FILINGS IN THE SUPREME COURT OF THE UNITED STATES

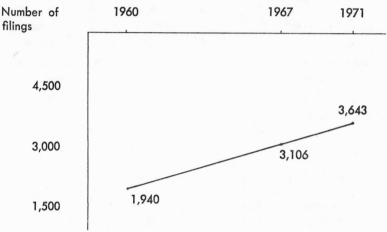

tionate increase in cases on the Appellate Docket—from 842 to 1,457.[159] Viewing the matter in another way, as the filings in the courts of appeals somewhat more than doubled, from 4,823 in 1962 to 10,248 in 1969,[160] petitions for certiorari to the courts of appeals nearly doubled, from 941[161] to 1,668.[162] Along with this, the grant ratio in applications to review decisions of the courts of appeals has declined from approximately 10% in 1962[163] to less than 6% in 1970.[164] If I am right in thinking that, unless the intake in the district courts is restricted, the filings in the courts of appeals will pass the 20,000 mark well before the end of the decade, the Supreme Court will then have some 3,400 petitions for certiorari from these courts alone,[165]—as many as the Court's entire filings for the 1969

159. A.O. ANN. REP., Table A1, at 204 (1970). If the figures were to be viewed from a longer time span, the conclusion would differ. *See* Mr. Justice Douglas' dissent in Tidewater Oil Co. v. United States, *supra*, — U.S. at —, 41 U.S.L.W. at 4060.

160. A.O. ANN. REP. 104 (1969).

161. A.O. ANN. REP., Table B2, at 184 (1962).

162. A.O. ANN. REP., Table B2, at 188 (1969).

163. *See* A.O. ANN. REP., Table B2, at 184 (1962).

164. *See* A.O. ANN. REP., Table B2, at 214 (1970).

165. I am indebted to E. Robert Seaver, Esq., then Clerk of the Supreme Court, for some of these computations. He has pointed out that for the years 1962–1970, the ratio of petitions for certiorari to the courts of appeals to filings in those courts has remained within a narrow range, from a low of 16% to a high of 19%.

Term. Since the number of full arguments the Court can hear is finite, this will mean a further decrease in the percentage of courts of appeals decisions in which certiorari can be granted. Yet this will not decrease the burden of picking out the cases to be reviewed.

A Study Group on the Caseload of the Supreme Court has recommended that the Court's burdens be eased by creation of a National Court of Appeals composed of seven circuit judges.[166] All matters now coming before the Supreme Court,[167] other than the few cases of original jurisdiction, would go to the National Court. It could take one of three courses: deny review, which would be the end of the road;[168] certify cases to the Supreme Court, of the order of 400 per year; or review with finality. The *Report* is a bit opaque on the point whether the National Court can follow the last course in any case or can only resolve conflicts among the circuits—indeed the *Report* strongly indicates the latter. The Supreme Court could dispose of the 400-odd cases as it saw fit, including a remand to the National Court in a case where the Supreme Court perceived a conflict among circuits but did not regard the issue as of sufficient comparative importance to warrant its hearing the matter. It seems curious that other cases certified by the National Court but denied review by the Supreme Court should wither on the vine as presumably they are more important than ones the National Court has decided to decide, unless, as appears to be intended, the National Court can only decide cases of conflicts among circuits. It is unfortunate that the Group did not put its proposal in statutory language. This "clears the mind wonderfully" and also would let the country know just what the proposal is. Conceding there are "objections that can be raised

---

166. SUPREME COURT REPORT 19.
167. This includes cases from state courts, whether by appeal, whose abolition the *Report* recommends, *id.* at 36–38, or by certiorari.
168. *Id.* at 21. This is qualified by allowing the Supreme Court to grant certiorari before judgment in a court of appeals, before denial of review in the National Court, or before judgment in a case set down for hearing or heard there, *id.* "The expectation would be that exercises of this power would be exceptional," *id.,* as the Court's exercise of the first power has been. However, nothing would prevent frequent application for such a grant, and the incentive would be much greater than now in view of possible preclusion of Supreme Court review by action of the National Court.

against this recommendation" but not truly measuring their extent and validity, the *Report* says "relief is imperative."

Is it? Before that can be determined, one should take account, apart from longer-range proposals made in these lectures, of two steps that could be made effective quite speedily. One is the Group's sound recommendation to abolish all mandatory Supreme Court appellate jurisdiction—by eliminating three-judge courts to review Interstate Commerce Commission orders and in cases challenging the constitutionality of state and federal statutes, by abolishing direct appeal in Government civil antitrust suits, and by making all review of state and federal court decisions discretionary.[169] While these reforms would not decrease the number of certioraris, the net saving of the Court's time would be substantial.

The other step would be changes in the Court's internal handling of certioraris. The *Report* says that "the tendency appears to be to allot the greater part of a clerk's time to the study of petitions for certiorari and the preparation of memoranda on them . . ." and, indeed, that some Justices require from their clerks "a memorandum concerning every petition for certiorari or other item to be considered by the Conference."[170] This seems unnecessary. There must be a good half of the petitions which a Justice could decide to deny on the basis of a few minutes talk with the clerk or "a memorandum" something like "The only substantial point raised is the sufficiency of the evidence to support submission of this criminal case to the jury." On the other hand, if the Justices, or most of them, have become afflicted with memorandumania, there is no reason why nine clerks need write memoranda on each petition. Justices desiring to participate in a joint program could pool their clerks;[171] others, who did not desire to do this, could be given a fourth clerk if they wished. Another possibility, dismissed by the *Report*, is for a small senior staff to summarize petitions and make recommendations;[172] I would

---

169. *Id.* at 25–38. Many of these proposals are discussed in other portions of these lectures.

170. *Id.* at 7, 43.

171. Apparently Mr. Justice Powell has suggested this, and five Justices have joined in the plan. *See* The National Observer, Nov. 11, 1972, at 14.

172. SUPREME COURT REPORT 15–16. Such a staff would be particularly valuable in the study of *in forma pauperis* petitions, where it may be necessary to obtain papers from lower courts.

add with instructions to recommend consideration of the grant of review in say three times the number of cases in which the Court could hear argument, something like the 400 that are to be forwarded by the National Court. While each Justice would read each staff memorandum and call for the papers when he desired, he and his own clerks would devote most of their attention to the cases, say 20% to 25% of the total, where consideration of review was recommended. Either program, or a combination of them, would save an enormous amount of time of the Justices and their clerks, yet would keep control of the Court's docket where it ought to be. The chance that, under such procedures, any truly worthy petition would escape the eye of every Justice seems minimal. If that should occur, the issue would surely arise again.

Rather than await the result of the recommended jurisdictional changes and altered administration, including such mundane things as increasing the efficiency of the law clerks by providing them with secretaries and modern office equipment,[173] the *Report* insists that, at whatever cost, the Justices must forthwith be relieved of any responsibility for the large number of petitions whose fate is foredoomed. Although the present system may waste some of the Justices' time, it is scarcely possible to engage in deep constitutional contemplation all day long, and there is no specific showing that the country has suffered from this diversion of energy. While the *Report* says that "[i]ssues that would have been decided on the merits a generation ago are passed over by the Court today,"[174] it does not cite any instances where a temporary passing over has really mattered; the impression I gain from thumbing the volumes of "a generation ago" is that the Court was deciding a good many cases not meriting its attention—as several Justices thought. In my view, if the Court's docket can be kept at or near its present size, the proposed cure is worse than the ailment.

The first problem which *saute aux yeux* is how rotating judges of the National Court of Appeals will manage better in sorting the mounting volume of certioraris into three piles than the abler and more experienced Justices of the Supreme Court can do in dividing them into two. The answer must be that the National Court will do

173. *Id.* at 45.
174. *Id.* at 6.

very little in *deciding* cases and thus will spend most of its time in screening; this must be why the *Report* lays such stress on the National Court's role in resolving intercircuit conflicts on issues of relatively minor importance, without ever quite saying this is all the National Court can decide. While the *Report* is full of talk about intercircuit conflicts, it contains no figures showing how many the Supreme Court resolves or leaves unresolved in a typical term. My own impression is that, with the exception of federal tax cases, for which a better solution has long been known,[175] and divergent views on constitutional issues, which the Court must handle in any event, resolved and unresolved conflicts in any term are relatively few.[176] If there are only a score or so of such cases each year, and say half of these are all the National Court of Appeals can decide, one can readily understand why service upon it should be deemed a sacrifice rather than a privilege,[177] and the court is badly misnamed. On the other hand, if the National Court were allowed to decide cases comparable with those decided by the Supreme Court in number although not in consequence,[178] the burden would simply have been transferred into less capable hands.

A second objection, important if the National Court were to engage substantially in decision making, goes to its composition. In an effort to avoid the possibility that a President might seek to stack the National Court in a manner that would lead it to keep cases away from the Supreme Court, the Study Group has come up with a proposal "for three-year staggered terms by a system of automatic rotation."[179] Apart from the undiscussed question whether this is constitutionally permissible, the method seems designed to insure that, instead of the National Court being served by the best qualified

175. *See* pp. 161–66 *infra*.
176. Review of the opinions of the 1971 Term indicates only eight (including two tax cases) where certiorari had been granted to resolve intercircuit conflicts on other than constitutional issues.
177. SUPREME COURT REPORT 19.
178. Some have thought there should be greater review of courts of appeals administrative law decisions, which frequently have large records. This was one of the motivations behind the proposal, rejected by the Study Group, *id.* at 16, for a new court "to hear and decide cases referred to it by the Supreme Court . . . ."
179. *Id.* at 19.

circuit judges, it will reflect only the average, and also that, as soon as a judge has gained real experience on the National Court, he will be sent back to his former post.[180] How can one believe that a court so constituted could have "the confidence of the profession, of the Supreme Court, and of the country" and, most important, of the courts of appeals and the state courts, as a decision making body?[181] While the proposed gadgetry could be replaced by a different method of appointment, we would then be back with the problem the gadgetry was designed to overcome.

A third objection, at least if the National Court were allowed to decide important questions of federal law where there was no conflict, is its effect on the prestige and morale of the courts of appeals. One does not like to imagine what Judge Learned Hand would have said about having his decisions reviewed by anything like the National Court. To be sure, not every circuit judge now regards each member of the Supreme Court as his intellectual superior, but all have a respect and reverence for the Court as an institution that they could never entertain for a body like the proposed National Court.[182]

Somewhat less important is the matter of delay. While the *Re-*

180. The problem created for the courts of appeals is glossed over with a single sentence. "It is to be noted that some additional circuit judgeships would have to be created." *Id.* at 19. The only feasible way of handling this would be a statute creating an additional temporary judgeship in any circuit from which a member had been drafted. This has several difficulties. A good part of the three-year term of the departing member might have passed before his replacement was nominated and confirmed, and had become familiar with his duties. If the circuit then lost its place on the National Court, it would have a possibly unwanted member when the departing brother returned. Also the balance among the states within the circuit would be altered.

181. *See id.* at 19.

182. The Report's lack of sensitivity to this problem is indicated by its suggestion, *id.* at 21 n.3, that the jurisdiction of the National Court "could be extended to cover also intra-circuit conflicts between panels and thus avoid the increasing problems of *en banc* hearings by the courts of appeals." It is hard to see how such problems are avoided by making the litigants go to Washington and placing decision in a body with no more than one member having any familiarity with the "law of the circuit."

port has the merit of avoiding the worst delays incident to a complete new level of appellate courts, an appreciable amount of time would be lost in the 400-odd cases which the National Court would send on to the Supreme Court. Although no new papers need be filed, there would be two sets of considerations whether or not to review, and still further delay in the cases remanded to the National Court for decision.

Finally, there is the stubborn fact that, despite the efforts made to insure that almost all meritorious cases will get to the Supreme Court, the proposal does impair the Supreme Court's control of its own docket. The Court would no longer be a body "in which every member is charged and properly charged with making an independent examination of the right of access to the court."[183] The thrust of the *Report* is that this principle now is served only in name and that the function of initial screening, presently performed with large aid from the clerks, had better be delegated to a court of seven circuit judges, with any three having the right to send a case forward, which would also engage in a very limited amount of decision making.

If the National Court is to do only this, the *Report* does not make a sufficient case for its creation at the present time. If it is to do more, along with the problem of burden, there would have to be a method of appointment designed to recruit and keep the best circuit judges—with the attendant dangers which the computerized method of selection and rapid rotation are meant to avoid. The greatest contribution made by the *Report* is in thus revealing the painful choices that will confront the country, at the Supreme Court level, if decisions by the courts of appeals and petitions to review them were to double, as they will unless fundamental corrective action is taken to prevent this.

183. Dick v. New York Life Ins. Co., *supra*, 359 U.S. at 460 (Frankfurter, J., dissenting).

PART III

The Minimum Model Today

THE FIRST STEP in determining the proper scope of lower federal court jurisdiction must be to consider that central core of cases over which such courts must have power. Only when we have perceived the magnitude of the tasks which these cases pose can we properly determine what cases must be eliminated as having too low an order of priority even if a federal forum possessed some modicum of value or what cases should be placed in specialized courts.

A good way to begin is to go back to the minimum model sketched in the first section, take up some of the heads of jurisdiction there listed, see what they amount to in this day and age, and consider whether, granted that generally they must remain in the federal courts, there should be changes in the way they are handled.

The very first subject, enforcement of federal criminal law, takes us into an area of acute controversy. While no one disputes the general proposition that enforcement of federal criminal law is a proper subject of federal jurisdiction, and indeed today that the federal courts should have exclusive jurisdiction over federal prosecutions,[1] there is much debate whether too many matters have not been swept into the federal penal code. There can be no controversy over what, until the Civil War, had been the exclusive subject of federal criminal jurisdiction—"acts directly injurious to the central government"[2]—revenue frauds, interference with or misdeeds by

---

1. For the contrary practice employed in some instances in earlier days, see pp. 8–9 *supra*. I perceive scant merit in the idea of a cession of jurisdiction to the state courts over minor federal crimes. If they are too minor to warrant federal court jurisdiction, they should not be federal crimes.

2. L. B. Schwartz, *Federal Criminal Jurisdiction and Prosecutors' Dis-*

federal officers, counterfeiting United States securities and coins,[3] espionage and treason. There can be equally little argument about the next step taken beyond this, the Civil Rights legislation prescribing criminal sanctions against those who refused to recognize the changes wrought by the Civil War and the three amendments of the Reconstruction period.[4] Again, there is no unreasonable expansion of federal criminal jurisdiction when Congress takes over substantive regulation of a field and decides that criminal as well as civil sanctions are desirable.[5] The antitrust laws and the securities laws are sufficient examples.

A very different question is posed when the primary basis for federal criminal jurisdiction is the use of facilities crossing state lines provided by the federal government or by private enterprises or, for that matter, when the defendant has crossed a state line on his own power. The progenitor appears to have been three provisions in the Post Office act of 1872, making the use of the mails to promote frauds[6] or lotteries,[7] or to disseminate obscenity,[8] federal crimes. The

cretion, 13 LAW & CONTEMP. PROB. 64, 65 (1948). This valuable article is updated by Abrams, *Consultant's Report on Jurisdiction*: Chapter 2, in I WORKING PAPERS OF THE NATIONAL COMMISSION ON REFORM OF FEDERAL CRIMINAL LAWS 33 (1970).

3. Indeed, the Constitution itself expressly authorizes Congress to punish counterfeiting. U.S. CONST. art. I, § 8, cl. 6.

4. Act of May 31, 1870, ch. 114, § 6, 16 Stat. 141, *as amended*, 18 U.S.C. § 241; Act of May 31, 1870, ch. 114, § 17, 16 Stat. 144, *as amended*, 18 U.S.C. § 242; Act of Mar. 1, 1875, ch. 114, § 4, 18 Stat. 336, *as amended*, 18 U.S.C. § 243.

5. This does not mean that the use of criminal sanctions is always desirable. Attorney General Mitchell in his address to the American Bar Association at London noted the increasing tendency of Congress to pass regulatory statutes dependent on enforcement by criminal proceedings, as distinguished from leaving the matter to a regulatory agency. *In Quest of Speedy Justice* 7 (July 16, 1971). Since the Department of Justice cannot possibly prosecute every violation, such statutes must require it to set up internal arrangements to determine which cases should be prosecuted. While something can and should be done by promulgating guidelines, a good deal must still be left to discretion, generally exercised in secret. See, as to the latter, DAVIS, DISCRETIONARY JUSTICE 17–19, 216–17 (1969) and, as to the propriety of the criminal sanction in one important area, AREEDA, ANTITRUST ANALYSIS 28–30 (1967).

6. Ch. 335, § 301, 17 Stat. 323, *as amended*, 18 U.S.C. § 1341.

7. Ch. 335, § 149, 17 Stat. 302, *as amended*, 18 U.S.C. § 1302.

8. Ch. 335, § 148, 17 Stat. 302, *as amended*, 18 U.S.C. § 1461.

progeny spawned by this statute is enormous; more than three closely printed pages of the index to the Criminal Code are required to list the federal offenses that can result from using the mails to transmit various things, ranging from articles designed for producing abortion to dangerous weapons. The similar development with respect to movement in interstate commerce seems to have begun in 1910 with the Mann Act,[9] followed shortly by the National Motor Vehicle Theft Act of 1919.[10] These statutes also have given rise to a population explosion, often sparked by a *cause célèbre* such as the Lindbergh kidnapping.[11] One might have thought the limit was reached in the so-called Travel Act of 1961,[12] but that was not to be so. Congress has since enacted statutes which make certain activities criminal on the basis of its determination that they *affect* interstate commerce, even though the acts in the particular case were entirely local, and the Supreme Court has sustained this.[13] Along with this has come an expanded notion of what constitutes interference with Government property; an example is the expansion of the statute against robbery of a national bank to include all banks which are members of the Federal Reserve System or whose deposits are insured by the Federal Deposit Insurance Corporation, any federal savings and loan association, any savings and loan association insured by the Federal Savings and Loan Insurance Corporation, and federal credit unions and certain other savings institutions.[14] This means almost all institutions in any way engaged in banking or the handling of savings. It is thus fair to say that today "[t]here is practically no offense within the purview of local law that does not become a federal crime if some distinctive federal involvement happens to be present"[15]—and the involvement may be exceedingly thin. The interest of the United

9. Ch. 395, 36 Stat. 825, *as amended*, 18 U.S.C. §§ 2421–24.

10. Ch. 89, 41 Stat. 324, *as amended*, 18 U.S.C. §§ 2311–13.

11. This led to the Act of June 22, 1932, ch. 271, 47 Stat. 326, *as amended*, 18 U.S.C. §§ 1201–02.

12. 75 Stat. 498, *as amended*, 18 U.S.C. § 1952.

13. *E.g.*, the loan-sharking statute, Consumer Credit Protection Act, tit. II, 82 Stat. 159 (1968), 18 U.S.C. §§ 891–96, upheld in Perez v. United States, 402 U.S. 146 (1971).

14. Act of Aug. 3, 1950, ch. 516, 64 Stat. 394; Act of April 8, 1952, ch. 164, 66 Stat. 46; Act of Sept. 22, 1959, § 2, 73 Stat. 639; Act of Oct. 19, 1970, § 8, 84 Stat. 1017; *all now codified at*, 18 U.S.C. § 2113.

15. Abrams, *supra* note 2, at 36.

States in the theft of $100 from a federally insured state savings and loan association is truly minimal.

In this respect as in others, the present condition of the federal criminal code is in utter disarray. Different jurisdictional tests are provided without any sensible basis for distinction. Sometimes the Government must establish that the defendant knew of the jurisdictional basis, sometimes not. Where it must, the prosecutor often relies on inferences, some created by statute, others (like that relating to possession of stolen property) going back to the common law. An enormous amount of the time of appellate courts has been spent in deciding whether allowance of these inferences is constitutional and whether the trial judge has charged them in exactly the right way. But these are problems that can be met by better drafting; the real issues lie deeper.

The question whether federal criminal prosecutions have not greatly outreached any true federal interest thus deserves the most serious examination, particularly in light of the tremendous increases in criminal filings in 1972. Why should the federal government care if a Manhattan businessman takes his mistress to sleep with him in Greenwich, Connecticut, although it would not if the love-nest were in Port Chester, N.Y.?[16] Why should it make a difference that a New York pimp chooses Newark, N.J., rather than Nyack, N.Y., as the place where his employees transact their business? If the house is in Nyack, why is the United States interested because the girls have traveled over the George Washington bridge and thence through New Jersey although it would not be if they crossed the Hudson over the New York Thruway? Why should the federal government be concerned with a $100 robbery from a federally insured savings bank although it is not if someone burned down Macy's? Is it right to have so many areas where local law enforcement officers can neglect their responsibilities on the basis of an expectation that the "federals" will do the job? On the other hand, is it right that there should be so many federal offenses which go unprosecuted because of secret administrative decisions, very likely sensible in most instances, that no sufficient federal interest is at stake? The Department of Justice has sought to enunciate some standards by instructions to United States Attorneys,

16. While ordinarily these cases are not prosecuted, the potential remains.

but generally these are not known to the public, surface only rarely,[17] are necessarily worded in rather general terms, and are not effectively policed.[18]

The Final Report of the National Commission on Reform of the Federal Criminal Laws, rendered in January 1971, is to be praised for having grasped the nettle. Whether it has done this successfully is another matter. So far as concerns what I have called the drafting difficulties, it has succeeded brilliantly. Section 201 sets up a series of "common jurisdictional bases," and the various substantive sections, except where the jurisdictional basis is obvious, designate just which of the series afford federal jurisdiction over a particular crime.[19] Furthermore, "culpability is not required with respect to any fact which is solely a basis for federal jurisdiction";[20] in other words, if goods have in fact been stolen from interstate commerce, it is not necessary for the Government to prove that the thief or a recipient who knows the goods are stolen also knows they were stolen from interstate commerce. A more controversial provision is the so-called "piggy-back" clause whereby in certain cases federal jurisdiction exists if "the offense is committed in the course of committing or in immediate flight from the commission of any other offense defined in this Code . . . ."[21] This would mean, for example, that persons killing civil rights workers could be prosecuted for homicide rather than merely for violations of the civil rights laws—a result which in that instance I would regard as highly desirable.

For the larger problems of creating standards that will keep

17. As in Redmond v. United States, 384 U.S. 264 (1966), where the Solicitor General successfully moved to have an obscenity conviction vacated because the United States Attorney had brought the prosecution in violation of a departmental memorandum.

18. *See* Abrams, *supra* note 2, at 58–60.

Decision whether the prosecution should be in federal or state court may be highly consequential to the accused. Sometimes the federal penalty is higher than the state's, sometimes lower. There may also be different attitudes with respect to plea bargaining.

19. *See, e.g.,* § 1616, dealing with menacing, which is a federal offense if any one of four of the jurisdictional bases of § 201 exists.

20. Section 204.

21. Section 201(b). This reform is supported by Note, *Piggyback Jurisdiction in the Proposed Federal Criminal Code*, 81 YALE L.J. 1209 (1972). For a *dubitante* view, see Note, *The Proposed Federal Criminal Code*, 47 N.Y.U.L. REV. 320, 325–32 (1972).

federal criminal jurisdiction within bounds and assure some uniformity in its application, the proposed Code relies on a section entitled "Discretionary Restraint in Exercise of Concurrent Jurisdiction."[22] This deserves quotation:

§ 207.   Discretionary Restraint in Exercise
of Concurrent Jurisdiction.

Notwithstanding the existence of concurrent jurisdiction, federal law enforcement agencies are authorized to decline or discontinue federal enforcement efforts whenever the offense can effectively be prosecuted by nonfederal agencies and it appears that there is no substantial federal interest in further prosecution or that the offense primarily affects state, local or foreign interests. A substantial federal interest exists in the following circumstances, among others:

(a) the offense is serious and state or local law enforcement is impeded by interstate aspects of the case; (b) federal enforcement is believed to be necessary to vindicate federally-protected civil rights; (c) if federal jurisdiction exists under section 201(b), the offense is closely related to the underlying offense, as to which there is a substantial federal interest; (d) an offense apparently limited in its impact is believed to be associated with organized criminal activities extending beyond state lines; (e) state or local law enforcement has been so corrupted as to undermine its effectiveness substantially.

Where federal law enforcement efforts are discontinued in deference to state, local or foreign prosecution, federal agencies are directed to cooperate with state, local or foreign agencies, by providing them with evidence already gathered or otherwise, to the extent that this is practicable without prejudice to federal law enforcement. The Attorney General is authorized to promulgate additional guidelines for the exercise of discretion in employing federal criminal jurisdiction. The presence or absence of a federal interest and any other question relating to the exercise of the discretion referred to in this section are for the prosecuting authorities alone and are not litigable.

With a few exceptions I find it hard to improve on this formulation. I would substitute "directed" for "authorized" in the first sentence. I would make it clear that any guidelines promulgated by the Attorney General shall be published. I would add requirements that before initiating a prosecution in the area of concurrent jurisdiction, the

22. The seeds of this formulation can apparently be found in a memorandum of Professor Herbert Wechsler, which led to a set of standards set forth in Schwartz, *supra*, 13 LAW & CONTEMP. PROB. at 73.

United States Attorney should report to the Attorney General what the substantial federal interest is; that the Attorney General should establish a section in the Department to review such reports and direct the prompt termination of any prosecutions not in accord with the standards; and that the Attorney General should report annually to Congress with respect to his administration of the section.

When all this is said, I still have an uneasy feeling that, even with the salutary restraints proposed by the new Code, federal criminal jurisdiction will be too frequently invoked. The Founding Fathers, I think, would have been surprised to find the federal courts trying cases of corruption in the New York City administration[23] simply because one of the participants had rowed across the Hudson in the course of the criminal venture. Yet would one want truly serious offenses to go unprosecuted because of corruption or even extreme slackness in state or local law enforcement if a basis for federal criminal jurisdiction exists?[24] Since I have been unable to think of any better solution of this dilemma than the Commission has proposed, save for the few suggestions just noted, I end on a note of applause, of hope that its recommendations in this respect will be enacted, and of prayer that the Attorney General and United States Attorneys will exercise a real sense of restraint, having in mind the over-burdened dockets of the federal courts.[25]

23. *See* United States v. Corallo, 413 F.2d 1306 (2d Cir.), *cert. denied*, 396 U.S. 958, 963 (1969); United States v. DeSapio, 435 F.2d 272 (2d Cir. 1970), *cert. denied*, 402 U.S. 999 (1971).

24. In the cases cited at note 23, *supra*, there was nothing to suggest corruption in "local law enforcement"; the New York County District Attorney's office, which under its present leadership has long been above any suspicion of corruption, had been active in both cases before the federal indictments were returned. Whether a state court conviction could have been obtained in the latter case may be more doubtful. But does that really justify the exercise of federal jurisdiction over an essentially local offense?

25. I have not attempted to deal with the broader subject of decreasing criminal business, both federal and state, by eliminating from the catalogue various "victimless" crimes, itself the subject for a lecture series. *See, e.g.*, PACKER, THE LIMITS OF THE CRIMINAL SANCTION 151–52 (1968). In the federal system the principal such offenses are gambling, narcotics and prostitution. My impression is that the United States does not generally prosecute under the various federal gambling statutes unless something more is suspected, even though it cannot be

The second item in the minimum model was civil suits by the United States. Here again there has been an enormous expansion. The Framers' conception was doubtless rather modest. They were thinking primarily of suits to collect the federal revenue; very likely they were also concerned with cases where a state would seek to thwart a federal officer in the performance of his duties, suits to protect the interest of the United States in public lands, and suits to enforce government contracts.

While such jurisdiction remains important, it is a small part of today's total picture. We can pass over the issue of how far the United States has non-statutory power to bring a civil suit to protect vital national interests.[26] Neither shall I take time to comment here on such obvious subjects for civil suits by the Government as actions to protect the navigability of streams and the safety of harbors.[27]

The two areas on which I wish to dwell are the roles of the civil suit by the United States or its agencies in the enforcement of regulatory statutes and in actions to protect civil rights. Of course, I do not question that issues arising under such statutes when enforcement is sought by the Government should at some point be presented to a federal court. But a crucial consideration—especially in terms of the workload of the lower federal courts—is *at what point* a federal court is to become involved.

Two early examples of suits by the United States to enforce

proved. I expect there would be little sentiment for removing the trafficking in "hard" narcotics from the list of federal crimes. Marijuana may be another matter. In 1971, only 36 prosecutions for "white slave traffic" were begun. A.O. ANN. REP., Table D2, at 321 (1971). One must question the usefulness of keeping on the books a statute so infrequently applied.

26. *See* United States v. American Bell Tel. Co., 128 U.S. 315 (1888); *In re* Debs, 158 U.S. 564 (1895); Sanitary Dist. of Chicago v. United States, 266 U.S. 405 (1925). While Justice Harlan properly raised this as an issue requiring decision in New York Times Co. v. United States, 403 U.S. 713, 753–54 (1971) (dissenting opinion), the answer could hardly be doubtful—even apart from the fact that Government property was involved. For an excellent discussion, see Note, *Nonstatutory Executive Authority to Bring Suit*, 85 HARV. L. REV. 1566 (1972).

27. *See* Rivers and Harbors Act of 1899, ch. 425, § 17, 30 Stat. 1153, *now* 33 U.S.C. § 413; Wyandotte Transp. Co. v. United States, 389 U.S. 191 (1967).

regulatory statutes are sections 12(1)[28] and 16(12)[29] of the Interstate Commerce Act and section 4 of the Sherman Act;[30] their successors have been too numerous for citation. I have cited these not only because of their importance and venerability but because they illustrate the different roles thrust upon the courts. When the United States sues to enforce an order of the Commission under section 16(12) of the Interstate Commerce Act, as the Commission itself could do, it is suing to enforce an order made after a trial and a report; the tasks of finding the facts and applying the law have been performed initially by an administrative agency and the role of the courts is not different from that in a suit by the defeated party to enjoin the order.[31] When the Government sues under section 12(1) of the Interstate Commerce Act[32] or, to take more familiar examples, the Department of Justice brings a civil suit under section 4 of the Sherman Act, or the SEC sues under section 20 of the Securities Act[33] or section 21 of the Securities Exchange Act,[34] where no previous administrative proceedings have been had, the entire task, including the laborious task of fact-finding, falls on the court. Everyone knows how substantial a burden this is in the typical Government civil antitrust suit, and I shall return to that point when I consider the possible desirability of a special court for antitrust cases. But the burdens of litigation initiated by other agencies can also be very heavy. *SEC v. Texas Gulf Sulphur Corp.*[35] is a sufficient example. Of course, I do not imply the slightest criticism of the

28. Ch. 104, § 12, 24 Stat. 383 (1887), *as amended*, 49 U.S.C. § 12(1).
29. Ch. 104, § 16, 24 Stat. 384 (1887), *as amended*, 49 U.S.C. § 16(12).
30. Ch. 647, § 4, 26 Stat. 209 (1890), *now* 15 U.S.C. § 4.
31. *Compare* City of New York v. United States, 337 F. Supp. 150, 151 (E.D.N.Y. 1972).
32. *See, e.g.*, United States v. New York, N.H. & H.R.R., 276 F.2d 525 (2d Cir.), *cert. denied*, 362 U.S. 961, 964 (1960).
33. 15 U.S.C. § 77t.
34. 15 U.S.C. § 78u.
35. 258 F. Supp. 262 (S.D.N.Y. 1966), *rev'd in part and aff'd in part*, 401 F.2d 833 (2d Cir. 1968) (en banc), *cert. denied*, 394 U.S. 976 (1969), *on remand*, 312 F. Supp. 77 (S.D.N.Y. 1970), *aff'd in part and remanded in part*, 446 F.2d 1301 (2d Cir.), *cert. denied*, 404 U.S. 1005, *on remand*, 331 F. Supp. 671 (S.D.N.Y. 1971). As is well known, the SEC's action stimulated a host of private suits; a settlement of those in the Southern District of New York has been approved by the district court.

Commission for having initiated this important and path-breaking case. Nevertheless, as a legislative matter, if we are to optimize the concentration of the federal courts on matters of true federal importance, the timing of when questions are heard by a federal court becomes nearly as important as the decision of what questions are to be heard. For this reason—and here I am also ranging into the realm of the private suit—I raise the issue whether it would not be wiser as a general rule to put the tasks of fact-finding and initial application of the law in executive or administrative agencies, not necessarily of the traditional type, rather than in the courts.

While the trend in the recent rash of congressional enactments is the other way, detailed examination of these enactments lends support to my view. For instance, why should enforcement of air quality standards under the Air Quality Control Act originate in the district courts?[36] If the administrative process is competent to establish such standards,[37] it is also capable of determining in the first instance, through agency adjudicatory process, whether those standards have been violated and what remedy or sanction should be imposed. Review of such findings by the courts would be narrow, and initial factual determinations by them, in a highly technical area, would be unnecessary.[38] Similarly, an administrative tribunal rather than a district court would be a more suitable forum for initial enforcement of the Wholesome Meat Act.[39] The technical and speedy determinations required in the enforcement of both these acts suggest the particular appropriateness of using in the first instance the more flexible and specialized administrative forum rather than the formal judicial process. On the other side of the coin, I see nothing to be lost by leaving the federal courts with only appellate jurisdiction in the context of such statutes as these. Proper design of the administrative process can ensure essentially as much impartiality as is

36. *See* Act of Nov. 21, 1967, § 108, 81 Stat. 491, 42 U.S.C. § 1857d(g).

37. *Id.* § 1857d(c)–(1)–(3).

38. For an illustration of the problems encountered by the courts in this type of litigation, see United States v. Bishop Processing Co., 287 F. Supp. 624 (D. Md. 1968), *aff'd*, 423 F.2d 469 (4th Cir.), *cert. denied*, 398 U.S. 904 (1970).

39. 21 U.S.C. §§ 673, 674.

available in the judicial process, while in important factors such as expertise and adaptability the administrative process is to be preferred.

Perhaps I would not feel so strongly that determinations under regulatory statutes normally should be lodged in the first instance in the administrative process if I could discern some meaningful standard which had guided Congress in making jurisdictional allocations between the courts and the agencies. But I cannot. In the long run, the choice has been haphazard. One looking only at recent history might be tempted to say that time provides a watershed. Certainly the statutes of the late 1960's and early 1970's reveal a pronounced tendency to bypass administrative agencies, born, no doubt, of legislative dissatisfaction with their performance. But the lack of any discernible standard for determining whether an issue should first be subjected to administrative processing goes back much further—at least to 1914 when Congress created the Federal Trade Commission and vested it with jurisdiction to enforce the antitrust laws by administrative proceedings followed by court order, while leaving unimpaired the power of the Department of Justice to bring the same issue directly before a court. Another striking instance can be found in the provisions of the Investment Company Act of 1940 relating to "control." An aggrieved person can either apply for a determination by the SEC[40] or proceed directly in court.[41] One would suppose that this was a subject in which the SEC would have expertise and that preliminary resort to that agency should always be required. In fact the SEC has been quite diffident about assuming the decision-making responsibilities ordinarily assigned to independent regulatory agencies. When it recommended to Congress that the management fees of investment companies should be subjected to a standard of "reasonableness,"[42] it proposed that this determination should be made initially, not by itself, but in a suit which it or a shareholder might institute.

40. Phillips v. SEC, 388 F.2d 964 (2d Cir. 1968).
41. Willheim v. Murchison, 342 F.2d 33 (2d Cir.), *cert. denied*, 382 U.S. 840 (1965).
42. REPORT OF THE SECURITIES AND EXCHANGE COMMISSION ON THE PUBLIC POLICY IMPLICATIONS OF INVESTMENT COMPANY GROWTH, H.R. REP. NO. 2337, 89th Cong., 2d Sess. 143–49 (1966).

How far this decision was of policy and how far of politics, I am uninformed.[43]

Beyond this, are we not placing the courts in danger when we ask them to decide essentially political controversies not only without adequate guidelines from Congress but also without action by an agency charged with executing Congress' policies?[44] An injunction issued by a district judge against the construction of a federally sponsored canal, even for the limited period he needed to determine its effects on the environment, drew a comment from the chairman of the Senate Judiciary Committee, through whose state the waterway was to pass, reminiscent of the attack on labor and utility rate injunctions in the early decades of the century.[45] The authors of a valuable comparative study of American and British administrative law have remarked of the tendency of American judges to overrule administrative agencies on policy grounds:[46]

Most British lawyers feel that any such activity must in the long run be damaging to the whole status of judges and the trust reposed in them.

It is equally damaging when the courts must decide in the first instance essentially legislative questions of priorities between economic and aesthetic considerations, where a great deal can be said on either side, and usually is.

Another point to be considered is this: When the fact-finding inevitably involved in initial enforcement is done by a regulatory agency, there is uniformity in approach, at least at any one time. When initial enforcement is entrusted to the courts, the parties are subject to the luck of the draw among hundreds of district judges. While their conclusions of law are subject to review by the courts of appeals and ultimately by the Supreme Court, their findings of

43. The outcome of the battle is § 36(b) of the Investment Company Act of 1940, ch. 686, 54 Stat. 841, 15 U.S.C. § 80a–35(b).

44. *See, e.g.,* District of Columbia Fed'n of Civic Ass'ns v. Volpe, 459 F.2d 1231 (D.C. Cir. 1971); Committee for Nuclear Repsonsibility, Inc. v. Seaborg, 463 F.2d 783 (D.C. Cir. 1971).

45. Senator Eastland of Mississippi accused the judge of "judicial tyranny" and said it was "deplorable that a Federal judge, with one stroke of the pen, has thrown a road block in the way" of the project. N.Y. Times, Sept. 22, 1971, at 34, col. 3.

46. SCHWARTZ & WADE 16. *See id.* 7, 15, 207.

fact enjoy the benefit of the "unless clearly erroneous" rule.[47] There is nothing about this to give concern so long as we are dealing with such "facts" as whether a particular act was or was not done. The problem in the area here being considered arises when the "unless clearly erroneous" rule is extended from basic facts to inferences therefrom.[48] It was doubtless of such findings that Chief Justice Hughes once said:[49]

An unscrupulous administrator might be tempted to say "Let me find the facts for the people of my country, and I care little who lays down the general principles."

A similar remark might be made concerning district judges who, though certainly not "unscrupulous," may be overly enthusiastic or unduly antagonistic with respect to a particular legislative program. I can think of widely differing inferences that might be drawn from the same set of facts by conscientious district judges in our own circuit. It has been suggested that, in order to meet this problem in antitrust cases decided by district courts,[50] the Supreme Court, despite contrary protestations,[51] does not in truth respect the inferences drawn by the trier of facts; the Court will not and probably should not allow its notions of proper antitrust policy to be obstructed by giving nearly conclusive weight to inferences drawn by district judges. Yet the Supreme Court simply cannot police the rulings of the district courts or the courts of appeals in all the new areas being entrusted to them. Even if the "unless clearly erroneous" rule is somewhat eroded by courts of appeals in this area, as I think it inevitably will be, we shall have taken a long step away from the ideal of uniform application of regulatory statutes limned in Mr. Justice White's historic opinion in the *Abilene* case.[52] Still, whether for better

47. F.R. Civ. P. 52(a).
48. *See* United States v. Yellow Cab Co., 338 U.S. 338, 341–42 (1949); CIR v. Duberstein, 363 U.S. 278, 291 (1960).
49. Address to Federal Bar Ass'n, *quoted in* Landis, The Administrative Process 136 (1938).
50. M. Shapiro, Law and Politics in the Supreme Court 293–95 (1964).
51. *See, e.g.*, United States v. Parke, Davis & Co., 362 U.S. 29, 44–45 (1960).
52. Texas & Pac. R.R. v. Abilene Cotton Oil Co., 204 U.S. 426 (1907).

or for worse, these statutes are with us, and we shall undoubtedly have more. They impose an enormous challenge to the federal courts in implementing congressional directives over almost every phase of life.

I pass now to the second category of civil suits by the United States mentioned some time back—suits to enforce statutes relating to civil rights. In 1961, the United States initiated 13 civil rights actions in federal district courts;[53] in 1971 it began 154.[54] The real upswing began to become evident in 1967.[55] This reflects the commencement of substantial enforcement of the initial civil rights legislation of the 1960's which ultimately included the Civil Rights Act of 1964,[56] the Voting Rights Act of 1965,[57] and the Housing Rights Act of 1968.[58] The federal courts could have no better business than this; Congress has made a clear and altogether appropriate policy determination that they are the proper forum for passing authoritatively upon official efforts to eradicate private discrimination in a variety of contexts, and the official nature of the suit safeguards against an inundation of trivial cases, although here again something could be said in favor of requiring prior administrative action. The work of the federal courts under such statutes has been extraordinarily valuable and will become more so. I might cite as one of many examples an opinion of one of my colleagues in a case dealing with whether a great steel producer, which had concededly engaged in racially discriminatory employment practices in the past, had taken sufficient steps to remove their effects.[59] On the other hand, this

See the remarks of Chief Justice Taft in his eulogy of his predecessor, 257 U.S. xi, xxv–xxvi (1922).

53. A.O. ANN. REP., Table C2, at 238 (1961).

54. A.O. ANN. REP., Table C2, at 262 (1971).

55. In 1965, 40 civil rights suits were initiated by the federal government; in 1966, the number was 60. In subsequent years, the figures for such suits are as follows: 1967—106; 1968—68; 1969—137; 1970 —126; 1971—154; 1972—132. All figures from A.O. ANN. REP., Table C2, for the respective year.

56. 78 Stat. 241, 42 U.S.C. §§ 2000a–2000h.

57. 79 Stat. 437, *as amended*, 42 U.S.C. §§ 1973–1973bb.

58. 82 Stat. 81, 42 U.S.C. §§ 3601–19.

59. United States v. Bethlehem Steel Corp., 446 F.2d 652 (2d Cir. 1971) (Feinberg, J.). For other fine opinions on this subject, see Robinson v. Lorillard Corp., 444 F.2d 791 (4th Cir.) (Sobeloff, J.), *cert. dismissed*, 404 U.S. 1006 (1971), and United States v. Jacksonville

lengthy and complex opinion is sufficient testimony to the fact that while even the present level of civil rights litigation by the federal government is not particularly large—especially in the context of the total business of the federal district courts—mere numbers do not by any means reflect the amount of judicial effort that such cases consume.[60] Opinions like this one are not written overnight.

The next category in my minimum model consisted of suits against the United States[61] or its officers. These also will increase, not merely by natural growth but as a result of statutory change. The Federal Tort Claims Act is overdue for overhaul to eliminate some exceptions and clarify others;[62] here we could well draw a leaf from the English book. Also, as stated by Professor Davis, "[j]urisdiction of the Court of Claims and of the district courts under the Tucker Act should be rounded out to terminate the uncertainty as to governmental liability for breach of contracts implied in law."[63] Jurisdiction over suits against federal officers has been expanded by the salutary 1962 enactment[64] giving the district courts "original jurisdiction of any action in the nature of mandamus to compel an officer of the United States or an agency thereof to perform a duty owed to the plaintiff," and the courts have displayed considerable ingenuity[65] in

Terminal Co., 451 F.2d 418 (5th Cir. 1971) (Dyer, J.), where a dissenting judge paid the unusual tribute of remarking on "the prodigious labor and the prolonged consideration which went into the production of the majority opinion . . . ." 451 F.2d at 460.

60. *See also Developments in the Law—Employment Discrimination and Title VII of the Civil Rights Act of 1964*, 84 HARV. L. REV. 1109, 1230–31 (1971).

61. The principal provision is 28 U.S.C. § 1346.

62. As to the extent of such overhaul, see the conflicting views in SCHWARTZ & WADE 194–98, and in 3 DAVIS, ADMINISTRATIVE LAW TREATISE § 25.08–.17, at 467–505 (1958), § 25.18, at 868–70 (Supp. 1970) and § 27.00–1, at 899 (Supp. 1970).

63. *Id.* § 27.00–1, at 899 (Supp. 1970).

64. 76 Stat. 744, 28 U.S.C. § 1361.

65. *See* Ashe v. McNamara, 355 F.2d 277 (1st Cir. 1965) (ordering reconsideration of prior Army discharge); Walker v. Blackwell, 360 F.2d 66 (5th Cir. 1966) (ordering reconsideration by prison officials of charges of religious discrimination); Feliciano v. Laird, 426 F.2d 424 (2d Cir. 1970) (ordering Army to reconsider hardship discharge application); *see* Byse and Fiocca, *Section 1361 of the Mandamus and Venue Act of 1962 and "Nonstatutory" Judicial Review of Federal Administrative Action*, 81 HARV. L. REV. 308 (1967).

eroding what the Department of Justice conceived to be limiting language.[66] The Administrative Conference and the ABA have joined in recommending a bill that would practically eliminate any issue of sovereign immunity in any federal action seeking relief other than money damages and stating a claim that an agency or an officer or employee thereof "acted or failed to act in an official capacity or under color of legal authority."[67] Whatever may be thought about a requirement of jurisdictional amount in federal question cases generally, it clearly has no proper place in actions against federal officers, as Professor Wechsler pointed out long ago.[68] The field of "unreviewable administrative action" seems bound to shrink.[69] Also the relaxation in the requirement of standing to which I have referred and will again discuss,[70] and similar judicial attitudes with respect to ripeness,[71] will bring many more cases of administrative action, or inaction, before the courts than in a former day. These new opportunities will be fullly used:[72]

> In recent years, indeed, Americans have more and more come to expect their courts to perform a virtual ombudsman function, turning to them to correct governmental malfunctioning which the political branches have proved unable or unwilling to correct.

Quite as important as the increased volume of review of the action of federal agencies is the heightened complexity of the problems on which the courts must rule. I do not mean to suggest that

---

66. 1962 U.S. CODE CONG. & AD. NEWS 2784, 2788–90.
67. *See* RECOMMENDATIONS AND REPORTS OF THE ADMINISTRATIVE CONFERENCE OF THE UNITED STATES, vol. 1, at 190 *et seq.*; DAVIS, ADMINISTRATIVE LAW TREATISE § 27.00–8, at 916 (Supp. 1970); Cramton, *Nonstatutory Review of Federal Administrative Action: The Need for Statutory Reform of Sovereign Immunity, Subject Matter Jurisdiction, and Parties Defendant*, 68 MICH. L. REV. 387 (1970).
68. Wechsler, *Federal Jurisdiction and the Revision of the Judicial Code*, 13 LAW & CONTEMP. PROB. 216, 225–26 (1948). The Administrative Conference has also recommended this change, *supra* note 67, at 169 *et seq.*
69. *See* DAVIS, ADMINISTRATIVE LAW TREATISE § 28 (Supp. 1970).
70. *See* p. 20 *supra* and pp. 113–16 *infra*.
71. An extreme example is Environmental Defense Fund, Inc. v. Ruckelshaus, 439 F.2d 584 (D.C. Cir. 1971). *See also* Medical Committee for Human Rights v. SEC, 432 F.2d 659 (D.C. Cir. 1970), *rev'd as moot*, 404 U.S. 403 (1972).
72. SCHWARTZ & WADE 207.

administrative review in the past was always a simple matter; one might instance the Supreme Court's review of an ICC "order that readjusts the class rates of the whole country barring only the territory west of the Rockies . . . ."[73] But, by and large, such cases were exceptional for the lower courts, save for the Court of Appeals for the District of Columbia Circuit. In the 1970's review has taken the federal courts far more deeply into the intricacies of federal action. In a well-known case our court had to consider whether the FPC had properly weighed, on the one hand, the needs of New York City for a quickly accessible supply of reserve electric power and the suitability of the method proposed for furnishing this, and, on the other side, a variety of adverse aesthetic effects, the invasion of a wilderness area, the impact on the Hudson River fishery, air pollution and, ultimately, danger to New York City's water supply.[74] Our brothers in the Third Circuit have held that the Department of Housing and Urban Development is under an affirmative obligation to utilize institutionalized methods to ascertain social and racial effects before authorizing federal mortgage guarantees and rent supplements for a project for moderate income tenants.[75] One could readily multiply examples. In the review of administrative determinations, as previously noted in the case of direct enforcement by the Government, the federal courts have become the arbiters of social policy in those frequent instances where Congress has not spelled out its intentions with sufficient precision and detail. I happen to think we have gone too far down this road. In the words of Edward H. Levi, President of the University of Chicago:[76]

But the concerns of a system of law cannot be limited to the work or reactions of courts. This overemphasis upon courts skews the question of

---

73. New York v. United States, 331 U.S. 284, 352 (1947) (dissenting opinion).
74. Scenic Hudson Preservation Conference v. FPC, 453 F.2d 463 (2d Cir. 1971), *cert. denied*, 407 U.S. 926 (1972). *See* Murphy, *The National Environmental Policy Act and the Licensing Process: Environmentalist Magna Carta or Agency Coup de Grace?*, 72 COLUM. L. REV. 963 (1972).
75. Shannon v. HUD, 436 F.2d 809 (3d Cir. 1970). *See* Comment, 46 N.Y.U.L. REV. 560 (1971).
76. Levi, *The Crisis in the Nature of Law*, 25 RECORD OF N.Y.C.B.A. 121, 139 (1970).

public policy and gives to the courts burdens which among the agencies of government and private life they are often least qualified to carry.

But neither President Levi nor I will arrest the trend whereby, as has been said:[77]

American judges tend to feel that they are no less qualified than the administrator to determine many questions of policy where they involve broad social considerations rather than narrow technical matters. This tendency has accelerated as the judges, like the citizenry generally, have become increasingly disenchanted with the claims of administrative expertise.

Courts charged with such delicate and important tasks—and here the burden falls most acutely on the courts of appeals—must have time for study, reflection and discussion and not feel compelled, as they now often do, to rush to decision on a production-line basis.[78]

The other items in my minimum model were admiralty, bankruptcy, patents and copyrights—the last three entirely and the first mainly subjects of exclusive federal jurisdiction. While aficionados of these subjects would doubtless find fertile ground for exploring them, I shall content myself at this point with the reminder that they are and, except as I shall later propose with respect to patents,[79] will remain heads of business for the federal courts that are sizeable in volume and difficulty, and often require a high degree of expertise. Since most federal judges do not possess this on their induction, they must have time to acquire it on the job.

In summary, even the minimum model supplies the federal courts today with a large and rapidly growing bundle of cases, a goodly number of which require an unusually large investment of judicial time. While this is an area where there cannot be retraction in the jurisdictional grant, two points have emerged from this discussion. The Department of Justice owes an obligation to the federal courts to take a considerably harder look at the initiation of federal prosecutions for acts that also constitute crimes against the states. The Administrative Conference should undertake a review of recent federal

77. SCHWARTZ & WADE 248.
78. There might well also be increasing need for consideration en banc. Determination of issues of such magnitude should not depend on the luck of the draw.
79. *See* pp. 154–61 *infra*.

legislation to see how far it may be feasible and desirable to interpose administrative determinations before proceedings are begun in the courts. It should keep a watchful eye over future legislation to the same end.[80]

80. In its most recent report, the Administrative Conference indicates that it has already undertaken this task in some degree. ADMINISTRATIVE CONFERENCE OF THE UNITED STATES, 1971–72 REPORT 4 (1972).

PART IV

Civil Rights Actions—and herein of Abstention, Comity and Exhaustion

WHILE the minimum model is thus by no means a modest grant of jurisdiction under conditions of the present day, there must be almost universal agreement that the federal courts should have large powers to entertain private as well as public actions involving questions arising under the Constitution, laws and treaties of the United States. It has long been a source of astonishment that, save for the ill-fated Federalist Judiciary Act of 1801,[1] there was no general grant of such jurisdiction until 1875.[2] Perhaps the outstanding category of federal question jurisdiction today consists of private actions charging violations of federal civil rights, a category where jurisdiction had been given, shortly after the war between the states, nearly a decade before the general grant.[3] But the proposition that the federal courts must have "large powers" to hear even civil rights cases is extremely general; ultimately we must confront the inevitable question, "How large?" While the answer is highly consequential with respect to the burdens on the federal courts since the volume of private civil rights litigation has grown tremendously in recent years,[4] the problem is not merely one of volume. A complete answer

1. Act of Feb. 13, 1801, ch. 4, § 11, 2 Stat. 92, *repealed by* Act of March 8, 1802, ch. 8, § 1, 2 Stat. 132.
2. Act of March 3, 1875, ch. 137, § 1, 18 Stat. 470, *as amended*, 28 U.S.C. § 1331. The development is traced in HART & WECHSLER 727–33.
3. *See* HART & WECHSLER 728–29.
4. In 1961, there were 270 private civil rights cases filed in federal district courts. A.O. ANN. REP., Table C2, at 238 (1961). By 1966, the number of such filings had risen to 1,154, A.O. ANN. REP., Table C2, at 171 (1966); three years later, in 1969, the figure was 2,180, A.O. ANN. REP., Table C2, at 206 (1969). In the past three

involves the appropriate reach of federal civil rights jurisdiction—
i.e., what subjects should be within it, the appropriate timing of the
exercise of the jurisdiction—*i.e.*, when should matters within it be
heard by a federal court, and, most important of all, accommodation
and reconciliation between the states and the nation. Initial reference
of private civil rights disputes to state administrative or judicial processes may either eliminate the need for any federal judicial action[5]
or significantly affect the posture of a dispute when it does appear
in federal court.[6] At the same time, it provides a means for permitting participation in the resolution of such disputes by bodies other
than the federal courts, which have a substantial and legitimate concern. Finally, in an area in which individual feelings often run high,
initial deferral to non-judicial processes may have the salutary consequence that a noncoercive resolution of a dispute is achieved.

Rather than proceed directly to the ubiquitous section 1983, of
which more hereafter, let me begin with two instances where Congress has made rather elaborate provision for the protection of civil
rights, Title VII of the Civil Rights Act of 1964,[7] the fair employment provisions, and Title VIII of the Civil Rights Act of 1968,[8]
the fair housing provisions.[9] As a prerequisite to suit under Title
VII, a private person must first give the Equal Employment Opportunity Commission (EEOC) 60 days in which to attempt voluntary
conciliation of any complaint of employment discrimination.[10] In

years, the figures have been 3,586, 4,609, and 5,482. A.O. ANN.
REP., Table C2 (1970, 1971 & 1972). These figures do not include
civil rights actions by prisoners.
5. *See* p. 92 *infra.*
6. *See* p. 101 *infra.*
7. 78 Stat. 253, 42 U.S.C. §§ 2000e to 2000e–15, *as amended by* Equal
Employment Opportunity Act of 1972, 86 Stat. 103.
8. 82 Stat. 81, 42 U.S.C. §§ 3601–19.
9. Federal jurisdiction over private actions to enjoin violations of Title
II of the 1964 Act, the public accommodations provision, was also
expressly established. 42 U.S.C. § 2000a–3(a). In Title IV of the
1964 Act, the school desegregation provision, which authorizes the
Attorney General to institute suits on the complaints of private
parties who are unable to sue themselves, 42 U.S.C. § 2000c–6, the
preexisting right of private parties to sue is expressly preserved, 42
U.S.C. § 2000c–8.
10. While the statute provides for only a 30-day waiting period, 42

addition, where a state or local authority capable of dealing with the alleged discrimination exists, the EEOC must defer to it for a period of 60 days.[11] Title VIII created no special commission to deal with housing discrimination; rather it authorized the filing of complaints with the Secretary of HUD[12] who has at least 30 days in which to attempt conciliation.[13] As in Title VII, reference to any available state authority is required before the federal administrative authority may act,[14] and here deferral is not for any fixed time period but can be indefinite.[15] Whether resort to these procedures was intended to be a prerequisite to suit under Title VIII—as is the case under Title VII—is unclear.[16] It has been said that the private enforcement

U.S.C. § 2000e–5(e), the EEOC, under authority contained in the law, has extended the waiting period to an automatic 60 days in all cases, 29 C.F.R. § 1601.25a(a) (1972). *See Developments in the Law—Employment Discrimination and Title VII of the Civil Rights Act of 1964*, 84 HARV. L. REV. 1109, 1201 n.43 (1971). *See generally id.* at 1202–04. The Supreme Court has already been obliged to deal with problems under these sections. Love v. Pullman Co., 404 U.S. 522 (1972). *See also* Vigil v. American Tel. & Tel. Co., 455 F.2d 1222 (10th Cir. 1972).

11. 42 U.S.C. § 2000e–5(b).
12. *Id.* § 3610(a).
13. *Id.* § 3610(d).
14. *Id.* § 3610(c).
15. So long as the state or local official "has, within thirty days from the date the alleged offense has been brought to his attention, commenced proceedings in the matter, or, having done so, carries forward such proceedings with reasonable promptness," the Secretary of HUD may not act. *Id.* There is, in other words, no time limit in which state or local authorities must achieve a result before federal officials may step in.
16. While 42 U.S.C. § 3610(d) conditions initiation of a federal judicial action on having allowed the Secretary of HUD 30 days to attempt conciliation, on having allowed any state or local action to be completed, and also on the absence of a substantial equivalent state and local judicial remedies, 42 U.S.C. § 3612 arguably provides an alternative jurisdictional basis for a private action, one essentially free of the prerequisites to suit under § 3610(d). *See* Note, *Discrimination in Employment and in Housing: Private Enforcement Provisions of the Civil Rights Acts of 1964 and 1968*, 82 HARV. L. REV. 834, 839, 855–59 (1969). Several district courts have so held. *See* Brown v. Lo Duca, 307 F. Supp. 102 (E.D. Wis. 1969); Johnson v. Decker, 333 F. Supp. 88 (N.D. Cal. 1971); Crim v. Glover, 338 F. Supp. 823 (S.D. Ohio 1972); Holmgren v. Little Village Community Reporter, 342 F. Supp. 512 (N.D. Ill. 1971). *See also* dicta

schemes under both Title VII and Title VIII are "the result of a political compromise, a product more of the desire for passage than the desire for a rational scheme for uprooting discrimination."[17] Whether the enforcement schemes were more imbued by a desire to impede access of individuals to the federal judiciary or by an effort to secure participation of state and local authorities in resolving disputes of local concern and to settle disputes by consent rather than by coercion whenever possible is not for me to say. Even if the enforcement schemes were political compromises, Congress was on the right track in endeavoring to accommodate the various interests involved before permitting resort to the federal courts.

There was some early concern that in the case of Title VIII, the fair housing statute, the congressional train was going to be derailed even before it got underway by the Supreme Court's decision in *Jones v. Alfred H. Mayer Co.*,[18] giving unsuspected meaning to the long quiescent section 1982,[19] the roots of which are in section 1 of the Civil Rights Act of 1866.[20] A classic example of poor timing, the Court's determination that section 1982 reached private racial discrimination in the sale or rental of housing came on the eve of the effectiveness of the anti-private discrimination provisions of Title VIII.[21] The decision was not received as a model of judicial crafts-

in Waters v. Wisconsin Steel Works of Int'l Harvester Co., 427 F.2d 476, 486 n.17 (7th Cir.), *cert. denied*, 400 U.S. 911 (1970); Trafficante v. Metropolitan Life Ins. Co., 446 F.2d 1158, 1161 (9th Cir. 1971), *rev'd*, 41 U.S.L.W. 4071 (Dec. 7, 1972). In addition, the United States Commission on Civil Rights assumes that § 3612 allows a complainant to "bypass the administrative process entirely and institute litigation in the first instance." *See* UNITED STATES COMMISSION ON CIVIL RIGHTS, FEDERAL CIVIL RIGHTS ENFORCEMENT EFFORT 146 (1971) [hereinafter cited as FEDERAL EFFORT].

17. Note, *supra*, 82 HARV. L. REV. at 835. *See generally* Vass, *Title VII: Legislative History*, 7 B.C. IND. & COM. L. REV. 431 (1966).

18. 392 U.S. 409 (1968).

19. 42 U.S.C. § 1982 reads as follows:

All citizens of the United States shall have the same right, in every State and Territory, as is enjoyed by white citizens thereof to inherit, purchase, lease, sell, hold, and convey real and personal property.

20. Act of April 9, 1866, ch. 31, § 1, 14 Stat. 27.

21. *Jones* was handed down on June 17, 1968; Title VIII's prohibition against private discrimination became effective January 1, 1969, *see* 42 U.S.C. § 3603(a)(2).

manship. The Court's reading of section 1982,[22] its review of the legislative history surrounding the statute's enactment,[23] and its analysis of relevant prior decisional law[24] were carefully weighed and found by most scholars to be wanting.[25] So far as history is concerned, the final blow has been struck by Professor Fairman in his definitive volume on the Reconstruction Court.[26] However, the Supreme Court can make history read as it wishes, and no purpose would be served by venturing here into this battle ground. There is, though, a further aspect of *Jones* which is highly relevant to my subject—the impact of the Court's exhumation of section 1982 on the deferral and administrative conciliation provisions of Title VIII.[27]

22. *See* Henkin, *The Supreme Court, 1967 Term, Foreword: On Drawing Lines*, 82 HARV. L. REV. 63, 85–86 (1968); Casper, *Jones v. Mayer: Clio, Bemused and Confused Muse*, 1968 SUP. CT. REV. 89, 96–99; *The Supreme Court, 1967 Term*, 82 HARV. L. REV. 63, 96 (1968).

23. *See* Casper, *supra*, 1968 SUP. CT. REV. at 111–22; *The Supreme Court, 1967 Term, supra*, 82 HARV. L. REV. at 97–101.

24. *See* Henkin, *supra*, 82 HARV. L. REV. at 87 & n.79; Casper, *supra*, 1968 SUP. CT. REV. at 125–29.

25. *But cf.* Kinoy, *The Constitutional Right of Negro Freedom Revisited: Some First Thoughts on* Jones v. Alfred H. Mayer Company, 22 RUTGERS L. REV. 537 (1968).

26. FAIRMAN, HISTORY OF THE SUPREME COURT OF THE UNITED STATES, VOL. VI: RECONSTRUCTION AND REUNION 1864–88, at 1207–58 (1971). See the writer's review in 87 POL. SCI. Q. 439, 445–47 (1972).

27. Perhaps of even greater concern was the fact that unlike Title VIII, § 1982 contains no exemptions of any sort for private clubs and religious organizations, *compare* 42 U.S.C. § 3607, or for owners of rental housing with less than five units or of one-family dwellings sold without the use of a real estate broker, *compare* 42 U.S.C. § 3603(b). *See* Casper, *supra*, 1968 SUP. CT. REV. at 130–32. This unfortunate conflict could be avoided if the Court would accept, and extend to the Fair Housing Provisions of the 1968 Act, the Fourth Circuit's holding that an exception to the ban on racial discrimination in the public accommodation provisions of the Civil Rights Act of 1964 "of necessity operates as an exception to the Act of 1866, in any cases where that Act prohibits the same conduct which is saved as lawful by the terms of the 1964 Act." Tillman v. Wheaton-Haven Recreation Ass'n, 451 F.2d 1211, 1214 (4th Cir. 1971), *cert. granted*, 406 U.S. 916 (1972) (No. 71-1136). It is useful to note that § 1982 reaches only racial discrimination whereas Title VIII reaches discrimination on the basis of not only race but also religion and national origin. 42 U.S.C. § 3604.

Moreover, if 42 U.S.C. § 3612(a) does indeed allow direct

If the decision posed serious threats on these scores, Congress should not shrink from overruling it, even with the near certainty that such action would be seriously misunderstood both by those seeking to end discrimination in housing and by those seeking to preserve it.

Experience up to this time does not indicate that *Jones* has had anything like the effect that might have been imagined. In the five years since *Jones* was decided, only twenty-eight decisions under section 1982 have been annotated in the U.S. Code. Such figures not only make quite doubtful that private suits under section 1982 have doomed the administrative conciliation and state and local participation provisions of Title VIII but raise a more important question. With the expansive reading given section 1982 in *Jones* and the generous remedial gloss subsequently imposed in *Sullivan v. Little Hunting Park, Inc.*,[28] one must wonder where the suitors are. The explanation does not lie in the fact that the actions are being instituted under Title VIII; only sixteen additional housing rights actions are annotated in the U.S. Code under the private enforcement provisions of Title VIII. Rather the important conclusion to be drawn from all of this is that private judicial action is not generally a very satisfactory mechanism for dealing with individual instances of housing discrimination. It requires an extraordinary amount of motivation on the part of an individual to pursue even nearly certain victory with respect to housing through the process of formal litigation. He must secure legal assistance, perhaps incur substantial expenses,[29] and await completion of extended litigation, when all the while what he is really seeking is housing and very likely he needs it immediately.[30] Consequently, other than perhaps in the context of

access to the courts for private actions, as has been held since the decision in *Jones*, *see* note 16 *supra*, that decision would be irrelevant insofar as the integrity of the administrative conciliation and deferral provisions are concerned.

28. 396 U.S. 229 (1969).

29. Title VIII does, to be sure, make provision for appointment of counsel, 42 U.S.C. § 3612(b), and for the award of counsel fees to a successful indigent plaintiff, 42 U.S.C. § 3612(c). An indication of the utility of these provisions may be that the annotations thus far reflect only one reported decision in which they have been granted, Williamson v. Hampton Mgmt. Co., 339 F. Supp. 1146 (N.D. Ill. 1972).

30. The United States Commission on Civil Rights has stated the mat-

large class suits, I believe, as earlier stated, that Congress—whether wittingly or unwittingly—was on the right course when it did not leave individual complainants with the courts as their only resort, but included provisions in Title VIII for initial efforts at administrative conciliation and the participation of state and local fair housing agencies.[31]

That is not to say we have an effective system at present.[32] HUD staff for dealing with private complaints remains grossly inadequate.[33] Consequently, HUD has been willing to undertake conciliation in only approximately 28% of the complaints filed with it.[34] Furthermore, of those cases which it does take, only about half are successfully settled, a figure representing only some 15% of the complaints originally filed.[35] And even where conciliation is successful, the delay between filing and completion of the process, some six months,[36] is such that it is questionable just how valuable the present administrative process is to an individual victim of discrimination in need of housing.[37]

ter thus: "In housing, where the need for relief is frequently urgent, the time involved in litigation, as well as the cost, make it a relatively ineffective enforcement mechanism." FEDERAL EFFORT 141–42.

31. In the overall campaign against discrimination in housing, the power of the Justice Department under Title VIII to institute "pattern or practice" suits, 42 U.S.C. § 3613, is, of course, of extreme importance. *See generally* FEDERAL EFFORT 160–62. But this power is not a substitute for an effective private complaint process. *See* p. 85 & n.46 *infra*.

32. "In the case of HUD . . . effective administration and enforcement of the various civil rights law relating to fair housing have not yet been achieved . . . . [It] has barely begun to use the variety of available enforcement techniques and strategies at its command." FEDERAL EFFORT 145.

33. *Id.*; UNITED STATES COMMISSION ON CIVIL RIGHTS, FEDERAL CIVIL RIGHTS ENFORCEMENT EFFORT: ONE YEAR LATER 41 (1971) [hereinafter cited as FEDERAL EFFORT: ONE YEAR LATER].

34. FEDERAL EFFORT: ONE YEAR LATER 43.

35. *Id.*

36. *Id.* at 41. Information on the performance of state and local authorities to which HUD refers complaints is not available. *See* FEDERAL EFFORT 147; FEDERAL EFFORTS ONE YEAR LATER 43. *But see* note 52 *infra*. By the end of 1970, 270 complaints, or about 13% of the total received by HUD, had been referred to such authorities. FEDERAL EFFORT: ONE YEAR LATER 43.

37. It has been pointed out that in contrast to the EEOC which received

In addition to substantial increases in staffing, the process would undoubtedly benefit from some form of enforcement powers in HUD —preferably cease and desist powers. Not only would this provide the agency with real muscle to deal with violators but, perhaps more important, it would encourage compliance with the law and settlement by offenders who are now faced with only a toothless administrative process and a slim chance of private suit.[38] An increased effort to inform the public of their rights and of the availability of federal assistance in securing them would also be beneficial, since relatively few victims of discrimination are now filing complaints.[39] While the courts should, without question, remain available to the individual, efforts should be concentrated on developing a more flexible and rapid administrative jurisdiction to deal with the mass of individual complaints about housing discrimination.

When we turn to employment discrimination, and Title VII of the Civil Rights Act of 1964, the ultimate conclusions are essentially the same. Initially we again find the courts confronted with the problems of reconciling Congress' recent legislation with a much older effort. Section 1981,[40] the codification of another part of sec-

more than 8,000 complaints in its first year, HUD received less than 1,500 in the first two years that it administered Title VIII. *See* FEDERAL EFFORT 146 & n.58. Explanations for this have included the cumbersome formalities required to file a complaint with HUD and the fact that the need for immediate relief in an area such as housing, where the complainant may have none or substantially none, is even more acute than in employment where public welfare affords an alternative to the destitute and the employee merely seeking a better job can afford to wait. *Id.* Added to this is an apparent lack of awareness on the part of the public concerning Title VIII and the administrative remedies available thereunder, a problem which at least some effort has been made to combat. *See* FEDERAL EFFORT: ONE YEAR LATER 42.

38. *See* FEDERAL EFFORT 146.

39. *See* note 37 *supra.*

40. 42 U.S.C. § 1981 provides:

All persons within the jurisdiction of the United States shall have the same right in every State and Territory to make and enforce contracts, to sue, be parties, give evidence, and to the full and equal benefit of all laws and proceedings for the security of persons and property as is enjoyed by white citizens, and shall be subject to like punishment, pains, penalties, taxes, licenses, and exactions of every kind, and to no other.

tion 1 of the Civil Rights Act of 1866,[41] guarantees, among other things, racial equality in the making of contracts. The Supreme Court has yet to say whether section 1981 provides individual victims of employment discrimination an alternative mode of proceeding distinct from the provisions of Title VII requiring initial resort to the EEOC and the participation of state and local authorities. While there is a split among the district courts that have considered whether section 1981 was repealed *pro tanto* by Title VII to the extent that the former may be addressed to employment relationships,[42] the courts of appeals which have considered the question have displayed at least a basic agreement that it was not.[43] Even if that should be the ultimate hold-

41. Act of April 9, 1866, ch. 31, § 1, 14 Stat. 27. There is some question whether § 1981 was derived from § 16 of the Enforcement Act of 1870, Act of May 31, 1870, ch. 114, § 16, 16 Stat. 144, instead of from § 1 of the 1866 Act. *Compare, e.g.,* Jones v. Alfred H. Mayer Co., *supra,* 392 U.S. at 422 n.28 & 442 n.78 (dicta), *with, e.g.,* Hurd v. Hodge, 334 U.S. 24, 30–31 n.7 (1948), *and* Cook v. Advertiser Co., 323 F. Supp. 1212, 1214–17 (M.D. Ala. 1971), *aff'd on other grounds,* 458 F.2d 1119 (5th Cir. 1972). The issue is not without significance since its resolution would affect the applicability to § 1981 of the reasoning in *Jones* that § 1 of the 1866 Act contemplated no state action requirement. A likely result, though, would seem to be that § 1981 will be deemed a single codification by the 1874 revisers of both § 16 of the 1870 Act and a portion of § 1 of the 1866 Act—although, to be sure, the derivation note to § 1981 mentions only the former. *See* Note, *Is Section 1981 Modified by Title VII of the Civil Rights Act of 1964,* 1970 DUKE L.J. 1223, 1237–38; New York v. Galamison, 342 F.2d 255, 260 (2d Cir.), *cert. denied,* 380 U.S. 977 (1965); Young v. International Tel. & Tel. Co., 438 F.2d 757, 759–60 (3d Cir. 1971); Brady v. Bristol-Meyers, Inc., 459 F.2d 621, 623 n.4 (8th Cir. 1972). *But see* Cook v. Advertiser Co., *supra.*

42. *Compare* Harrison v. American Can Co., 61 CCH Lab. Cas. ¶ 9353 (S.D. Ala. 1969), *and* Smith v. North Am. Rockwell Corp., 50 F.R.D. 515, 518–21 (N.D. Okla. 1970) (holding that § 1981 was effectively repealed to the extent it applied to employment relationships) *with* Washington v. Bough Constr. Co., 313 F. Supp. 598, 605 (W.D. Wash. 1969), Rice v. Chrysler Corp., 327 F. Supp. 80, 86–87 (E.D. Mich. 1971) (holding that § 1981 was not so repealed).

43. Waters v. Wisconsin Steel Works of Int'l Harvester Co., 427 F.2d 476 (7th Cir.), *cert. denied,* 400 U.S. 911 (1970); Sanders v. Dobbs Houses, Inc., 431 F.2d 1097 (5th Cir. 1970), *cert. denied,* 401 U.S. 948 (1971); Young v. International Tel. & Tel. Co., 438 F.2d 757 (3d Cir. 1971); Johnson v. City of Cincinnati, 450 F.2d 796 (6th Cir. 1971); Brady v. Bristol-Meyers, Inc., 459 F.2d 621 (8th Cir.

ing, its practical significance will probably be small. Here again the striking fact is how few attempts have been made to circumvent the deferral and administrative conciliation provisions of Title VII by way of section 1981 in order to proceed directly in the federal courts. The annotations I have been able to find show only four such instances.[44] Although employment may offer greater opportunity than housing for class actions, it is still an area in which initial jurisdic-

1972). Of the courts of appeals decisions, however, only in *Young* and in Caldwell v. National Brewing Co., 443 F.2d 1044 (5th Cir. 1971), *cert. denied,* 405 U.S. 916 (1972), had the plaintiffs not initially pursued the administrative remedies available under Title VII to some extent. In *Young,* the Third Circuit indicated that although it would not require exhaustion of Title VII administrative remedies as a prerequisite to suit under § 1981, district courts could in the exercise of equitable discretion determine on a case-by-case basis whether judicial action should be stayed pending resort to administrative remedies. 438 F.2d at 761–64. The Fifth Circuit agreed in *Caldwell, supra,* 443 F.2d at 1046. In *Waters,* the Seventh Circuit went further, holding that, absent exhaustion of Title VII administrative remedies, suit under § 1981 is barred unless the plaintiff "pleads a reasonable excuse for his failure to exhaust EEOC remedies." 427 F.2d at 487. The Eighth Circuit in *Brady* considered the two remedies to be parallel.

　　While the courts finding no repeal understandably have relied heavily on the decision in *Jones,* there are a number of factors here which make a stronger case for implied repeal than in *Jones.* Although in enacting Title VIII, Congress was well informed that § 1982 might provide an alternative mode of proceeding in cases of housing discrimination, *see* Jones v. Alfred H. Mayer Co., *supra,* 392 U.S. at 415–16, Congress was unaware in enacting Title VII that § 1981 might provide an existing means of initiating private actions for employment discrimination, *see Developments in the Law, supra,* 84 HARV. L. REV. at 1202 n.46; Note, *supra,* 1970 DUKE L.J. at 1228 & n.36. The decision in Hodges v. United States, 203 U.S. 1 (1906), that § 1981—because of the then prevailing conception of the scope of the Thirteenth Amendment—did not reach a racially motivated private conspiracy to interfere with contracts of employment, still stood; it was not until some four years later in *Jones* that *Hodges* was cast aside, 392 U.S. at 441–43 n.78. Finally, unlike Title VIII, 42 U.S.C. § 3615, Title VII contains no saving clause of any sort with regard to previous legislation of similar coverage.

44. *See* Young v. International Tel. & Tel. Co., *supra,* 438 F.2d at 761–63; Caldwell v. National Brewing Co., *supra,* 443 F.2d at 1045–46; Washington v. Bough Constr. Co., *supra,* 313 F. Supp. at 605; Harrison v. American Can Co., *supra,* 61 CCH Lab. Cas. ¶ 9353.

tion to deal with complaints of discrimination is best lodged elsewhere than in the courts. Essentially the same factors—need for immediate employment, not litigation; lack of education and experience; and a sense of futility in combating what for most of those affected is just another discriminatory incident in a life filled with them—again severely limit the utility of the judicial process for the individual victim of employment discrimination.[45] Effective relief must be readily available to the individual in an administrative process if it is to be available at all.[46]

Here also we have not had such an effective process up to now. It has taken the EEOC almost two years to complete conciliation efforts[47] in complaints in which it finds "reasonable cause."[48] Nevertheless, the vast majority of individual complainants allowed the administrative process to run its course,[49] rather than secure the necessary notice of right to sue[50] from the EEOC after the requisite 60 day waiting period has passed and initiate court action. Indeed, less than 10% of the complaints in which the EEOC found reasonable cause but did not successfully conciliate were ever the subject of private judicial actions.[51]

As with HUD, the obvious importance of the administrative process to the individual victim of job discrimination does not alter

45. *Developments in the Law, supra,* 84 HARV. L. REV. at 1252–53.
46. Of course, the use by the Attorney General of his power under Title VII to initiate "pattern or practice" suits, 42 U.S.C. § 2000e, is also essential to the eradication of employment discrimination in our country.

Nonetheless, the pattern or practice authority can only be effective as a supplement to the private complaint process. The consideration of individual grievances is essential for two reasons. First, no one is in a better position to detect and report violations of the Act than the persons affected . . . . Secondly, there are important private interests which Title VII was enacted to protect.

Developments in the Law, supra, 84 HARV. L. REV. at 1269.
47. *Developments in the Law, supra,* 84 HARV. L. REV. at 1201–02. Indeed, as of September 1971, there were 23,642 charges pending in EEOC. FEDERAL EFFORT: ONE YEAR LATER 28. This represented a 25% increase in the number of pending charges in a period of just 6½ months. *Id.*
48. 42 U.S.C. § 2000e–5(a).
49. *Developments in the Law, supra,* 84 HARV. L. REV. at 1246.
50. *See id.* at 1207–08.
51. *Developments in the Law, supra,* 84 HARV. L. REV. at 1252.

the fact that up until recently the scheme has been unsatisfactory. This is self-evident from the fact that it has taken the EEOC almost two years to complete conciliation efforts. Moreover, the EEOC was able to achieve even partially successful conciliation in something less than half of the complaints in which it found reasonable cause[52] —a record to be contrasted with the NLRB's 90% settlement rate with respect to the charges that it takes.[53] The causes of this were much the same as with HUD. In addition to the problems of inadequate staffing and funding, the EEOC has had no real enforcement powers of its own.[54]

Recent legislation[55] has changed this in an important way. Apparently recognizing that the lack of power to enforce sanctions denied the EEOC any effective bargaining tool in conciliation nego-

52. *Id.* at 1200. The results of deferral to state and local fair employment authorities were even less satisfactory. In 1970, 4,201 charges were deferred to state and local authorities; in 1971, 8,516 were deferred. Only 18% of the charges deferred in 1971 were successfully resolved by the state or local authority. "The deferral process has generally meant additional delay to the complainant, without a countervailing benefit in the form of increased chances for favorable settlement." FEDERAL EFFORT: ONE YEAR LATER 36. It has been argued that automatic deferral should be eliminated in favor of a procedure whereby private complainants would make a binding election between the state and federal administrative processes; that by so doing states would be encouraged to upgrade their own fair employment authorities so that they would not be bypassed by local citizens in favor of federal authorities. See *Developments in the Law*, *supra*, 84 HARV. L. REV. at 1274–75. Of course, it is not possible at this point to determine what effect the 1972 amendments—permitting the Commission to initiate civil actions—will have on the conciliation rate. Hopefully, the amendments will produce a dramatic increase. See pp. 86–87 *infra*.

53. *Developments in the Law*, *supra*, 84 HARV. L. REV. at 1200 n.39. To this should be added the fact that the EEOC Chairman has stated that he believes approximately 80% of the charges filed with the EEOC to be valid. FEDERAL EFFORT: ONE YEAR LATER 29.

54. For an explanation of the congressional maneuvering, at the time Title VII was enacted, which saw the EEOC stripped successively of cease and desist powers similar to those of the NLRB and then of power to bring legal action in its own name on the basis of individual complaints, *see Developments in the Law*, *supra*, 84 HARV. L. REV. at 1196 nn.7 & 8.

55. Equal Employment Opportunity Act of 1972, 86 Stat. 103, *amending* 42 U.S.C. §§ 2000e *et seq.*

tiations, Congress has provided that the Commission is no longer limited to merely certifying a complainant's case as proper for private litigation in the district court but may now itself bring such an action[56] in which the complainant may intervene.[57] While giving the Commission cease and desist powers would have been preferable, such a solution apparently was not politically acceptable. Hopefully the middle road that Congress has chosen will force a higher rate of conciliation agreements in a shorter period of time, and the potentially great involvement of the federal courts in this area of the law will be correspondingly diminished.

The general civil rights statute, 42 U.S.C. § 1983, derived from the Civil Rights Act of 1871,[58] presents a different range of problems. The familiar words of the statute bear repeating:

> Every person who, under color of any statute, ordinance, regulation, custom, or usage, of any State or Territory, subjects, or causes to be subjected, any citizen of the United States or other person within the jurisdiction thereof to the deprivation of any rights, privileges, or immunities secured by the Constitution and laws, shall be liable to the party injured in an action at law, suit in equity, or other proper proceeding for redress.

The recent enormous growth of private civil rights litigation[59] is largely attributable to this simple provision. One indication of the extent of this is the some 425 pages of annotations in the U.S. Code. As has been wittily said, "A judge is tempted to conclude that the chief weapon expected to forestall Orwell's *1984* is the United States Code's § 1983."[60]

Mere numbers, though, cannot adequately convey the variety

56. *Id.* § 4, *amending* 42 U.S.C. § 2000e–5.
57. *Id.*
58. Act of April 20, 1871, ch. 22, § 1, 17 Stat. 13. Although 42 U.S.C. § 1983 includes state action violating a federal statute, the jurisdictional statute, 28 U.S.C. § 1343(3) uses the narrower phrase, "any Act of Congress providing for equal rights of citizens or of all persons within the jurisdiction of the United States," which presumably has the same restricted meaning ascribed to the similar language in 28 U.S.C. § 1443(1). *See* Georgia v. Rachel, 384 U.S. 780, 792 (1966); City of Greenwood v. Peacock, 384 U.S. 808, 831 (1966).
59. *See* note 4 *supra.*
60. Coffin, *Justice and Workability: Un Essai,* 5 SUFFOLK U.L. REV. 567, 570 (1971).

and importance of the claims coming before the courts under section 1983. For that purpose, I cannot do better than quote in the margin the catalogue of such cases heard by the First Circuit at a single term.[61] Yet this list, for the smallest of the circuits, does not contain the host of complaints of racial discrimination that fill the dockets of most. We must remember also the tendency of each path-breaking civil rights decision to engender hundreds of other actions for similar relief. Litigation in this area grows in exponential progression.

A particularly apt illustration is the Fifth Circuit's decision requiring a municipality to furnish a variety of services—paving, street lighting, surface water drainage, sewers, water mains and fire hydrants —to black neighborhoods on an equal basis to white.[62] It would be

---

61. —Do indigent tenants have to post a bond for costs and disbursements to remove an eviction case to federal court?

—Do low income tenants alleging that their landlord seeks to evict them for reporting building code violations state a cause of action under the Civil Rights Act?

—Do tenants in a federally subsidized housing project have a right to a hearing on a proposed rent increase?

—Must indigents pay the statutorily required filing fee to secure a discharge in bankruptcy?

—Do welfare mothers have an unlimited right to demonstrate at welfare offices?

—Must hot lunches be furnished at all of a city's schools if they are furnished at some?

—Must surplus foods be distributed to the poor in all communities if they are distributed in a few?

—May a university dismantle an "embarrassing" corridor art exhibit?

—May a high school suspend a teacher for discussing a magazine article exploring current obscenities?

—May a high school arbitrarily suspend a student for having long hair?

—Does a prisoner committed to solitary confinement have any due process rights?

—Under what circumstances does a person committed to a mental institution for observation have a Civil Rights action?

Coffin, *supra*, 5 Suffolk U.L. Rev. at 569–70 (footnotes omitted).

62. Hawkins v. Town of Shaw, 437 F.2d 1286 (5th Cir. 1971), *adhered to on rehearing en banc*, 461 F.2d 1171 (1972).

A decision under the Civil Rights Act which, if followed, could be an even larger breeder of litigation and producer of federal-state tension is Littleton v. Berbling, — F.2d —, 41 U.S.L.W. 2215 (7th Cir., Oct. 6, 1972), holding that federal courts have jurisdiction over

an insensitive person, indeed, who did not experience a thrill on reading the court's opinion, appropriately written by former Chief Judge Tuttle, the hero of the struggle for desegregated schools in the South, rejecting the Town's transparent attempts to paper over what everyone knew to be the facts.[63] One recalls the remark Professor Paul Freund made somewhere in defense of *Brown v. Board of Education*, "Can you imagine it having been decided the other way?" Yet the decision created serious problems with respect to the remedy, even as to this town of 2,500 inhabitants. Moreover, *Hawkins* will be a tremendous litigation breeder—in some cases where the discrimination is equally serious and indefensible, in others where the objections are trivial or captious, and in still others that lie between.[64] The decision also suggests such questions as the constitutional validity of discrimination in services based on financial considerations, without the added invidious component of race; the extent to which local government bodies can avoid the thrust of such decisions by resorting to special property assessments as the basis for financing improvements in various areas; and, ultimately, just what a court can do if a municipality refuses to put up the necessary funds.[65] It would be altogether wrong to characterize *Hawkins* as opening a Pandora's

claims that state judges have discriminated, on racial or economic grounds, in setting bond, sentencing and assessing the costs of a jury trial, and that state prosecutors have discriminated in their treatment of black as against white citizens.

63. As a perceptive comment has noted, "this was a case where these judges of the Deep South could not be ignorant as judges of what they knew as men." Ellington & Jones, Hawkins v. Town of Shaw: *The Court as City Manager*, 5 GEORGIA L. REV. 734, 739 (1971).

64. Complaints based on the *Hawkins* decision will not be confined to the South. *See* Beal v. Lindsay, — F.2d —, slip op. p. 23 (2d Cir., Oct. 5, 1972).

65. Compare the problems with respect to the enforcement of bonds issued by towns and counties to finance railroad development in the 1870's, vividly recounted in FAIRMAN, *supra* note 26, at 918–1116. Similar problems may arise out of decisions condemning historic methods for financing schools. *See, e.g.,* Rodriguez v. San Antonio Independent School Dist., 337 F. Supp. 280 (W.D. Tex. 1971) (three-judge court), *prob. juris. noted*, 406 U.S. 966 (1972) (No. 71-1332). *See also* Wyatt v. Stickney, 344 F. Supp. 373 (M.D. Ala. 1972), in which the court made detailed specifications as to the accommodations and staffing of state mental hospitals and said that lack of financial resources would not be deemed an excuse.

box; the box badly needed to be opened. But it would be equally wrong to blind our eyes to the burdens on judicial time and the federal-state frictions it will create, or to refuse even to consider whether any limits can properly be placed on section 1983.

In approaching the subject of private litigation under the general civil rights statute, I must own a Faustian conflict. It is hard to conceive a task more appropriate for federal courts than to protect civil rights guaranteed by the Constitution against invasion by the states. Yet we also have state courts, whose judges, like those of the federal courts, must take an oath to support the Constitution[66] and were intended to play an important role in carrying it out. As Hamilton wrote:[67]

[T]he national and State systems are to be regarded as ONE WHOLE. The courts of the latter will of course be natural auxiliaries to the execution of the laws of the Union, and an appeal from them will as naturally lie to that tribunal which is destined to unite and assimilate the principles of national justice and the rules of national decisions.

In the areas of housing and employment we have seen how Congress, recognizing the tensions in our federal system, attempted in recent legislation to strike a balance of relevant interests with the inclusion of provisions for state and local participation. Under section 1983 the courts have little in the way of congressional guidance, but the tensions are equally great and cannot properly be ignored. I thus have qualms about developments whereby almost all challenges to the constitutionality of state action, save those arising in the trial of criminal cases, take the form of suits for declaratory judgments or injunctions in the federal courts, often brought almost before the ink on a new state statute is dry. Surely it must be more acceptable if a state statute is struck down as offending the Federal Constitution by state judges, often elected by the people, than by federal judges owing their appointment to Washington. My remarks about actions under the general civil rights statute reflect this conflict between my sense that substantial state and local participation in this area is essential and my belief that no business is more appro-

---

66. U.S. CONST. art. VI, para. 3.
67. THE FEDERALIST No. 82, at 517 (B. Wright ed. 1961). *See also* Martin v. Hunter's Lessee, 14 U.S. (1 Wheat.) 304, 340–42 (1816) (Story, J.).

priate for the federal courts than suits to protect such federal constitutional rights against invasion by the states—some will say my inability to resolve it.

One method for narrowing the area of conflict has recently gone by the board. A literal reading of the civil rights statute would embrace every case where state action was claimed to violate any provision of the Federal Constitution, including such provisions as the commerce clause and the prohibition of impairment of the obligations of contracts. Believing that the Reconstruction Congress did not intend to go so far, Mr. Justice Stone, joined by Mr. Justice Reed and apparently by Chief Justice Hughes, announced a formulation[68] whereby the civil rights statute would apply only "whenever the right or immunity is one of personal liberty, not dependent for its existence upon the infringement of property rights . . . ." The endorsement of Justice Stone's view by our circuit and others[69] did not meet with favor in the Supreme Court.[70] Despite the "law-office history"[71] in the opinion, I cannot help thinking that Justice Stone came closer to capturing the spirit of the Civil Rights Act and that the framers of that statute, whose concern, as the references show, was with the rights of the freedmen in the south, would have been no end surprised to find that it encompassed an attack on a Connecticut garnishment statute and still more so to find it applicable to a creditor's claim of impairment of the obligation of a contract. The Court's reference to "the virtual impossibility of applying" the per-

---

68. Hague v. CIO, 307 U.S. 496, 531 (1939).
69. Eisen v. Eastman, 421 F.2d 560, 566 (2d Cir. 1969), *cert. denied*, 400 U.S. 841 (1970) (suit to challenge allegedly unconstitutional rent control law); Fuller v. Volk, 351 F.2d 323, 327 (3d Cir. 1965) (suit to enjoin allegedly unconstitutional use of state funds); Gray v. Morgan, 371 F.2d 172, 175 (7th Cir. 1966), *cert. denied*, 386 U.S. 1033 (1967) (suit to enjoin allegedly unconstitutional state income tax); Howard v. Higgins, 379 F.2d 227, 228 (10th Cir. 1967) (suit to recover property seized by sheriff); Bussie v. Long, 383 F.2d 766, 769 (5th Cir. 1967) (suit to enjoin alleged non-feasance of State Tax Commission); Weddle v. Director, 436 F.2d 342, 343 (4th Cir. 1970), *vacated and remanded in light of Lynch v. Household Fin. Corp.*, 405 U.S. 1036 (1972) (suit to recover property seized by state officials).
70. Lynch v. Household Fin. Corp., 405 U.S. 538 (1972).
71. *See* Kelly, *Clio and the Court: An Illicit Love Affair*, 1965 SUP. CT. REV. 119.

sonal liberty-property rights distinction[72] was a considerable hyperbole. Although I do not understand the Court's zeal to expand section 1983 to include the sort of property rights case that had been quite satisfactorily handled by review of state court decisions,[73] this subject would cease to have practical importance as regards getting into federal court if, as recommended below,[74] jurisdictional amount should be abolished as a requirement to the invocation of federal jurisdiction in all federal question cases. However, the destruction of the "personal liberty" limitation on the breadth of Civil Rights Act jurisdiction enhances the importance of considering other means for lessening federal-state tensions in this sensitive area.

One such means is the doctrine of abstention.[75] In 1967, a writer pronounced that "the retirement of Mr. Justice Frankfurter in 1962 left the abstention doctrine a judicial orphan."[76] However, like other orphans, the doctrine has shown it can survive a parent's decease.[77] There must be some merit in a principle with such staying power. Despite this, one must agree with another statement of the same writer:[78]

72. 405 U.S. at 550–52.
73. *Cf.* Sniadach v. Family Fin. Corp., 395 U.S. 337 (1969).
74. *See* pp. 120–24 *infra.*
75. Although a civil rights case, Railroad Comm'n v. Pullman Co., 312 U.S. 496 (1941), gave birth to the doctrine, the problem is not confined to such cases. Indeed, it was once suggested that they be excluded from it, *see* Wechsler, *Federal Jurisdiction and the Revision of the Judicial Code,* 13 LAW & CONTEMP. PROB. 216, 230 (1948), although I doubt that the author would take that view today. However, this is a convenient place to discuss the problem in general.
76. Note, *Federal-Question Abstention: Justice Frankfurter's Doctrine in an Activist Era,* 80 HARV. L. REV. 604 (1967).
77. For recent cases applying the doctrine, see Reetz v. Bozanich, 397 U.S. 82 (1970); Fornaris v. Ridge Tool Co., 400 U.S. 41 (1970); Askew v. Hargrave, 401 U.S. 476 (1971). *Contrast* Wisconsin v. Constantineau, 400 U.S. 433 (1971), refusing to apply the doctrine, over the dissent of three Justices. In Lake Carriers' Ass'n v. MacMullan, 406 U.S. 498 (1972), the Court took the somewhat extraordinary course of indicating various factors that would not have justified a three-judge court in abstaining, and then going on to affirm its decision to abstain because of ambiguity in the Michigan statute under constitutional attack.
78. Note, *supra,* 80 HARV. L. REV. at 621.

"No clear-cut statement of the doctrine has emerged; standards remain confused."

The American Law Institute has endeavored to fill the void.[79]

One type of case almost universally recognized as appropriate for abstention is that of a state statute, not yet construed by the state courts, which is susceptible of one construction that would render it free from federal constitutional objection and another that would not.[80] A federal court should not place itself in the position of holding the statute unconstitutional by giving it the latter construction, only to find that the highest court of the state will render the decision futile and unnecessary by adopting the former. Such a decision not only is a waste of judicial resources but provokes a needless collision between state and federal power.

Abstention is also generally felt to be justified when a state statute is subject to fair challenge under state constitutional provisions having no counterpart in the Federal Constitution.[81] Here also abstention may save the federal courts from a needless task and unnecessary confrontation with a state. On the other hand, a divided Court has held abstention to be improper where the state statute was clear and the state constitutional attack would be on the same basis as the federal.[82] Some may find this distinction to be of dubious tenability.[83]

79. *See* ALI STUDY § 1371(c), and commentary, *id.* at 282–90.
80. *E.g.,* the Puerto Rican statute in Fornaris v. Ridge Tool Co., *supra,* 400 U.S. at 43–44, and the Michigan statute in Lake Carriers' Ass'n v. MacMullan, *supra,* 406 U.S. at 510–12.

   Abstention has not been considered appropriate when the statute is attacked as overbroad and the limiting construction that might render it constitutional could be achieved only as the result of a series of cases in which the statute is applied to various sets of facts. *See* Dombrowski v. Pfister, 380 U.S. 479, 490–92 (1965); *cf.* Zwickler v. Koota, 389 U.S. 241, 249–52 (1967). At least a shadow of doubt, however, has been cast across this principle by Mr. Justice Black's opinion for the Court in Younger v. Harris, 401 U.S. 37, 52–53 (1971).
81. *See* Reetz v. Bozanich, *supra,* 397 U.S. 82. This was also the situation in Askew v. Hargrave, *supra,* 401 U.S. 476, where, in addition, a state court suit attacking the state statute on the state constitutional ground had in fact been instituted subsequent to the filing of the federal case.
82. Wisconsin v. Constantineau, 400 U.S. 433 (1971).
83. The Court stated, 400 U.S. at 438, that "the abstention rule only

Although originally favoring the ALI proposal, I have come to question the wisdom of attempting to codify abstention;[84] I now tend to think the courts can work this out better on a case-by-case basis. The problem generally arises in suits for an injunction or a declaratory judgment, as to which Mr. Justice Frankfurter rightly observed in the path-breaking opinion on the subject:[85]

The history of equity jurisdiction is the history of regard for public consequences in employing the extraordinary remedy of the injunction. There have been as many and as variegated applications of this supple principle as the situations that have brought it into play. . . . Few public interests have a higher claim upon the discretion of a federal chancellor than the avoidance of needless friction with state policies . . . .

We need to listen to both parts of Justice Stone's wise remark:[86]

Courts of equity may, and frequently do, go much farther both to give and withhold relief in furtherance of the public interest than they are accustomed to go when only private interests are involved.

> applies where 'the issue of state law is uncertain'," quoting Harman v. Forssenius, 380 U.S. 528, 534 (1965). But the issue of "state law" was just as uncertain as in *Reetz v. Bozanich*, authored by the same Justice, namely whether the state statute was valid under the state constitution.

84. One great virtue in the ALI proposed codification is the provision that if a federal court abstains, all questions shall be determined in the state court, subject only to Supreme Court review, unless the federal court vacates the stay because "the State proceeding proves ineffective in reaching a prompt and final disposition on the merits . . . ." ALI STUDY § 1371(d). This would avoid the bifurcation of issues proposed in England v. Louisiana State Bd. of Medical Examiners, 375 U.S. 411 (1964), as a method of preventing the state court from deciding constitutional issues, with consequent res judicata effect, *see* pp. 101–02 *infra*. I see no reason why Congress could not enact a statute covering only this phase of the ALI abstention proposal.

85. Railroad Comm'n v. Pullman Co., *supra*, 312 U.S. at 500.

86. Virginian Ry. v. System Fed'n No. 40, 300 U.S. 515, 552 (1937). See also his well-known discussions in Douglas v. City of Jeannette, 319 U.S. 157, 162–64 (1943), and his statement in Meredith v. Winter Haven, 320 U.S. 228, 235 (1943): "An appeal to the equity jurisdiction conferred on federal district courts is an appeal to the sound discretion which guides the determinations of courts of equity." *See also* Eccles v. Peoples Bank, 333 U.S. 426, 431 (1948) (Frankfurter, J.).

Much may depend on the strength of the federal interest involved; I would be considerably more willing to abstain in a case, even not within well-marked traditional categories, where the issue was the permissible length of hair of high school students[87] than when it concerned the rights of black citizens to equal education, housing or employment opportunity. Another relevant consideration is the degree to which abstention might avoid continuous federal supervision of state functioning. Also, there are cases where a federal court might properly refuse to enjoin or grant declaratory relief with respect to new state legislation until there has been sufficient experience for an informed judgment concerning its effect. Abstention would likewise be proper in the many instances where the particular grievance sparking the suit has been settled but "public service" lawyers wish to make a "federal case" by bringing a class action for declaratory or injunctive relief.[88] Even though the matter cannot properly be ruled to be moot, there is no sufficient justification in such cases for provoking a federal-state conflict. These are suggestive illustrations only; they by no means exhaust the instances where a federal court might decide, in the exercise of sound discretion, that the state tribunals will afford full justice, subject, of course, to Supreme Court review.[89]

87. *See, e.g.,* Richards v. Thurston, 424 F.2d 1281 (1st Cir. 1970); Gfell v. Rickelman, 441 F.2d 444 (6th Cir. 1971); King v. Saddleback Junior College Dist., 445 F.2d 932 (9th Cir. 1971); Freeman v. Flake, 448 F.2d 258 (10th Cir. 1971); Bishop v. Colaw, 450 F.2d 1069 (8th Cir. 1971); Gere v. Stanley, 453 F.2d 205 (3d Cir. 1971); Arnold v. Carpenter, 459 F.2d 939 (7th Cir. 1972); Karr v. Schmidt, 460 F.2d 609 (5th Cir. 1972) (en banc) (hair grooming rules presumptively valid). The Supreme Court's disinterest in hair length is illustrated by its denial of certiorari despite a clear conflict among the circuits. *See* Olff v. East Side Union High School Dist., 404 U.S. 1042 (1972); Freeman v. Flake, 405 U.S. 1032 (1972); Karr v. Schmidt, 41 U.S.L.W. 3254 (Nov. 6, 1972). If the Court does not regard the subject as sufficiently important to reconcile so plain a conflict, why should not the lower federal courts leave decision to the courts of the respective states?

88. *Compare* Negron v. Wallace, 436 F.2d 1139 (2d Cir.), *cert. denied,* 402 U.S. 998 (1971); Calloway v. Briggs, 443 F.2d 296, 299 (6th Cir.) (O'Sullivan, J., dissenting), *cert. denied,* 404 U.S. 916 (1971); Kerrigan v. Boucher, 450 F.2d 487 (2d Cir. 1971).

89. If it be said by way of objection that this will impose an added

Should it be said that so flexible an approach leaves too large an area for discretion on the part of the lower courts, the answer is that the ruling does not go to the merits but merely determines where the initial decision shall be made.

Another source of conflict arising with particular frequency in the civil rights area is when a state court proceeding is pending and a federal court is asked to enjoin it. The principle of comity inherent in our federal system creates strong pressure against this, which has found both legislative and judicial expression. Section 2283 of the Judicial Code, which can be traced back to 1793,[90] forbids a federal court to "grant an injunction to stay proceedings in a State court except as expressly authorized by Act of Congress, or where necessary in aid of its jurisdiction, or to protect or effectuate its judgments." At the same time, the courts have evolved their own equitable doctrine of non-interference in state court proceedings[91]—a doctrine which, though distinct from the statute, has sometimes been thought to be reflected in it.[92]

In view of what was to befall section 2283 at the 1971 Term,

burden on the Supreme Court, at least a partial answer is that many such cases come before three-judge courts with consequent direct appeal, and that, when they do not or if that outmoded institution should be abolished, this is the type of case in which certiorari from a judgment of a court of appeals is almost invariably sought.

Judge Hufstedler has supplied a thoughtful analysis of relevant considerations, *The Changing Role of the Federal Judiciary*, N.Y.L.J., Nov. 3, 1972, at 4, cols. 1 & 2, although her general attitude toward abstention is considerably more negative than mine.

90. Act of March 2, 1793, ch. 22, § 5, 1 Stat. 334–35, *as amended*, 28 U.S.C. § 2283.

91. *See, e.g.*, Fenner v. Boykin, 271 U.S. 240 (1926); Douglas v. City of Jeannette, 319 U.S. 157 (1943); Younger v. Harris, 401 U.S. 37 (1971).

92. *See, e.g.*, Machesky v. Bizzell, 414 F.2d 283, 287 (5th Cir. 1969); Sheridan v. Garrison, 415 F.2d 699, 704 (5th Cir. 1969), *cert. denied*, 396 U.S. 1040 (1970). The view taken in these decisions, that § 2283 was merely a codification of judicially-recognized principles of comity, and as such subject to judicially-recognized exceptions thereto, was rejected in Atlantic Coast Line R.R. v. Brotherhood of Locomotive Eng'rs, 398 U.S. 281, 286–87, 294–95 (1970).

it must be regarded as fortunate that in the preceding term the Court delivered a sextet of opinions placing strict limits, under the comity principle, upon both federal injunctions and declaratory judgments with respect to pending state criminal prosecutions.[93] The precise holdings are not easily ascertainable. Although Mr. Justice Black's opinion in the *Younger* case was presented as that of the Court, two Justices, Stewart and Harlan, whose concurrence was necessary for a majority, added a separate statement[94] in which they spoke in narrower terms. According to Justice Black a federal court may generally not issue either an injunction or a declaratory judgment with respect to a pending state criminal prosecution. However, after stating the three exceptions in the anti-injunction statute, he referred to a "judicial exception" covering a case where "a person about to be prosecuted in a state court can show that he will, if the proceeding in the state court is not enjoined, suffer irreparable damages." While the meaning of that phrase was not illumined, I have little doubt that, as indicated in *Perez*, it covers cases where state court prosecutions, at least those infringing First Amendment rights, have been initiated "in bad faith without hope of obtaining a valid conviction."

Apart from this ambiguity, what is bothersome about the sextet as a policy matter is in making so much turn on whether the federal injunction is obtained before or after the state proceeding is formally begun. The effect is to encourage the state to race to its courthouse with a possibly ill-founded prosecution and the prospective defendants to run to the federal courthouse to prevent a prosecution that might never be initiated.[95] Granted that the offense to the state is greater when the prosecution has been formally initiated, the force of Justice Black's admonition that federal courts should not "survey the statute books and pass judgment on laws before the courts are called upon to enforce them"[96] goes beyond prosecutions already begun. There

93. Younger v. Harris, 401 U.S. 37 (1971); Samuels v. Mackell, 401 U.S. 66 (1971); Boyle v. Landry, 401 U.S. 77 (1971); Perez v. Ledesma, 401 U.S. 82 (1971); Dyson v. Stein, 401 U.S. 200 (1971); Bryne v. Karalexis, 401 U.S. 216 (1971).

94. 401 U.S. at 54–56.

95. *See* Krahm v. Graham, 461 F.2d 703, 708 (9th Cir. 1972).

96. Younger v. Harris, *supra*, 401 U.S. at 52.

would thus be merit in a statute which provided that, whether state proceedings be pending or impending, a federal court shall not issue an injunction or a declaratory judgment against the enforcement of a state criminal statute unless there is no other means of avoiding grave and irreparable harm or where a prosecution would be instituted in bad faith, *i.e.*, with knowledge that there was no reasonable expectation that a valid conviction could be obtained.[97]

As indicated, the 1971 Term was a bad one for section 2283. The first blow was struck in a decision, already discussed in another context,[98] where the Court held the anti-injunction act inapplicable when a federal court was asked to enjoin a garnishment "more than seven months after the writ had been executed, the summons and complaint served, process returned, and the case docketed in Connecticut court."[99] How the holding that this was not within the terms of section 2283 can be reconciled with previous decisions[100] is beyond my comprehension; moreover, the creation of this confusion was quite unnecessary in view of the later holding,[101] in a case *sub judice* at the time, that the Civil Rights Act is an exception to section 2283. This indentation was followed by the direction of injunctions against the execution of prejudgment replevin writs, without even so much as mention of section 2283.[102]

A still more important blow fell when, after many years of

97. In effect this would combine Justice Black's statements in *Younger v. Harris* and *Perez v. Ledesma* with the ALI's proposal, ALI STUDY § 1372, but would extend the prohibition to prosecutions not yet begun. In another sense it represents a return to the wisdom of Chief Justice Stone in Douglas v. City of Jeannette, *supra*, 319 U.S. at 162–64.

98. Lynch v. Household Fin. Corp., *supra*, 405 U.S. 538.

99. *Id.* at 558 (White, J., dissenting).

100. Notably Hill v. Martin, 296 U.S. 393, 403 (1935).

101. Mitchum v. Foster, 407 U.S. 225 (1972).

102. Fuentes v. Shevin, 407 U.S. 67 (1972). This decision came only a week before Mitchum v. Foster, *supra*, which would have afforded an easy rationale. Mr. Justice White, who, joined by the Chief Justice and Mr. Justice Blackmun, had strongly dissented in *Lynch* on the basis of § 2283, argued in a dissent in *Fuentes*, 407 U.S. at 97–99, also joined in by the Chief Justice and Mr. Justice Blackmun, that consideration should be given to the "sextet" of the previous term. The *Mitchum* opinion leaves open the question whether the sextet applies at all to civil actions, 407 U.S. at 243–44.

endeavor to avoid a decision, the Court held the Civil Rights Act constituted an exception to the anti-injunction statute.[103] What makes this decision especially devastating to proper federal-state relations is its combination with the decision a few months earlier which abandoned any attempts to limit the Civil Rights Act to what the Reconstruction Congress had in mind.[104] Those seeking amusement could do worse than to consider the legislative history relied upon in both these opinions as applied to an action by a business to enjoin a pending state suit under a regulatory statute on the ground that the latter violated the commerce clause. While, as stated above, the *Lynch* decision would cease to have significance as regards *getting into* the federal courts if jurisdictional amount were abolished in all federal question cases, its combination with *Mitchum* makes the anti-injunction act almost a dead letter wherever a plaintiff asserts a claim based on the Constitution, as distinguished from a federal statute.

The uncertainties, and worse, which the Court has managed to create by this series of decisions cry out for new legislation. Under the ALI's proposal, the section conferring jurisdiction in civil rights cases was to be repealed as no longer needed in view of the proposed abolition of jurisdictional amount. The exceptions to the anti-injunction statute were set forth in detail; it was proposed that true civil rights cases be handled by one of these, namely, that an injunction may be issued "to restrain a criminal prosecution that should not be permitted to continue either because the statute or other law that is the basis of the prosecution plainly cannot constitutionally be applied to the party seeking the injunction or because the prosecution is so plainly discriminatory as to amount to a denial of the equal protection of the laws."[105] Presumably, in the light of *Mitchum*, the legislative history would have to make clear that this was intended to be the sole civil rights exception; if that were not deemed sufficient, the first exception, namely, where "(1) an Act of Congress authorized such relief or provides that other proceedings shall cease" would have to be amended to read "authorizes an injunction against state court proceedings or provides," etc. An alternative and possibly preferable course might be to build on the

103. Mitchum v. Foster, *supra*, 407 U.S. 225.
104. Lynch v. Household Fin. Corp., *supra*, 405 U.S. 538.
105. ALI STUDY § 1372; *see* commentary, *id.* at 299–312.

proposal of Professor David Currie,[106] that "the federal courts shall not enjoin pending or threatened proceedings in state courts unless there is no other effective means of avoiding grave and irreparable harm," and couple this with the ALI's exceptions (1), modified as suggested in the text, and (2)–(6) inclusive. Such a solution would comprehend the sextet, eliminate the distinction between pending and threatened proceedings, cover civil as well as criminal actions, allow injunctions in the rare cases when they are needed, effect a better division of civil rights litigation between state and federal courts, and undo the damage created by the combination of *Lynch* and *Mitchum*.[107]

The final point for discussion with respect to federal-state relationships in the civil rights area is whether there should be a requirement of exhaustion of state remedies under the general statute, such as exists by explicit congressional enactment with respect to habeas corpus for state prisoners.[108]

It is clear that the Supreme Court has not sanctioned any general requirement of exhaustion of state *judicial* remedies as a prelude to federal suits for damages or for injunctive or declaratory relief against unconstitutional state action.[109] Until recently it was equally clear that exhaustion of state *administrative* remedies was required;[110] I have undertaken to show in an opinion that this is still the law except when the administrative remedy is inadequate or resort to it is certainly or probably futile.[111] There is no justification for

---

106. Currie, *The Federal Courts and the American Law Institute* (Part II), 36 U. CHI. L. REV. 268, 329 (1969).
107. Very likely new legislation should also repair the holes created by the other aspect of *Lynch,* discussed at p. 98 *supra,* and by *Fuentes.*
108. 28 U.S.C. § 2254(b).
109. Bacon v. Rutland R.R., 232 U.S. 134 (1914); Monroe v. Pape, 365 U.S. 167 (1961); McNeese v. Board of Educ., 373 U.S. 668 (1963). The situation may be different when the plaintiff seeks to sue in federal equity and there is an adequate state remedy at law. *Cf.* Potwora v. Dillon, 386 F.2d 74 (2d Cir. 1967). *But see* DiGiovanni v. Camden Fire Ins. Ass'n, 296 U.S. 64, 69–70 (1935).
110. Prentis v. Atlantic Coast Line Co., 211 U.S. 210 (1908).
111. Eisen v. Eastman, *supra,* 421 F.2d at 567–69. The per curiam opinion in Carter v. Stanton, 405 U.S. 669 (1972), may further confuse the matter; I read it as being based, like Damico v. California, 389 U.S. 416 (1967), on the futility of the administrative remedy

leaving the matter in doubt. Congress should provide that a federal court faced with a challenge to the constitutionality of state action, whether under the Civil Rights Act or otherwise, *may* abstain pending exhaustion of state administrative remedies and *shall* do so whenever these remedies are plain, adequate and effective. The reasons have been so well stated in a note in this University's law review as to render their repetition in text supererogatory.[112]

If this step were taken, should Congress enact still further legislation to establish a general requirement of exhaustion of state *judicial* remedies in civil rights cases? Although there are arguments for this, I am not persuaded by them. For one thing, it is misleading in most instances to speak as if, after litigating his federal constitutional claims in state court, the plaintiff could then come to federal court to litigate them again. Under present law, if the federal claims have been raised in a state court and decided against plaintiff on the merits, such a judgment would be res judicata and bar a subsequent federal suit on the same issue.[113] Of course, insofar as such

in light of the Indiana regulation. The disapproval of another phase of *Eisen* in Lynch v. Household Fin. Corp., *supra*, 405 U.S. 538, has no bearing on this issue.

112. Note, *Exhaustion of State Remedies under the Civil Rights Act*, 68 COLUM. L. REV. 1201, 1206 (1968) (footnotes omitted):

A strong state interest is reflected in the establishment of a comprehensive scheme of regulation; authority over the subject matter of the dispute has been vested in an expert supervisory body, far more familiar than a federal court with local factors that legitimately affect administration.

. . . Moreover, the states, as well as the federal government have an interest in providing a means whereby official abuse can be corrected without resort to lengthy and costly trial. Thus, the same considerations which support an exhaustion requirement in suits against a federal agency in federal court or a state agency in state court are relevant.

Note also Judge Wisdom's statement, "[t]here are good reasons in favor of requiring exhaustion of administrative remedies which are not applicable to exhaustion of state judicial remedies." Moreno v. Henckel, 431 F.2d 1299, 1306–07 (5th Cir. 1970) (footnote omitted).

113. Norwood v. Parenteau, 228 F.2d 148 (8th Cir. 1955), *cert. denied*, 351 U.S. 955 (1956); Goss v. Illinois, 312 F.2d 257 (7th Cir. 1963); Rhodes v. Meyer, 334 F.2d 709 (8th Cir.), *cert. denied*, 379 U.S. 915 (1964); Frazier v. East Baton Rouge Paris School Bd., 363 F.2d 861 (5th Cir. 1966); Brown v. Chastain, 416 F.2d 1012 (5th Cir. 1969), *cert. denied*, 397 U.S. 951 (1970); Paul v. Dade County,

actions raise questions of both state and federal law, one could introduce in the context of an exhaustion requirement the kind of saving procedure now employed in abstention[114] whereby the private litigant would carefully preserve his federal claim, litigating only issues of non-compliance with state law. As has been the case in abstention,[115] some state courts would undoubtedly decline even to participate in this piecemeal method of litigation. Moreover, in abstention, such complexity, entailing as it does substantial hardships for the litigant who desires a federal forum, is justified by the countervailing considerations of federalism which arise when a federal court is faced *in a particular case* with an unsettled question of state law, the resolution of which might make decision of a federal constitutional question unnecessary, or with other special circumstances. Since such circumstances clearly do not exist in *every* private civil rights action, it does not seem proper to require every such litigant who desires that a federal court should decide his federal constitutional question to shuttle between state and federal courts. Congress could simply withdraw res judicata effect from state determinations of federal issues in such cases; but we would again encounter arguments such as delay, expense, and lesser receptivity of some state courts to federal constitutional claims.

A general exhaustion requirement would thus mean, in practical effect, that all private civil rights litigants would be left to the state courts with the attendant possibility of Supreme Court review of the state court judgment. The inadequacies of such a procedure from a federal perspective are self-evident. The Court is in no better position to correct constitutional errors in all civil rights judgments of 50 state courts than it was with respect to their judgments in criminal cases; it was this bursting of the dikes that led to the efflorescence of federal

419 F.2d 10 (5th Cir. 1969), *cert. denied*, 397 U.S. 1065 (1970); Howe v. Brouse, 422 F.2d 347 (8th Cir. 1970); Scott v. California Supreme Court, 426 F.2d 300 (9th Cir. 1970); Lackawanna Police Benevolent Ass'n v. Balen, 446 F.2d 52 (2d Cir. 1971). *But see* dissenting opinions in Brown v. Chastain, *supra*, 416 F.2d at 1017–23 and in Florida State Bd. v. Mack, 401 U.S. 960 (1971).

114. *See* England v. Louisiana State Bd. of Medical Examiners, 375 U.S. 411 (1964).

115. *See* C. WRIGHT, HANDBOOK OF THE LAW OF FEDERAL COURTS 199 (1970).

habeas corpus for state prisoners.[116] To be sure, in my discussion of abstention, I indicated that in certain circumstances a federal court, in the exercise of its equitable discretion, would be justified in declining jurisdiction and leaving the parties to state court proceedings and the possibility of Supreme Court review. But the circumstances in which such action is appropriate are narrow and should not be expanded into a general rule. In short, I would consider it a serious mistake to impose a general requirement of "exhaustion" of state judicial remedies in civil rights cases.[117]

A requirement of exhaustion for a more limited class of cases —namely, state prisoner civil rights actions—is another matter. The power of federal courts to deal with the federal constitutional claims of state prisoners has long been a subject of controversy. Until recently, though, this has focused upon federal court jurisdiction to entertain the habeas corpus petitions of state prisoners challenging the validity of their convictions. It seems appropriate to consider this by way of introduction—though I shall not say very much since I have expressed my views elsewhere.[118] I there noted how the volume of petitions for such relief had grown from the 541 which Mr. Justice Jackson in 1953 had characterized as the "floods of stale, frivolous and repetitious petitions [which] inundate the docket of the lower courts and swell our own"[119] to 7,359 in 1969.[120] After a further rise to 9,063 in 1970, these dropped to 8,372 in 1971 and 7,949 in 1972.[121] While this downturn is gratifying, it should not

---

116. Brown v. Allen, 344 U.S. 443 (1953); *see* Friendly, *Is Innocence Irrelevant? Collateral Attack on Criminal Judgments*, 38 U. CHI. L. REV. 142, 154–55, 164–65 (1970).

117. For a good statement on this, see Judge Wisdom's opinion in Moreno v. Henckel, *supra*, 431 F.2d 1299.

118. *Supra*, 38 U. CHI. L. REV. 142.

119. Brown v. Allen, *supra*, 344 U.S. at 536 & n.8 (concurring opinion).

120. A.O. ANN. REP. 141 (1969).

121. A.O. ANN. REP., Table 17 (1972). The baselessness of prophecies that such petitions will phase themselves away because the Supreme Court has run out of new constitutional doctrines in criminal procedure is demonstrated by the death penalty decision, Furman v. Georgia, 408 U.S. 238 (1972). This will give rise to two new series of cases—one dealing with death penalty statutes seeking to come within the views expressed by Justices Stewart and White, the other complaining of excessive penalties on the basis of dicta in the opinions of Justices Douglas, Brennan and Marshall.

obscure the facts that these petitions still compromise 8.3% of the "civil" filings[122] and that they are largely, and increasingly, a waste of judicial time. The figures for 1971 indicate that 96% of the petitions failed to attain even the limited success of winning a new trial or appeal.[123] These figures emphasize the need for legislation that would limit such petitions, save for certain exceptions which I have noted, to cases where the alleged constitutional error may be causing the punishment of an innocent man.[124]

We come then to the new area of controversy with respect to state prisoners—civil rights complaints. The moderate downturn in petitions by state prisoners attacking their convictions has been accompanied by a violent upswing in complaints by state prisoners attacking the conditions of their confinement and the denial of good-time credits. These rose from 218 in 1966 to 2,915 in 1971[125] and 3,348 in 1972.[126] The handling of such a complaint imposes burdens on the district judge considerably greater than the usual habeas corpus petition attacking the validity of a state conviction. Whereas most of the latter can be decided without an evidentiary hearing on the basis of the record of state proceedings, the new breed of prisoner complaints generally involves disputed issues of fact. Unless such complaints are to be subjected to higher standards of specificity than are complaints in general[127] or the Rules of Civil Procedure should be amended to broaden the use of summary judgment in such cases, oral hearings would seem necessary in the great bulk; indeed, it is quite likely that this factor itself enhances the attractiveness of such complaints.

No one can deny, however, that some of these complaints have revealed serious denials of federal constitutional rights,[128] although

122. A.O. ANN. REP., Table C2 (1972).
123. A.O. ANN. REP. 132 (1971).
124. For proposals along these lines, see S. 895, 92d Cong., 2d Sess. (1972); S. 3833, 92d Cong., 2d Sess. (1972).
125. A.O. ANN. REP. 135 (1971).
126. A.O. ANN. REP., Table 17 (1972).
127. Mr. Justice Rehnquist has suggested this. *See* Cruz v. Beto, 405 U.S. 319, 326–28 (1972) (dissenting opinion).
128. *See, e.g.*, Wright v. McMann, 387 F.2d 519 (2d Cir. 1967), 460 F.2d 126 (2d Cir. 1972), *cert. denied*, 41 U.S.L.W. 3188 (Oct. 10, 1972); Jackson v. Bishop, 404 F.2d 571 (8th Cir. 1968) (Blackmun, J.); Holt v. Sarver, 309 F. Supp. 362 (E.D. Ark. 1970), *aff'd*, 442

many are exceedingly trivial. There could be no more thought of suggesting that such wrongs should go without a remedy than of proposing such a course with respect to state prisoners attacking the validity of their convictions. It would be equally improper to deny a "final federal say." The serious question is what, if anything, state prisoners must do within the state system before getting this.

My first proposition is that if a state has provided suitable administrative remedies for hearing prisoner complaints, these must be exhausted. While, as stated, I favor a general requirement of exhaustion of state administrative remedies,[129] the reasons for this are particularly compelling here. Such a step would help substantially to stem the rising tide of prisoner civil rights complaints, *provided* that the states develop adequate administrative schemes. It is in everyone's interest that they should, as was the case with the development of state post-conviction remedies. The state, which has a special concern with the rehabilitation or incapacitation of persons convicted of violating its penal laws, also has a special responsibility to give them decent treatment and to impose only such restrictions on rights accorded other citizens as are necessary to prevent disorder and escape.[130] Moreover, the administrative process is far better suited than the judicial to deal with complaints, many of them minor, emanating from such large government run institutions as the prisons.

F.2d 304 (8th Cir. 1971), *noted in* 84 HARV. L. REV. 456 (1970); Landman v. Royster, 333 F. Supp. 621 (E.D. Va. 1971); Anderson v. Nosser, 456 F.2d 835 (5th Cir. 1972) (en banc), *cert. denied,* 41 U.S.L.W. 3184 (Oct. 10, 1972). For a description of prison horrors, see Mattick, *The Prosaic Sources of Prison Violence,* Occasional Papers of the University of Chicago Law School 5–6 (1972). Contrast the procedures with respect to solitary confinement now prevailing in Texas, as described in Novak v. Beto, 453 F.2d 661, 666–69 (5th Cir. 1971). On the other hand, it is to be hoped that in the process of remedying serious deprivations of federal constitutional liberties in the context of prison facilities, judges can maintain a balanced perspective. Thus, what appears to be an otherwise sensible decision that prison officials could not forbid a prisoner to engage in amorous correspondence with his sister-in-law scarcely gains adherents by a statement, "I am persuaded that the institution of prison probably must end." Morales v. Schmidt, 340 F. Supp. 544, 548 (E.D. Wis. 1972).

129. *See* pp. 100–01 *supra.*
130. *See* Coffin v. Reichard, 143 F.2d 443, 445 (6th Cir. 1944), *cert. denied,* 325 U.S. 887 (1945).

A sweeping federal injunction, which leaves state prison officials to struggle with the day to day problems it creates, is generally not a satisfactory means of dealing with the issues that arise in this context. Rather, complaints concerning the action of prison officials should be handled in the first instance by state administrative machinery, which should provide for hearing officers independent of the prison administration, review of their reports by a senior state official not connected with the particular prison, and, to the extent feasible, assistance to prisoners by lawyers or volunteer law students.

Beyond this, prisoner complaints seeking declaratory or injunctive relief constitute a category that should be governed by the same formula applied in prisoner petitions attacking their convictions—initial resort to the state courts if effective state corrective process exists, with a right to return to the federal courts if satisfaction has not been obtained—rather than that applicable in civil rights cases generally. I have contended that this, in fact, has always been required since, under the broad scope the Supreme Court has given to the Great Writ as enacted by the Act of 1867,[131] all such petitions by state prisoners for injunctive relief with respect to the length or the conditions of their custody are, in fact, petitions for habeas corpus and are thus governed by the exhaustion requirement,[132] but are not subject to *res adjudicata* as a result of adverse state determination.[133] While that view has seemingly been rejected by the Supreme Court in summary dispositions that gave no real consideration to the arguments,[134] a recent grant of certiorari[135] may indicate that the issue has not been foreclosed. Whatever the Court may decide on this point which is now before it, nothing stands in the way of legislation assimilating such petitions to those attacking convictions. Whether such legislation should encompass actions for damages is another

---

131. Act of Feb. 5, 1867, ch. 28, 14 Stat. 385.

132. 28 U.S.C. § 2254(b).

133. Rodriguez v. McGinnis, 456 F.2d 79, 80 (2d Cir. 1972) (en banc) (concurring opinion), *cert. granted sub nom.* Oswald v. Rodriguez, 407 U.S. 919 (1972) (No. 71-1369).

134. Wilwording v. Swenson, 404 U.S. 249 (1971); Haines v. Kerner, 404 U.S. 519 (1972). *See also* Houghton v. Shafer, 392 U.S. 639 (1968).

135. *See* note 133 *supra*.

matter; I think it should if the state provides an adequate remedy, as most do not.

The relationship of the state to prisoners in its institutions is sufficiently different from its relations to other persons complaining of denial of civil rights guaranteed by the Constitution to warrant a requirement of initial invocation of state judicial remedies not usually imposed. These are people who have been adjudged guilty of breaking state criminal laws, often with very grave consequences to others. The state is in contact with them not merely daily but throughout the day—and the night as well. Their grievances are frequently of a sort that cannot be cured by prescription of a general rule but require determination of the facts of a specific incident. There are serious physical problems in hearing these cases in a federal court, usually many miles away, as distinguished from hearing by a state judge in a nearby county courthouse or in the prison itself.[136] While state officials may not precisely welcome federal interference in education, welfare, or public housing,[137] I believe there is particular resentment—and substantial ground for it—when a far-off federal judge issues declaratory or injunctive orders on behalf of a prisoner who has bypassed a nearby state judge ready and willing to hear him. Although one or more of these factors favoring prior resort to the state court may be found in other categories of civil rights litigation, I know of no other that combines them all. I realize that this is an unpopular position since prisoner complaints now lie so close to the hearts of civil rights lawyers. But that attitude will pass if Congress legislates a sensible system for dealing with state prisoner complaints and the states do their job.

136. This is well put in Judge Mansfield's concurring opinion in Rodriguez v. McGinnis, *supra,* 456 F.2d at 84. While a federal judge can also come to the prison or to a nearby town, he lacks the time to do so.
137. *See* Judge Kaufman's concurring opinion in Rodriguez v. McGinnis, *supra,* 456 F.2d at 82.

PART V

Other Federal Question Litigation— and herein of Standing, Class Actions, Jurisdictional Amount, and Federal Defense Removal

OTHER private litigation over federal questions includes a host of suits, of every conceivable sort, against other citizens and state governmental authorities.[1] When we add such litigation, together with civil rights actions, to the many heads of federal question litigation within the minimum model, 1972 style, we find, without going further, that the federal courts today are occupied with a set of legal problems unparalleled in variety and difficulty. While many of these actions could also be brought in state courts, they rarely are.

The jurisdictional bases for such litigation are too numerous to catalogue. Besides such sweeping provisions in Title 28 as that establishing the general federal question jurisdiction[2] and others[3] that would be rendered unnecessary if jurisdictional amount were to be abolished, substantive federal statutes often provide specifically for federal court jurisdiction over private actions.[4] There is little doubt that, to the extent that private parties are allowed to maintain such actions anywhere, access to the federal courts is appropriate.[5] However, the questions raised by litigation in this area are numerous;[6] I will limit my discussion to a number of basic ones.

1. When there is a claim of constitutional violation, actions against state authorities can now be brought under the Civil Rights Act. Lynch v. Household Fin. Corp., 405 U.S. 538 (1972). The reference here is to actions claiming, *e.g.*, that a state business regulatory statute runs counter to a federal act, or that state handling of federally assisted welfare programs does not comply with federal statutes or regulations.
2. 28 U.S.C. § 1331(a).
3. *See, e.g., id.* §§ 1337, 1338, 1348.
4. *E.g.*, Securities Act of 1933, § 22, 15 U.S.C. § 77v(a); Securities Exchange Act of 1934, § 27, 15 U.S.C. § 78aa; Consumer Credit Protection Act, § 130, 15 U.S.C. § 1640.
5. *See* ALI STUDY 164–68.
6. Some of them have been mentioned previously; indeed, there is in-

109

In Parts II and III, I noted the currently predominating trend in new federal regulatory laws to provide for initial enforcement by suit by the Government in federal district courts, and the heavy impact of such actions on available judge-power.[7] Here we deal with a concomitant having an even larger portent, efforts of private parties to maintain actions under many of these laws, although the statutes provide in terms only for suit by the Government. Ten years ago I was "bold enough to predict" that the development of bodies of federal common law in the context of private actions, based sometimes on asserted violation of a statute providing in terms only for enforcement by the Government, was "a young man with a future."[8] Only a year later I indicated that the future might already have become the present.[9] In 1972 it surely has. There is no occasion for me to replough the fields covered in these earlier lectures with respect to the growth of federal common law.[10] Yet insofar as that development has occurred in the context of legislation containing no express provision for private action, it is of considerable significance with respect to the substantial body of recent regulatory legislation. One need only consider the explosion of litigation under the SEC's Rule 10b-5, the

evitably some duplication in this Part of material more summarily stated in Parts II and III. The doctrines of abstention and of exhaustion of administrative and state judicial remedies, discussed in Part IV, are often relevant here. *See, e.g.,* Chemical Specialties Mfrs. Ass'n v. Lowery, 452 F.2d 431, 433 (2d Cir. 1971) (abstention).

7. *See* pp. 21, 61–62 *supra.*

8. Friendly, *The Gap in Lawmaking—Judges Who Can't and Legislators Who Won't,* 63 Colum. L. Rev. 787, 789 (1963), *reprinted in* Benchmarks 41, 44 (1967).

9. Friendly, *In Praise of Erie—and of the New Federal Common Law,* 39 N.Y.U.L. Rev. 383, 412–21 (1964), *reprinted in* Benchmarks 155, 185–94 (1967).

10. Two developments, both salutary in my view, should be noted. One is the stimulus to actions to enjoin strikes allegedly prohibited by contracts providing for arbitration, which was afforded by the Supreme Court's ruling that such actions are not within the ban previously held to have been established by the Norris-LaGuardia Act. Boys Markets, Inc. v. Retail Clerks Local 770, 398 U.S. 235 (1970). The other is the near certainty of legislation that will confer on the federal courts exclusive jurisdiction over airplane accidents giving rise to multiple claims. *See* Farrell v. Piedmont Aviation, Inc., 411 F.2d 812, 815 n.3 (2d Cir.), *cert. denied,* 396 U.S. 840 (1969).

proxy rules, and the new sections dealing with tender offers[11] added in 1968 to the Securities Exchange Act to realize the impact that any such regulatory law can have once a right of private action is implied. As already indicated, one of the most important of these will lie in efforts to establish implied private actions under federal environmental legislation, both new[12] and old.[13] Indeed, the Supreme Court has held that interstate interests in the environment are governed by federal common law even in the absence of a pertinent statute.[14]

Growth in such regulatory legislation is bound to continue. Many of our most aggravated problems, notably those relating to the environment, cannot be handled by a single state. It does no good for a state on the lower reaches of a great river to enact stern measures to prevent pollution if nothing is done by the state on the other side or a state upstream. Even when one state is able to take effective action, it can hardly be expected to impose a burden on its industries from which their competitors in other states are free. For this reason also it will no more be possible for a single state or group of states to deal successfully with many phases of protection of the environment than it was to deal with child labor. Thus, there is force in Judge J. Skelly Wright's view that in this area "Mr. Justice Brandeis' wonderful laboratory theory for state government experimentation has shipwrecked on the contemporary fact of industrial mobility; no state dares impose sweeping new regulations on industry, for their imposition would drive away business concerns whose presence in the state opens up employment opportunities and accounts for vital tax revenues."[15] At the very least the federal government must set

---

11. §§ 2, 3, 82 Stat. 454–57, *as amended,* 15 U.S.C. §§ 78m(d), 78n(d)–(f).

12. *See* Water and Environmental Quality Improvement Act of 1970, § 102, 84 Stat. 94, 96, 33 U.S.C. §§ 1161(e), 1163(i).

13. *See* Rivers and Harbors Act of 1899, ch. 425, § 13, 30 Stat. 1152, *now* 33 U.S.C. § 407.

14. Illinois v. City of Milwaukee, 406 U.S. 91, 99–100 (1972), *quoting with approval from* Texas v. Pankey, 441 F.2d 236, 240 (10th Cir. 1971).

15. J. S. Wright, *The Federal Courts and the Nature and Quality of State Law,* 13 WAYNE L. REV. 317, 331–32 (1967). In his zeal to demolish Justice Brandeis, Judge Wright did not mention that the "wonderful laboratory theory" was enunciated with respect to a state statute requiring a license to engage in the manufacture, sale or distribution of

minimum standards.[16] I have already noted the use of this model in the welfare field.[17]

With respect to such future legislation, as well as some already enacted, one might wonder whether Congress ought not to spell out more clearly whether and, if so, under what circumstances it intends to allow private persons to bring enforcement proceedings.[18] Where to strike the balance depends on a number of factors in addition to the burden of private suits on the federal courts. Pointing in one direction is the adverse effect of such suits on a well-considered policy of enforcement and the likelihood of settlements by governmental agencies which may be more productive than long litigation. On the other side are the aid furnished by such actions to understaffed government agencies and the safeguard they afford against bureaucratic sluggishness. Much depends also on whether the defendant's acts have caused such serious economic wrong to a person or persons that relief looking only to the future will not be adequate. These are factors that should be weighed by Congress whenever it considers legislation.[19]

ice, where the factors emphasized by Judge Wright would hardly exist. New State Ice Co. v. Liebmann, 285 U.S. 262, 311 (1932) (Brandeis, J., dissenting). There are still a good many such cases.

16. *See* Freund, *The Supreme Court and the Future of Federalism*, in THE FUTURE OF FEDERALISM 37, 47–48 (S. Schuman ed. 1968), citing the unemployment insurance law.

17. *See* pp. 25–26 *supra.*

18. For example, in The Clean Air Amendments of 1970, § 12(a), 84 Stat. 1706, 42 U.S.C. § 1857h-2, Congress specifically spelled out when and under what conditions a private party could sue in a federal district court to enforce federal air quality standards.

19. These factors would seem very relevant in the evaluation of a number of bills pending before the last Congress which would authorize citizen suits against public bodies and private persons to protect the environment. *See* S. 1032, 92d Cong., 1st Sess. (1971); H.R. 49, 92d Cong., 1st Sess. (1971); H.R. 5074, 92d Cong., 1st Sess. (1971); H.R. 5075, 92d Cong., 1st Sess. (1971); H.R. 5076, 92d Cong., 1st Sess. (1971); H.R. 8331, 92d Cong., 1st Sess. (1971). With the single exception of H.R. 49, the legislative drafters neatly attempted to avoid any Article III problems with respect to the expansive right of action which these bills would create by limiting such actions to those instances in which the challenged "activity and [the] action for relief constitute a case or controversy"—thereby passing the buck to the courts.

Assuming that the statute is silent or speaks only in Delphic terms, we reach the topic of standing. When the suit, although founded on a federal statute, is solely between private persons, there seems to be little doubt that a plaintiff must show economic injury in traditional terms. This is eminently sound policy even if the "case or controversy" requirement did not compel such a result, as it very well may. As Judge Oscar Davis has said, "To allow any citizen to perform that function, normally fulfilled by the Government," of representing the public in seeking to confine private individuals within the law, would "raise grave problems for equal, fair, and consistent law enforcement."[20] None of the cases implying private rights of action, of which *J. I. Case Co. v. Borak*[21] is typical, goes so far. Again to quote Judge Davis, "The claimant in each of those cases had been or could be financially injured by the unlawful conduct, and the court also thought that the statute on which he relied was designed to protect his particular group, as distinguished from the general public. *Borak* would only be in point if it had permitted a plaintiff owning no stock in the corporation to sue the company for false and misleading proxy statements because, as a matter of personal conviction, he strongly disapproved of tainted proxy solicitations and, as a matter of public policy, believed that misleading proxy solicitations are a general menace to the free enterprise system."[22] However, this limitation will not stem the torrent of actions between private persons if Congress should move further in authorizing actions by consumers who have been the victims of some unfair business practice. We already have four permanent pieces of legislation on consumer protection, the Consumer Credit Protection Act,[23] the Fair Credit Reporting Act,[24] and the Interstate Land Sales Full Disclosure Act,[25] and now the Consumer Product Safety Act,[26] and one supposedly temporary one, the 1971 Economic Stabilization Act

20. Connecticut Action Now, Inc. v. Roberts Plating Co., 457 F.2d 81, 90 (2d Cir. 1972).
21. 377 U.S. 426 (1964).
22. *Supra,* 457 F.2d at 90.
23. 15 U.S.C. §§ 1601 *et seq.*
24. *Id.* §§ 1671 *et seq.*
25. *Id.* §§ 1701 *et seq.*
26. 86 Stat. 1207 (1972).

Amendments,[27] whose impact has yet to be felt. Yet these statutes, except perhaps the last, would be as nothing when compared to the proposals that suits for all kinds of unfair practices upon consumers may be brought in the federal courts.

In contrast to suits against private persons, where traditional notions of standing are relatively intact, there has been a substantial relaxation of this requirement when the complaint challenges acts or failures to act by federal administrative officials. Although I shall speak in terms of actions against federal officials, similar considerations apply in actions against state officers, except for the bearing of the Administrative Procedure Act.

In addition to its traditional regulatory activities, the federal government has long been involved in a variety of managerial functions of direct concern to large segments of the private sector. For example, it manages forests which private interests are allowed to mine and lumber;[28] it controls navigable rivers and their use;[29] it authorizes the construction of highways to which federal funds are contributed.[30] With the growth in federal regulatory and grant legislation, the conduct of federal officials undoubtedly affects the lives of more people more directly than ever before in our nation's history. Some federal statutes provide for suits by persons "aggrieved" by the actions of administrative authorities;[31] others do not.[32]

In 1953, Mr. Justice Frankfurter described the standing doctrine as a "complicated specialty of federal jurisdiction, the solution of whose problems is . . . more or less determined by the specific circumstances of individual situations . . . ."[33] In recent decisions the Supreme Court has taken considerable strides toward eliminating complexity.

---

27. 85 Stat. 743 (1971).
28. *See, e.g.*, Sierra Club v. Hardin, 325 F. Supp. 99 (D. Alas. 1971).
29. *See, e.g.*, Citizens Committee for the Hudson Valley v. Volpe, 425 F.2d 97 (2d Cir. 1970), *cert. denied*, 400 U.S. 949 (1971).
30. *See, e.g.*, Citizens to Preserve Overton Park, Inc. v. Volpe, 401 U.S. 402 (1971).
31. *E.g.*, Federal Water Power Act, 16 U.S.C. § 825*l*(b), *as added by* Act of Aug. 26, 1935, ch. 687, § 213(b), 49 Stat. 860–61.
32. *E.g.*, Bank Service Act of 1962, §§ 1–5, 76 Stat. 1132, 12 U.S.C. §§ 1861–65.
33. United States *ex rel.* Chapman v. FPC, 345 U.S. 153, 156.

The distance we have traveled can be discerned by going back to the 1939 decision in *Tennessee Electric Power Co. v. TVA*.[34] When confronted with a challenge by private power companies to the constitutionality of the TVA, the Court said:[35]

The appellants invoke the doctrine that one threatened with direct and special injury by the act of an agent of the government which, but for statutory authority for its performance, would be a violation of its legal rights, may challenge the validity of the statute in a suit against the agent. The principle is without application unless the right invaded is a legal right—one of property, one arising out of contract, or one founded on a statute which confers a privilege.

The view thus prevailed that, as a general matter, Article III's requirement of "case or controversy" demanded a "substantive legally protected interest" for a private party to have standing to challenge federal action.[36] Thirty years later the Court rendered two decisions which swept such learning aside. In *Association of Data Processing Service Organizations, Inc. v. Camp*,[37] its main opinion, the Court said:[38]

The "legal interest" test goes to the merits. The question of standing is different. It concerns, apart from the "case" or "controversy" test, the question whether the interest sought to be protected is arguably within the zone of interest to be protected or regulated by the statute or constitutional guarantee in question.

If "the plaintiff alleges that the challenged action has caused him injury in fact, economic or otherwise,"[39] he both satisfies the constitutional test and has "standing."

However, the Supreme Court still insists on a showing of injury of some sort. In *Sierra Club v. Morton*, it disapproved decisions of inferior courts "conferring standing upon organizations that have

34. 306 U.S. 118.
35. *Id*. at 137–38 (footnotes omitted).
36. *See, e.g.*, Associated Indus. of New York State, Inc. v. Ickes, 134 F.2d 694, 700 (2d Cir.), *vacated as moot*, 320 U.S. 707 (1943).
37. 397 U.S. 150 (1970). The companion case decided the same day was Barlow v. Collins, 397 U.S. 159.
38. *Id*. at 153.
39. *Id*. at 152. The Court emphasized the "or otherwise" by adding "[t]hat interest, at times, may reflect aesthetic, conservational, and recreational as well as economic values." *Id*. at 154.

demonstrated 'an organizational interest in the problem' of environmental or consumer protection."[40] If their members are injured, such organizations have standing and can assert public as well as private claims. "But a mere 'interest in a problem,' no matter how longstanding the interest and no matter how qualified the organization is in evaluating the problem, is not sufficient by itself to render the organization 'adversely affected' or 'aggrieved' within the meaning of the APA"[41]—or presumably to give it standing to attack state administrative action. In a sense the Court's opinion may seem trivial at least with respect to environmental cases, in view of its indications that the Sierra Club could have achieved standing by sending a single member on a hike into the Mineral King Valley[42] and that the Club's defeat came from its stiff-necked determination to establish that not even such a minimal effort was required. Still the opinion is to be applauded for putting some limits on a development that would have given standing to anyone objecting to governmental action, whether he would suffer any injury or not.[43] While I see no basis for believing that new legislation with respect to "standing" could improve on what the Court has done, it must be realized what a vast expansion of federal jurisdiction the Court has wrought.

A related question in this area is the relationship between standing to seek judicial review and intervention in formal administrative processes, where available. It was held long ago that "[t]he mere fact

40. 405 U.S. 727, 738–39 (1972). Among the leading decisions thus condemned were Citizens Committee for the Hudson Valley v. Volpe, 425 F.2d 97, 105 (2d Cir. 1970); and Environmental Defense Fund, Inc. v. Hardin, 428 F.2d 1093, 1096–97 (D.C. Cir. 1970).

41. 405 U.S. at 739. The Court took occasion to dispel confusion created by a dictum in Scripps-Howard Radio, Inc. v. FCC, 316 U.S. 4, 14 (1942), where economic injury was clear. Similarly in Associated Indus. of New York State, Inc. v. Ickes, *supra*, 134 F.2d 694, where Judge Jerome Frank gave birth to the "private attorney general" phrase, *id.* at 704, the plaintiff's members were major consumers of coal who were faced with the prospect of substantial economic harm from the minimum coal price orders they sought to challenge, and thus had an interest at stake discernibly different from that of the public at large.

42. 405 U.S. at 735–36 & n.8.

43. The "organizational interest" notion was impossible of rational application. How large would the organization have to be—five hundred, one hundred or ten? And if ten would suffice, why not one?

that [a party] was permitted to intervene before [an agency] does not entitle it to institute an independent suit to set aside [the agency's] order in the absence of resulting actual or threatened legal injury to it . . . ."[44] Whatever the shifts in the law of judicial standing since Mr. Justice Brandeis wrote those words in 1930, his basic proposition —that judicial standing does not automatically accrue from the fact of administrative intervention—necessarily continues to be true.[45]

44. Pittsburgh & W. Va. Ry. v. United States, 281 U.S. 479, 486 (1930) (citation omitted). In saying this, Mr. Justice Brandeis effectively qualified his perhaps overbroad statements, made some six years earlier, that "plaintiffs may challenge the order because they are parties to it. . . . [T]he fact of intervention, allowed as it was, implied a finding by the Commission that plaintiffs have an interest." Chicago Junction Case, 264 U.S. 258, 267–68 (1924).

45. *See, e.g.,* Moffat Tunnel League v. United States, 289 U.S. 113, 120–21 (1933); Perkins v. Lukens Steel Co., 310 U.S. 113 (1940); Boston Tow Boat Co. v. United States, 321 U.S. 632 (1944); Jersey City v. United States, 101 F. Supp. 702 (D.N.J. 1950) (three-judge court); North Carolina Natural Gas Corp. v. United States, 200 F. Supp. 745, 751–52 (D. Del. 1961) (three-judge court); National Motor Freight Traffic Ass'n, Inc. v. United States, 205 F. Supp. 592, 593 (D.D.C.) (three-judge court), *aff'd,* 371 U.S. 223 (1962), *rehearing denied and opinion clarified,* 372 U.S. 246 (1963) (affirming on the merits, but disagreeing with district court's determination that appellants lacked standing, although not with its statement that intervention before the agency did not assure right to seek judicial review).

Of course, there may be instances in which the scope of the right to intervene at the administrative level and the scope of the right to seek judicial review coincide. Such appears to be the case with respect to the FCC. Thus, Chief Justice Burger, while still on the Court of Appeals for the District of Columbia Circuit, wrote in the context of an action challenging a denial of intervention before the FCC:

All parties seem to consider that the same standards are applicable to determining standing before the Commission and standing to appeal a Commission order to this court. We have, therefore, used the cases dealing with standing in the two tribunals interchangeably.

Office of Communication of the United Church of Christ v. FCC, 359 F.2d 994, 1000 n.8 (D.C. Cir. 1966) (citations omitted). Whatever the appropriateness of looking to cases involving judicial standing, and to a party's right ultimately to seek judicial review in determining the party's right of administrative intervention, *compare, e.g.,* American Communications Ass'n v. United States, 298 F.2d 648, 650–51 (2d Cir. 1962); National Welfare Rights Organization v. Finch, 429 F.2d 725, 732–38 (D.C. Cir. 1970), courts should exercise completely independent judgment in deciding the question of standing to seek judicial review in such "mirror image" situations.

The need for a "case or controversy" to seek judicial review but not to intervene in an administrative hearing; the differences between statutes and agency rules controlling intervention and statutes controlling judicial review; and the differing characters of administrative and judicial proceedings[46]—all of these negate any general rule linking a person's standing to seek judicial review to the fact that he has been allowed to intervene before the agency.

Another development which has greatly augmented the volume of private litigation of the type here considered is the expanded concept of the class action resulting from the 1966 amendment of Rule 23 of the Federal Rules of Civil Procedure.[47] When the action is against a government official, this creates few problems, and indeed may provide substantial benefits. To be sure, there may be some question of the need for a class action in such cases. The relief sought is generally an injunction or a declaratory judgment and, although in strict theory such a decree in an action brought by an individual plaintiff binds the government officer only with respect to him, normally the government—federal, state or local—will regard a decision by the highest court to which the question can be taken as controlling, at least for the future, with respect to all persons similarly situated. However, this may not invariably be true. Also the class action may in some instances assist a plaintiff in surmounting a hurdle of jurisdictional amount, and it can benefit a successful defendant in preventing further litigation—a point that may be of particular interest to government agencies in environmental litigation. Putting the matter in more technical terms, I perceive few grounds for serious criticism of Rule 23(b)(2).[48]

The difficulty has arisen largely from Rule 23(b)(3) or, more accurately, from the judicial gloss that a prime purpose of this sec-

---

46. *See* 3 Davis, Administrative Law Treatise § 22.08, at 241 (1958).
47. An interesting by-product of this is the rule of the Second Circuit that denial of class action status is appealable if this would ring a "death-knell" in prosecution of the action. See Eisen v. Carlisle & Jacquelin, 370 F.2d 119 (1966), *cert. denied*, 386 U.S. 1035 (1967), and the contrary decision in Hackett v. General Host Corp., 455 F.2d 618 (3d Cir.), *cert. denied*, 407 U.S. 925 (1972). Some day the Supreme Court will have to resolve this conflict. Why not now?
48. So far as I am aware there has also been no criticism of Rule 23(b)(1).

tion was to provide "small claimants with a method for obtaining redress for claims which would otherwise be too small to warrant individual litigation."[49] While this has a fine ring, its practical consequences may not have been sufficiently appreciated. In the case where this goal was announced by the court of appeals, the district judge later estimated that the average recovery for the 6,000,000 members of the class might be as low as $1.30 or, when trebled since this was an antitrust case, $3.90.[50] Since it is obviously impracticable to send 6,000,000 notices, the requirements for the sending of notice and the consequent possibility of "opting-out"[51] were largely ignored. The benefit to any individual plaintiff often is minimal, considerably less than the cost of ascertaining his identity, establishing his damages, and preparing and mailing a check for the few dollars to which he is entitled. Since many members of the class and their damages often cannot be ascertained, it has been proposed that there should be a "fluid class recovery,"[52] meaning that the portion belonging to claimants who have not presented themselves and proved their damages should be devoted to a purpose that would benefit generally the class which was harmed by the defendant's unlawful conduct. As Professor Handler has pointed out, whatever the propriety of this when the action has been settled for a lump sum and the defendant no longer has any interest in the apportionment of the fund, it is radically new law for purposes of litigation; in what would have been a "spurious" class action "[t]he class as a whole has no right to recover anything."[53] While the benefits to the individual class members are usually minuscule, the possible consequences of a judgment to the defendant are so horrendous that these

49. Eisen v. Carlisle & Jacquelin, 391 F.2d 555, 560 (2d Cir. 1968).
50. *See* Eisen v. Carlisle & Jacquelin, 52 F.R.D. 253, 265 (S.D.N.Y. 1971); AMERICAN COLLEGE OF TRIAL LAWYERS, REPORT AND RECOMMENDATIONS OF THE SPECIAL COMMITTEE ON RULE 23 OF THE FEDERAL RULES OF CIVIL PROCEDURE, at 15 & n.38 (1972).
51. F.R. CIV. P. 23(c)(2). It is understood that in one case the cost of mailing notices, there charged against the budget of the federal judiciary, exceeded $450,000.
52. *Supra*, 52 F.R.D. at 264–65.
53. Handler, *Twenty-Fourth Annual Antitrust Review*, 72 COLUM. L. REV. 1, 36–41 (1972). For an opposing view see Note, *Damage Distribution in Class Actions: The Cy Pres Remedy*, 39 U. CHI. L. REV. 448 (1972).

actions are almost always settled. Generally this is for a figure constituting a small fraction of the amount claimed but large enough to yield compensation to the plaintiffs' lawyers which seems inordinate even in these days of high legal fees.[54] It is thus not surprising that the suits designated as class actions in the Southern District of New York grew from 118 in 1967 to 410 in 1971.[55] And mere figures give no idea of the burdens such actions impose.

Something seems to have gone radically wrong with a well-intentioned effort. Of course, an injured plaintiff should be compensated, but the federal judicial system is not adapted to affording compensation to classes of hundreds of people with $10 or even $50 claims.[56] The important thing is to stop the evil conduct. For this an injunction is the appropriate remedy, and an attorney who obtains one should be properly compensated by the defendant, although not in the astronomical terms fixed when there is a multi-million dollar settlement. If it be said that this still leaves the defendant with the fruits of past wrong-doing, consideration might be given to civil fines, payable to the government, sufficiently substantial to discourage engaging in such conduct but not so colossal as to produce recoveries that would ruin innocent stockholders or, what is more likely, produce blackmail settlements.[57] This is a matter that needs urgent attention.

Another problem in the federal question area is whether there should be any requirement of jurisdictional amount, either for initial invocation of jurisdiction or for removal. There is obvious appeal in the position that a person claiming a right conferred by the Constitution or a law or a treaty of the United States should be able to

54. The supposed justification is the contingent nature of the fee. But there is little real contingency with respect to achieving a substantial settlement once designation as a class suit has been attained in these gargantuan actions.

55. REPORT, *supra* note 50, at 13. As of June 30, 1972, there were 3,148 class actions pending in the district courts—some 3% of the total civil litigation. 1972 A.O. REPORT, II–96–97.

56. See Judge Gibbons' remark in Hackett v. General Host Corp., *supra*, 455 F.2d at 625–26.

57. Handler, *The Shift from Substantive to Procedural Innovations in Antitrust Suits—the Twenty-Third Annual Antitrust Review*, 71 COLUM. L. REV. 1, 9 (1971). *See also* Judge Lumbard's dissenting opinion in Eisen v. Carlisle & Jacquelin, *supra*, 391 F.2d at 572.

have that claim passed upon by a federal tribunal, no matter how small its amount. However, we must recall that, but for a single exception of one year's duration,[58] eighty-six years elapsed before Congress conferred general federal question jurisdiction at all;[59] that when it did, it imposed a jurisdictional amount; and that the only change in this provision in the last 97 years has been to increase it.[60] Yet, while this is the truth, it is not the whole truth. Chapter 85 of the Judicial Code specifies a large number of matters in which federal question jurisdiction exists without jurisdictional amount. Today the most important of these is section 1343(3), conferring federal jurisdiction over suits "[t]o redress the deprivation, under color of any State law, statute, ordinance, regulation, custom or usage, of any right, privilege or immunity secured by the Constitution of the United States or by any Act of Congress providing for equal rights of citizens or of all persons within the jurisdiction of the United States," and, as noted above,[61] the Supreme Court now reads this and its jurisdictional supplement so as to include every conceivable attack on state action violating a specific provision of the Constitution other than the supremacy clause.

The area where a jurisdictional amount for federal question cases has long been recognized to be most offensive[62] is one considered in the discussion of suits against the United States,[63] namely, suits against federal officers or agencies to enjoin or require action alleged to be forbidden or required by federal law. Such actions do not differ, except in form, from the review which most statutes specifically permit regardless of the amount involved. A pertinent example of the latter is the provision for review of actions of the Social Security Administration[64] with respect to disability pensions, where

58. Act of Feb. 13, 1801, ch. 4, § 11, 2 Stat. 92, *repealed by* Act of March 8, 1802, ch. 8, § 1, 2 Stat. 132.
59. Act of March 3, 1875, ch. 137, § 1, 18 Stat. 470.
60. *See* Act of March 3, 1887, ch. 373, § 1, 24 Stat. 552 ($2,000); Act of March 3, 1911, ch. 231, § 24, 36 Stat. 1091 ($3,000); Act of July 25, 1958, § 1, 72 Stat. 415 ($10,000).
61. *See* pp. 91–92 *supra*.
62. *See* Wechsler, *Federal Jurisdiction and the Revision of the Judicial Code*, 13 LAW & CONTEMP. PROB. 216, 220 (1948).
63. *See* pp. 69–70 *supra*.
64. 42 U.S.C. § 405(g).

the amount involved often does not approach $10,000. But there are instances where Congress has neither provided for nor excluded such review, and it is in these that the problem of jurisdictional amount still arises. There can thus be no sound objection to the recommendation of the Administrative Conference that Title 28 should be amended "to eliminate any requirement of a minimum jurisdictional amount before U.S. district courts may exercise original jurisdiction over any action in which the plaintiff alleges that he has been injured or threatened with injury by an officer or employee of the United States or any agency thereof, acting under color of Federal law."[65]

The remaining general federal question cases fall into two principal classes: suits by citizens against state officers and suits between private citizens. Under the Supreme Court's recent ruling the former are now cognizable in federal court without regard to amount, under the jurisdictional implementation of the Civil Rights Act, if the state action is alleged to have violated the Constitution even as regards property rights. However, the $10,000 amount is required if the complaint alleges merely that the state has violated a federal statute, unless the statute be one providing for equal rights of citizens, a phrase that has properly been given a rather narrow meaning.[66] Suits between private citizens generally will not be cognizable in the absence of the jurisdictional amount unless there is a specific provision for such suits in the relevant statute or they arise under one of the types of statute described in various sections of Chapter 85, notably "any Act of Congress regulating commerce or protecting trade or commerce against restraints and monopolies."[67]

---

65. 1 RECOMMENDATIONS AND REPORTS OF THE ADMINISTRATIVE CONFERENCE OF THE UNITED STATES 169 (1970). The amendment would be unnecessary if, as contended by Professor Davis, ADMINISTRATIVE LAW TREATISE § 23.02, at 791 (Supp. 1970), § 10(a) of the Administrative Procedure Act, *now* 5 U.S.C. § 702, was itself a jurisdictional grant. But the courts have been slow either to affirm or to deny this proposition.

66. *Cf.* Georgia v. Rachel, 384 U.S. 780, 789–90 (1966); City of Greenwood v. Peacock, 384 U.S. 808, 824–25 (1966).

67. 28 U.S.C. § 1337.

One thing which seems plain is that the present patch-work structure is indefensible; Congress should move in one direction or the other. It is impossible, for example, to comprehend why there should be no requirement of jurisdictional amount with respect to actions arising under federal regulatory statutes drawing in part on the commerce clause[68] but should be one under regulatory statutes exclusively based on other powers. A good example of what seems to be the absurdity of the present regime is a recent case where our circuit was constrained to dismiss for lack of jurisdictional amount an action raising an important question of the validity of New York and New Jersey legislation under the congressionally approved compact establishing the Port of New York Authority.[69] The distinction whereby no jurisdictional amount is required for actions challenging acts of state officers as violating the Constitution but is required when they are claimed only to have violated a statute has proved particularly troublesome in the growing field of welfare litigation. In one opinion of mine,[70] the discussion of jurisdictional problems required six printed pages which must be as tiresome to read as they were to write; when we finally reached the merits, only half a page was needed to sustain the plaintiffs' claim that New York's practices with respect to terminating benefits under federally assisted programs, although not unconstitutional, violated valid federal regulations. Clearly the case was appropriate for a federal court, and we should have been able to reach the substantive issue without delay.

Since Congress must move in one direction or the other, I would favor its moving to abolish the requirement of jurisdictional amount for initial invocation of jurisdiction in general federal question cases.[71] These cases must be tried somewhere, and the federal courts possess

---

68. The courts have gone a long way in stretching this. *See, e.g.,* the writer's opinion in Murphy v. Colonial Fed. Sav. & Loan Ass'n, 388 F.2d 609, 614 (2d Cir. 1967).

69. Kheel v. Port of New York Authority, 457 F.2d 46 (2d Cir. 1972), *cert. denied,* 41 U.S.L.W. 3248 (Nov. 7, 1972).

70. Almenares v. Wyman, 453 F.2d 1075 (2d Cir. 1971), *cert. denied,* 405 U.S. 944 (1972).

71. This would be in line with the views stated long ago by Professor Wechsler, *supra,* 13 LAW & CONTEMP. PROB. at 225–26, and recommended in the ALI STUDY § 1311(a).

greater expertise. Although precise figures are lacking, I believe the added load, though substantial,[72] would not be serious; moreover, it would be somewhat counterbalanced by avoiding the difficult jurisdictional problems arising under the present system.

On the other hand, I have serious question how far it is advisable to introduce federal defense removal in civil cases on a broad scale, as recommended by the American Law Institute,[73] when the federal courts are under such severe pressure. We have too little notion what its burdens would be, and there has been no empirical showing for its need. There was substantial difference of opinion within the Institute on whether removal should be allowed on the basis of a constitutional as contrasted with a federal statutory defense.[74] The view that a constitutional defense should not be a ground for removal was not based, of course, on any lack of respect for the Constitution, but rather on a fear that the provisions of that great instrument are necessarily so open-ended that imaginative defense lawyers would manage to contrive the assertion of a constitutional defense in a great number of cases which could be perfectly well handled in the state courts. Even if the federal court were subsequently to hold the assertion unsubstantial and to remand, much time and expense would be incurred, both by the parties and by the courts —indeed, these are the cases where removal is at its worst.

Perhaps the largest class of cases where removal would be effected on the basis of a constitutional defense under the ALI proposal would be actions for defamation or loss of privacy. The defendant would almost always assert a violation of *New York Times v. Sullivan*[75] and its progeny, and even if the proposed $10,000 requirement for removal were retained, it would not be effective in such cases, where complaints generally seek astronomical amounts. Federal courts have more important functions today than trying defamation suits not otherwise within federal jurisdiction. If there is evidence that state courts have not been properly applying the *New York Times* doctrine, I have not seen it. Another type of action that would be

72. For an example, see Kiernan v. Lindsay, 334 F. Supp. 588 (S.D.N.Y. 1971) (three-judge court), *aff'd mem.*, 405 U.S. 1000 (1972).
73. ALI STUDY § 1312(a)(2).
74. *Id.* at 198.
75. 376 U.S. 254 (1964).

rather regularly removed if the jurisdictional amount requirement for federal defense removal were abolished would be eviction suits by public housing authorities, by owners of publicly assisted housing, or even, in some cases, by private citizens. Proceedings for civil commitment would be another fertile ground for a constitutional defense; proceedings for civil contempt for refusal to answer questions would be another. We are witnessing the development of a new set of due process concepts that have wide implications on such subjects as conditional sale contracts, distraint, garnishment, replevin and cognovit judgments. We thus cannot predict what the added burden from removal on the basis of a federal constitutional defense would be, and we cannot now afford to take risks that some might have regarded as not unreasonable in 1968.

I am by no means convinced that state judges cannot be relied upon to enforce constitutional rights when asserted as defenses, subject to Supreme Court review. Indeed, as indicated above,[76] I think it unfortunate that we may be drifting into a state of affairs where, except in criminal cases, state judges are being largely deprived of a role in enforcing the Constitution they have sworn to support. If there is concern over allowing removal where the state court plaintiff asserts a constitutional claim but not where the defendant asserts a constitutional defense, I would solve the dilemma by denying removal in both instances; statistics cited in the *ALI Study*[77] show that the right to remove where the plaintiff has asserted a federal claim of any sort has been rarely exercised, and the number of such removals based on the plaintiff's assertion of a constitutional claim would be smaller still. On the other hand the argument that the small number of such cases shows there is no danger in federal constitutional defense removal does not parse. The plaintiff with a constitutional claim will normally sue in the federal court in the first place and the question of removal therefore does not arise.

Removal for a defense based on a federal statute stands differently. Unlike the Constitution many such statutes are rather technical; probably most state judges would be happy to be relieved of the need to deal, for example, with the occasional case where a de-

76. *See* pp. 90–92 *supra*.
77. ALI STUDY 192.

fense is predicated on federal securities legislation. While I have no serious objection to removal in civil cases on the basis of a substantial defense under a federal statute, it might be well for Congress, in the absence of a greater demonstration of need than now exists, to consider confining this to three categories for the time being.

The first would be where the defense, if it had been stated as a claim, would be one over which the federal courts would have exclusive jurisdiction, typically a defense based on the antitrust laws. Here we have a legislative judgment that litigation may properly be carried on only in a federal court, and while thus far Congress has provided this only for the assertion of claims, the same policy should apply with respect to defenses. Furthermore, removal in such cases would solve the vexing problem whether rejection of the defense in a state action precludes subsequent consideration of the same issue in a federal action where the lineup of the parties is reversed.[78] A second type of case for removal would be where the defendant alleged that the entire area in which the plaintiff's claim rested had been preempted by federal legislation. The "arguably subject" doctrine in labor disputes[79] is a prime example. I would also allow removal where the defendant relied upon a treaty. Such cases are few and there is a peculiar fitness in having a court of the United States pass on a claim that allowing a plaintiff to recover would involve this country in a breach of its international obligations.

If objection is made to allowing removal for a defense based on a federal statute only in these three instances whereas there is a broader right of removal if a statute is the basis for plaintiff's claim, I would answer that we know the latter has not been a significant burden and we do not know what the former would be, and there has been no demonstration of its need. However, as indicated, I would not strongly oppose federal defense removal in civil cases if

---

78. Judge L. Hand held it would not in his well-known opinion in Lyons v. Westinghouse Elec. Corp., 222 F.2d 184, 188–90 (2d Cir.), *cert. denied*, 350 U.S. 825 (1955). The decision may have been right, but it is certainly troubling and any way to avoid the problem should be welcomed. *See generally* Note, *The Effect of Prior Nonfederal Proceedings on Exclusive Federal Jurisdiction over Section 10(b) of the Securities Exchange Act of 1934*, 46 N.Y.U.L. Rev. 936 (1971).

79. *See, e.g.*, Amalgamated Ass'n of St. Elec. Ry. & Motor Coach Employees v. Lockridge, 403 U.S. 274 (1971).

this were limited to statutes and treaties as distinguished from constitutional defenses.[80]

80. If federal defense removal is to go beyond the three categories I have
mentioned, I would retain the requirement of a $10,000 jurisdictional
amount. One purpose of this would be to prevent removal of some of
the types of cases noted in the discussion of constitutional defense
removal, which might be removable under the Supreme Court's construction of 42 U.S.C. §§ 1981 and 1982 as applying to private, as
well as state authorized, discrimination.

PART VI

Claims of Railway Workers and Seamen, and Automobile Accident Litigation

THE DISCUSSION up to this point has developed how much and what difficult litigation must remain in the general federal courts and how hard this will be to handle even if all available means for improving the judicial machinery are adopted. These courts must thus be relieved of unnecessary burdens if they are effectively to discharge the tasks that are properly theirs. There are two principal methods for accomplishing this. One is restriction of intake into the federal system; the other is the allocation to specialized courts of certain types of cases admittedly appropriate for federal cognizance. This and the next section will examine what can be done by the former method; the two following sections will consider the latter.

In attempting to direct the work of the federal courts to cases where their special qualifications can be used to best advantage, the first step is to eliminate certain types of cases that do not belong in the courts at all. I shall identify three: injuries to railroad workers in the course of their employment, similar injuries to most maritime workers, and—a problem of concern to both state and federal courts —motor vehicle accident litigation.

The most obvious and compelling instance for change from a judicial to an administrative remedy is afforded by the Federal Employers' Liability Act.[1] The purpose of this 1908 statute, relating to employees of railroads engaged in interstate commerce, was wholly salutary. Its principal objectives, as stated in the Report of the House Judiciary Committee,[2] were to abrogate the fellow-servant rule and

1. Ch. 149, 35 Stat. 65 (1908), *now* 45 U.S.C. §§ 51–60.
2. *Reprinted in* W. THORNTON, A TREATISE ON THE FEDERAL EMPLOYERS'

the doctrine of assumption of risk, and to replace the common law principle making contributory negligence a complete defense with a rule of comparative negligence. The reports and debates afford no indication that Congress gave any consideration to the alternative of a workmen's compensation law.[3] That was by no means so unnatural as would now appear. Three years after enactment of the FELA, the New York Court of Appeals held a workmen's compensation law to be a denial of due process, even though it was applicable to a very limited number of specially hazardous activities;[4] the validity of such laws under the Federal Constitution was not established until 1917.[5]

If there is any good reason why, in contrast to almost all other workers in the United States, this particular group should still be put to the burden of maintaining a court action or have the benefit of an unlimited recovery, I have not heard of it. To be sure, workmen's compensation, like other institutions, has its faults, but it is hard to quarrel with the assessment by the head of the program in one of our largest industrial states:[6]

It is a means through which prompt and reasonable compensation is paid to victims of work-produced injuries and to their dependents; it is a means of freeing the courts of the delays and costs inherent in the hearing of such a common situation; it is a method of relieving the public welfare agencies of a tremendous financial drain which would otherwise result if such injured individuals and their families did not have this system of compensation; it provides through its case files ample evidence for those interested in learning the causes and the possible preventions of the most typical industrial accidents.

LIABILITY AND SAFETY APPLIANCE ACTS 557 (3d ed. 1916). *See also* the explanation by Senator Dolliver on the floor of the Senate, *id.* at 1–3, 42 CONG. REC. 4526–27 (1908).

3. *See* W. THORNTON, *supra* note 2, *at* 557–98; 42 CONG. REC. 4526–51 (1908).

4. Ives v. South Buffalo Ry., 201 N.Y. 271 (1911).

5. New York Cent. R.R. v. White, 243 U.S. 188 (1917); Arizona Employers' Liab. Cases, 250 U.S. 400 (1919).

6. Kelly, *Workmen's Compensation—Still a Vehicle for Social Justice,* 55 MASS. L.Q. 251, 252 (1970). For a sampling of criticisms, see Johnson, *Can Our State Workmen's Compensation System Survive?,* 3 FORUM 264 (1968); Colvin, *Workmen's Compensation—Its Moment of Truth,* 4 FORUM 151, 152–54 (1969); Horowitz, *Worldwide Workmen's Compensation Trends,* 59 KY. L.J. 37, 87–92 (1970).

There does not seem even to be any real need that the compensation scheme for railway workers should be federal; workers in other forms of interstate transportation, such as bus lines, truckers, and airlines, have been handled quite satisfactorily under the workmen's compensation law of the states.[7] However, with the political difficulties such as they are, a federal railway worker's compensation act might be more acceptable, as well as furnish a model for the upgrading of outmoded state statutes.

A second category of business to be partially eliminated from the courts consists of injuries to certain maritime workers. Here one must begin by distinguishing between the shore-based worker, who is protected by the Longshoremen's and Harbor Workers' Compensation Act[8] and the true seaman, who is not, or, in Professor Lucas' phrase, the oyster and the shrimp.[9] With respect to the oyster, this lecture had originally included a highly critical analysis of Mr. Justice Rutledge's discovery[10] that a longshoreman was a seaman, entitled to the benefits of the warranty of seaworthiness, and of the series of decisions in which the Supreme Court seemed obsessed in demonstrating its ability to press a principle not only to the limits of its logic but beyond them, by finding unseaworthiness in a condition created by the longshoreman's employer or even by himself.[11] This spawned the well-known three-party action,[12] wherein the ship became merely a conduit for enabling the longshoreman to recover from

7. The principal difficulty lies in the disparity of benefits and the consequent maneuvering to take advantage of the most favorable law that might be applicable. *See* RESTATEMENT (SECOND) OF THE CONFLICT OF LAWS §§ 181–82 (1971); 3 LARSON, THE LAW OF WORKMEN'S COMPENSATION § 84.10 (1971).

8. Ch. 509, 44 Stat. 1424–46 (1927), *now* 33 U.S.C. §§ 901–50.

9. Lucas, *Flood Tide: Some Irrelevant History of Admiralty*, 1964 SUP. CT. REV. 249, 260.

10. Seas Shipping Co. v. Sieracki, 328 U.S. 85 (1946).

11. Landmarks along this path were Alaska S.S. Co. v. Petterson, 347 U.S. 396 (1954), Gutierrez v. Waterman S.S. Corp., 373 U.S. 206 (1963), and Mascuilli v. United States, 387 U.S. 237 (1967). A return toward sanity began in Usner v. Luckenbach Overseas Corp., 400 U.S. 494 (1971), and Victory Carriers, Inc. v. Law, 404 U.S. 202 (1971).

12. Here the landmark is Ryan Stevedoring Co. v. Pan-Atlantic S.S. Corp., 350 U.S. 124 (1956).

his employer, thereby frustrating the intent of the Compensation Act and often producing results that were truly ludicrous.[13]

Happily it has become unnecessary to elaborate upon this. In its closing days the 92d Congress made substantially the reform I intended to advocate.[14] This increased the benefits under the Longshoremen's and Harbor Workers' Compensation Act but provided that while an injured harbor worker may bring an action against the ship for negligence, in accordance with standard workmen's compensation practice,[15] the action must be for that and not for breach of a warranty of seaworthiness, and that negligence of the ship cannot be predicated upon negligence of the persons providing the shore-based services. Congress has thus put the law back where it was before the ill-starred *Sieracki* decision and has relieved the federal courts of much unnecessary litigation, while making needed adjustments in the level of compensation benefits. When a reform like this can be effected, we should not lose optimism over others.

The problem of the true seaman, the free-swimming shrimp, is easier in one sense, more difficult in another. So far as concerns seamen on vessels of American registry, I perceive no reason why a new system of compulsory workmen's compensation should not be an exclusive remedy against the ship and its owner, as is now the case with seamen employed by the United States.[16] No more than in the case of railway workers should this change be regarded as adverse to the employee.[17] If desired for good measure, maintenance

13. *See, e.g.*, McLaughlin v. Trelleborgs Angfartygs A/B, 408 F.2d 1334 (2d Cir.), *cert. denied*, 395 U.S. 946 (1969).
14. Longshoremen's and Harbor Workers' Compensation Act Amendments, § 18, 86 Stat. 1251 (1972).
15. *See* 2 LARSON, *supra* note 7, §§ 71.00–77.30. In all jurisdictions but two, actions against third parties are allowed. *Id.* § 71.00.
16. Federal Employees Compensation Act of 1916, ch. 458, 39 Stat. 742, *as amended*, 5 U.S.C. §§ 8101 *et seq. See* Johansen v. United States, 343 U.S. 427 (1952).
17. A recent case in the Second Circuit illustrates the unconscionable delay frequently attendant on reliance on negligence actions to compensate needy seamen or their representatives. The Marine Sulphur Queen disappeared, with all hands, on February 4, 1963. A Coast Guard investigation ensued, as well as lengthy discovery proceedings by the parties. Not until June 1969 was a trial held on the issue of liability. The lower court found liability in a decision handed down in May 1970. *In re* Marine Sulphur Transp. Corp., 312 F. Supp. 1081

and cure could also be retained, with appropriate provisions against doubling up the two remedies.

This leaves the problem of the seaman, whether an American or a foreigner, injured on a foreign-flag ship, whether in American waters, on the high seas, or in a foreign port, under circumstances making it proper to allow him to sue in an American court.[18] Here, it would seem to me, the right course would be that instead of allowing an action for unseaworthiness and disallowing one for negligence,[19] recovery should be only for negligence, although, of course, this will include many, indeed most, cases of unseaworthiness since the owner is bound to use due care to provide a seaworthy vessel. The reasons for such a policy are set forth in the dissents of Mr. Justice Frankfurter and Mr. Justice Harlan in *Mitchell v. Trawler Racer, Inc.*,[20] and need not be repeated. Here again Congress might wish to relieve against the common law principle that contributory negligence is a total bar.

The third category of cases that I would banish is not a matter of exclusively federal concern; I refer, of course, to actions arising out of motor vehicle accidents. While the subject is substantially less important to the federal courts than to the states, it is nevertheless appropriate for brief mention here. Although there are other ways for eliminating these cases from the federal courts, one great advantage of the no-fault route, apart from its intrinsic merit, is that the relief this would give the state courts would eliminate one argument often used against the abolition of diversity jurisdiction although, as I will later show, it lacks validity even now.

(S.D.N.Y. 1970). Our court affirmed as to the liability of the ship's owner and demise charterers in April 1972. *In re* Marine Sulphur Queen, 460 F.2d 89 (2d Cir. 1972). Certiorari on that issue was denied on Nov. 6, 1972, 34 L. Ed. 2d 246. As of this writing, there has not as yet been a trial or settlement of the amount of the wrongful death claims. Thus, over ten years—half a generation—will have elapsed before the families of the deceased seamen will have received any compensation for their loss.

18. Here the "landmark" decision is Lauritzen v. Larsen, 345 U.S. 571 (1953).

19. The Osceola, 189 U.S. 158, 175 (1903); Chelentis v. Luckenbach S.S. Co., 247 U.S. 372, 383–85 (1918).

20. 362 U.S. 539, 550, 570 (1960).

The topic is the subject of a large literature,[21] and I shall limit myself to the highlights. I have heard no valid argument against the point that there is need for a remedy that will compensate the vast number of persons injured in such accidents swiftly, surely and inexpensively, and that our system in its present form is incapable of doing that. While there may be controversy over the precise figures, there can be no real doubt that the accident liability insurance system overcompensates for small injuries, where the costs of litigation promote liberal settlements, and undercompensates for large ones,[22] and that it involves more than a dollar of expense to deliver a dollar of benefits.[23] Yet these miserable results have been accompanied by precipitate increases in liability insurance costs.[24] Motor vehicle accident litigation requires over 11% of the time of federal district

21. *See, e.g.,* W. BLUM & H. KALVEN, JR., PUBLIC LAW PERSPECTIVES ON A PRIVATE LAW PROBLEM: AUTO COMPENSATION PLANS (1965); DEPARTMENT OF TRANSPORTATION, THE ORIGIN AND DEVELOPMENT OF THE NEGLIGENCE ACTION (1970); *id.,* CONSTITUTIONAL PROBLEMS IN AUTOMOBILE ACCIDENT COMPENSATION REFORM (1970); R. KEETON & J. O'CONNELL, BASIC PROTECTION FOR THE TRAFFIC VICTIM (1965); Blum & Kalven, *The Empty Cabinet of Dr. Calabresi,* 34 U. CHI. L. REV. 239 (1967); Calabresi, *The Decision for Accidents: An Approach to Nonfault Allocation of Costs,* 78 HARV. L. REV. 713 (1965); Calabresi, *Fault, Accidents and the Wonderful World of Blum and Kalven,* 75 YALE L.J. 216 (1965); Conard, *The Economic Treatment of Automobile Injuries,* 63 MICH. L. REV. 279 (1964); James, *An Evaluation of the Fault Concept,* 32 TENN. L. REV. 394 (1965); *Symposium on Nonfault Automobile Insurance,* 71 COLUM. L. REV. 189 (1971).

22. DEPARTMENT OF TRANSPORTATION, MOTOR VEHICLE CRASH LOSSES AND THEIR COMPENSATION IN THE UNITED STATES: A REPORT TO THE CONGRESS AND THE PRESIDENT [hereinafter VOLPE REPORT] 35–37 & Table 8 (1971). *See also* 117 CONG. REC. 3741 (1971) (statement of Senator Hart of Michigan).

23. VOLPE REPORT at 51 & Table 22. Another analysis of the automobile accident liability insurance system indicated that only 44 cents out of every premium dollar went to compensate victims and that, of this, only 14 1/2 cents went to compensate for otherwise uncompensated economic losses. P. KEETON & R. KEETON, COMPENSATION SYSTEMS: THE SEARCH FOR A VIABLE ALTERNATIVE TO NEGLIGENCE LAW 57–63 (1971). Another study, for 1969, developed a figure of 42 cents per dollar, 117 CONG. REC. at 3748 (1971) (Table 3).

24. 117 CONG. REC. at 3749 (1971) (Table 8).

judges and approximately 17% of the time of judges of state courts of general jurisdiction.[25]

Since both motor vehicles and insurance are traditionally subjects for state regulation, state statutory solutions to this highly visible problem seem most desirable. After years of inaction, fostered by an alliance of personal injury lawyers and insurance companies, many insurers have seen the light and the log-jam has started to break. As of this writing, nine states[26] have enacted various reforms to their automobile accident law, ostensibly designed to promote a more rapid settlement of claims, remove the bulk of cases from the courts, reduce insurance costs, and channel a higher percentage of the insurance premium to benefits. Although most of the state plans permit too much litigation of claims[27] and at least half of them seem intended to

25. FEDERAL JUDICIAL CENTER, AUTOMOBILE ACCIDENT LITIGATION: A REPORT TO THE DEPARTMENT OF TRANSPORTATION 44 (1970).
26. Massachusetts Personal Injury Protection Act of 1970, Mass. Gen. Laws Ann. ch. 90, §§ 34A,D,M,N; ch. 175, §§ 22E–H, 113B–C; ch. 231, § 6D (Supp. 1971); Florida Automobile Reparations Reform Act, Fla. Stat. Ann. §§ 627.730–627.741 (Supp. 1972); Ore. Rev. Stat. §§ 743.786–743.792 (1971); Ill. Ann. Stat. ch. 73, §§ 1065.150–1065.163 (Smith-Hurd 1971); Del. Laws 1971, ch. 98, *as amended by* Del. Laws 1972, chs. 353, 443 (to be codified at Del. Code Ann. tit. 21, § 2118); [Minn.] Laws 1971, ch. 581 (to be codified at Minn. Stat. § 72A.1494); S.D. Laws 1972, H.B. No. 65 (to be codified at S.D. Compiled Laws Ann. §§ 58-23-6 to –8); [Conn.] Pub. Act No. 273 (1972); New Jersey Automobile Reform Reparation Act, 1972 Laws, ch. 70 (to be codified at N.J. Stat. Ann. §§ 39:6A-1 to –18); [Md.] Laws 1972, ch. 73 (to be codified at Md. Ann. Code art. 48A, subtit. 35, §§ 538–46). However, the Illinois statute has been held to violate the state constitution. Grace v. Howlett, 51 Ill. 2d 478, 283 N.E.2d 474 (1972) (Schaefer, J.). The Commonwealth of Puerto Rico has also enacted a limited "no fault" statute, P.R. Laws Ann. tit. 9, §§ 2051–65 (Supp. 1972), which is of special interest because it involves both no fault insurance and state involvement in the administration of benefits. The plans in Oregon, Delaware, Minnesota, South Dakota, Maryland, and, to some extent, the now defunct plan in Illinois, are not really "no fault" plans at all, in that they do not preclude court action in most cases. These plans are more accurately described as "mandatory first party benefit" plans, which seem intended to get funds to the victims more quickly and yet leave the final resolution of liability to the courts.
27. Even the arguably successful Massachusetts Plan permits actions for pain and suffering when, among other things, "reasonable and neces-

impair rather than enhance their own effectiveness,[28] some at least are moving in the proper direction.[29] While the Department of Transportation initially favored uniform legislation at the state level,[30] President Nixon has later declared himself in favor of experimentation by the states.[31] I agree with this, provided—and the proviso is important—that a genuine and general effort toward reform can be discerned. Though normally such a movement continues in the states once it has attained a critical mass, the invalidation of the Illinois statute under the state constitution,[32] although on grounds rather easily met, and the failure in 1972 of what had seemed promising efforts in New York and California, only partially compensated by successes in New Jersey, Connecticut, and Maryland, and the tendency to water down such laws as are passed, now cast doubt on whether most of the states will move at the requisite speed and effectiveness.

sary" expenses incurred for medical and related services exceed $500. Mass. Gen. Laws Ann. ch. 231, § 6D (Supp. 1971). The original plan of Keeton and O'Connell would have allowed actions for pain and suffering only when such damages exceeded $5,000. R. KEETON & J. O'CONNELL, *supra* note 21, at 274–75. *See* Note, *The Massachusetts "No Fault" Automobile Insurance Law: An Analysis and Proposed Revision*, 8 HARV. J. LEGIS. 455, 484–87 (1971). Contrast the clean lines of the *Report of the Special Committee on Automobile Insurance Plans of the Association of the Bar of the City of New York*, dated January 4, 1972, chaired by Hon. David W. Peck, former Presiding Justice of the Appellate Division for the First Department. 27 RECORD OF N.Y.C.B.A. 245 (1972).

28. *E.g.*, the Delaware plan, Del. Laws 1971, ch. 98, contains no threshold below which an injured party may not sue for pain and suffering. Thus, while suits may not be maintained for which mandatory first party benefits are receivable, it would seem that a party could sue for "pain and suffering," regardless of the size of the claim. While some of the first party benefits might arguably absorb potential pain and suffering claims, only time will demonstrate whether the Delaware plan significantly reduces litigation.

29. The first year of operation of the Massachusetts plan has resulted in cuts of about 54% in bodily-injury premiums. N.Y. Times, Dec. 22, 1971, at 24, col. 1. While the validity of these statistics, and their ultimate meaning, are subjects of great debate, the initial results are heartening.

30. *Id.* at 24, col. 3.

31. N.Y. Times, June 8, 1972, at 1, col. 8.

32. *See* Grace v. Howlett, 51 Ill. 2d 478, 283 N.E.2d 474 (1972).

A sharp spur to action by the states is furnished by the threat of federal legislation. House and Senate committees have considered bills which would preempt the field with a federal "no fault" law.[33] The plaintiffs' personal injury trial bar would not have quite the same influence in Congress, especially in the Senate, that it has in state capitols. While action by the states would be preferable, the possibility of federal legislation should be preserved and, if necessary, implemented.

However all this may be, Congress should remove automobile accident litigation from the federal courts, and do it now. Even though there has been a slight decline in the number of these cases, nearly 8,000[34] are still too many for courts overburdened with peculiarly federal tasks, when state judges, familiar with applicable state law, can handle them sufficiently well. This reform could be accomplished either by the abolition of diversity jurisdiction[35] or, doubtless more speedily, by simply removing automobile accident litigation from the federal courts.[36]

To conclude this section, I will try to estimate the impact of the three proposals here made. Of the 96,173 civil cases filed in the district courts in 1972, there were 1,391 FELA cases, 7,700 motor vehicle cases, and 6,534 cases labelled only as "Personal Injury: Marine."[37] The statistics do not enable us to tell how many of the latter would disappear under legislation enacted or proposed; it would be conservative to estimate that half would do so. This would mean a 13% reduction in the civil caseload. The beauty of this is that while it would constitute appreciable relief to the federal courts, it would not create a substantial added burden for the states. The

33. S. 945, 92d Cong., 1st Sess. (1971) (introduced by Senators Hart and Magnuson); H.R. 7514, 92d Cong., 1st Sess. (1971) (introduced by Representative Moss). The latter would seemingly close the pain and suffering door to litigation by forcing insurance companies to put a pain and suffering coverage clause in the policy. While such an approach might have an unfortunate effect on premium levels, it bears consideration as the most promising attempt to keep such controversies out of the courts.

34. A.O. ANN. REP., Table C2 (1972).

35. *See* Part VII *infra.*

36. For a similar proposal, see Meador, *A New Approach to Limiting Diversity Jurisdiction*, 46 A.B.A.J. 383 (1960).

37. A.O. ANN. REP., Table C2 (1972).

changes proposed for railway and marine workers would create none;[38] indeed, they would eliminate a number of such cases now heard by state courts. Changed treatment of motor vehicle accidents would likewise be without consequences for the state courts to the extent that the states took these out of their own judicial machinery. Even if the remedy were to take the form of excluding motor vehicle accident litigation from the federal courts without reform in the state liability system, the increase in the business of the state courts would be negligible in proportion to their existing volume.[39]

38. This assumes that railway workers would be covered under a *federal* compensation act, so that the few cases where review would be sought would be in the federal courts.

39. In 1970 there were filed in the four federal district courts in New York 304 personal injury motor vehicle cases. A.O. ANN. REP., Table C3, at 235 (1970). During the same period, 24,661 cases of the same type were filed in the New York State Supreme Court, Trial Division, alone. SIXTEENTH ANNUAL REPORT OF THE ADMINISTRATIVE BOARD OF THE JUDICIAL CONFERENCE OF THE STATE OF NEW YORK, at A58 (1971). Transfer of all federal motor vehicle cases to the New York courts would thus increase *the volume of such cases* by only 1.2%.

PART VII

Diversity Jurisdiction

UP TO THIS POINT, save for the brief excursion into motor vehicle accident litigation, I have been dealing entirely with categories where federal jurisdiction is predicated upon the federal nature of the claim. We come now to the one area where it rests upon the identity of the parties—the long controverted subject of diversity jurisdiction. As Professor Wechsler wrote in 1948, diversity and alienage jurisdiction "pose the deepest issue of the uses of the federal courts. In these instances the jurisdiction is employed not to vindicate rights grounded in the national authority but solely to administer state law."[1] Urging a thorough re-examination of the jurisdiction but recognizing the lack of political attractiveness in such an effort, he thought "[s]upport must come . . . from the disinterested sources, the judiciary and the bar—including the law members of the Congress—content to view the issue in its right dimensions as a problem of the uses of the federal courts."[2] The increase in "rights grounded in the national authority" during the last quarter-century has affected the issue of diversity jurisdiction in two ways: The new tasks given the federal courts have heightened the required showing of justification for retaining diversity; and many cases that could previously have come within federal cognizance only because of diversity are now subject to federal jurisdiction by virtue of this growth of federal law.[3]

1. Wechsler, *Federal Jurisdiction and the Revision of the Judicial Code*, 13 LAW & CONTEMP. PROB. 216, 235 (1948).
2. *Id.* at 240.
3. Professor Wechsler called attention to the possibility of this development, *id.* at 239. Judge J. Skelly Wright has recognized that "the prominence of diversity as a legal institution is dwindling today because of the rapidly expanding coverage of federal law," *The Federal Courts and the Nature and Quality of State Law*, 13 WAYNE L.

I am not certain that I qualify as "disinterested" on the issue of diversity jurisdiction; at the very least I would be subject to a peremptory challenge. My first signed piece of legal writing, nearly forty-five years ago, concluded by noting that the growth in the work of the federal courts in administering federal law would "not abate, since it is responsive to deep social and economic causes," that only diversity jurisdiction "is out of the current of these nationalizing forces," and that "[t]he unifying tendencies of America here make for a recession of jurisdiction to the states . . . ."[4] Some might regard that statement as showing remarkable prescience, others as indicating that I never learn. Although I do not like to be cast in the role of a Cato, I cannot but affirm my deep conviction that these thoughts, believed to be true in 1928, are *a multo fortiori* so in 1972.

We may begin by considering the dimensions of the problem. Of the 96,173 civil cases filed in the district courts in 1972, 24,109 were predicated on diverse citizenship.[5] Ten years ago they comprised 18,359 out of 61,836 civil filings.[6] While their proportion and ratio of increase have thus been less than for civil filings as a whole, a head

Rev. 317, 329–30 (1967), but curiously refuses to draw the conclusion that this substantially weakens the case for diversity jurisdiction. While he thinks that diversity jurisdiction will ultimately shrivel as a result of "the rapidly expanding coverage of federal law," *id.*, there is no evidence as distinguished from relative terms. *See* pp. 140–41 *infra.* On grounds I am unable to comprehend, Professor Moore also considers the extension of federal law to be an argument in favor of retaining diversity, *see* Moore & Weckstein, *Diversity Jurisdiction: Past, Present, and Future,* 43 Texas L. Rev. 1, 20 (1964).

4. Friendly, *The Historic Basis of Diversity Jurisdiction,* 41 Harv. L. Rev. 483, 510 (1928). The article called attention to a 1914 report of a distinguished committee including such now legendary figures as Charles W. Eliot, Louis D. Brandeis and Roscoe Pound, which had stated that "the concurrent jurisdiction of state and federal courts on the ground of diversity of citizenship often causes much delay, expense and uncertainty." Preliminary Report on Efficiency in the Administration of Justice 28 (1914). While one source of the "uncertainty" was removed by Erie R.R. v. Tompkins, 304 U.S. 64 (1938), another was substituted. *See* pp. 142–43 *infra.*

5. A.O. Ann. Rep., Table C2 (1972). The largest categories are insurance, "other contract actions," motor vehicle personal injury, and "other personal injury." These comprise 82% of the total.

6. A.O. Ann. Rep., Table C2, at 196 (1962).

of jurisdiction constituting 25% of the civil filings cannot be ignored as *de minimis* or as of sharply decreasing significance. Opponents of diversity are not required to shoulder the burden of showing it is "working badly"[7] which some have tried to cast upon them. Rather the proponents have the burden of showing sufficient reasons for its retention at a time when the federal court system is severely pressed.

The first and greatest single objection to the federal courts entertaining these actions is the diversion of judge-power urgently needed for tasks which only federal courts can handle or which, because of their expertise, they can handle significantly better than the courts of a state. There is simply no analogy between today's situation and that existing in 1789 when, in the words of the ALI Study, "[s]ince diversity of citizenship was one of the major heads of federal judicial business, it contributed to the expansion of the federal courts throughout the nation" and thus "enhanced awareness in the people of the existence of the new and originally weak central government."[8] Without diversity jurisdiction, the circuit courts created by the First Judiciary Act would have had very little to do. Perhaps this is as good an explanation as any why the statute made a broad grant of diversity jurisdiction, although this had been hotly contested and not very staunchly supported in the ratifying conventions,[9] including the invocation of a jurisdiction supposedly based on prejudice against out-of-staters by a citizen of the state where the suit was brought.

As indicated in an earlier portion of these lectures, the problem of the volume of cases filed is not simply in the district courts, where the addition of judges may afford opportunity for relief, but in the courts of appeals and the Supreme Court. In 1972 diversity accounted for 18% of civil appeals to the courts of appeals; if habeas corpus and other types of federal and state prisoner petitions were excluded from the "civil" category, the proportion would be 24%.[10] A significant number of these cases must translate themselves into petitions for certiorari, although almost none are granted.[11] For the moment I

---

7. J. P. Frank, *For Maintaining Diversity Jurisdiction*, 73 YALE L.J. 7, 8 (1963).

8. ALI STUDY 101.

9. Friendly, *supra*, 41 HARV. L. REV. at 487–99.

10. A.O. ANN. REP., Table B7 (1972).

11. Although the Supreme Court does not record the number of petitions

shall defer discussing whether *anything* is accomplished by having these cases in federal court. Certainly the accomplishment is materially *less* than when a federal question is present, and if anything must be eliminated from the business of the federal courts, beyond the categories discussed in the preceding section, diversity cases are the prime candidate. Mr. Justice Frankfurter said that "[a]n Act for the elimination of diversity jurisdiction could fairly be called an Act for the relief of the federal courts."[12] Twenty-three years after that statement, the time for such relief has come.

A second difficulty with diversity jurisdiction is that in such cases federal courts cannot discharge the important objective of making law. When the state law is plain, the federal judge is reduced to a "ventriloquist's dummy to the courts of some particular state."[13] Much worse are the cases where, in Judge Wright's phrase, "state law on the point at issue is less than immaculately clear."[14] Whereas the highest court of the state can "quite acceptably ride along a crest of common sense, avoiding the extensive citation of authority,"[15] a federal court often must exhaustively dissect each piece of evidence thought to cast light on what the highest state court would ultimately decide.[16] In

for certiorari where jurisdiction is based solely on diversity of citizenship, the following data on full opinions by the Court shows how few are deemed worthy of the Court's attention:

Term	Total Dispositions with Full Opinions	Diversity Case Dispositions with Full Opinions
1966	119	4
1967	127	3
1968	120	4
1969	94	0
1970	122	2
1971	151	2

These statistics appear in the annual Supreme Court Note in the *Harvard Law Review*.

12. National Mut. Ins. Co. v. Tidewater Transfer Co., 337 U.S. 582, 651 (1949) (dissenting opinion).
13. Richardson v. CIR, 126 F.2d 562, 567 (2d Cir. 1942) (Frank, J.).
14. J. Skelly Wright, *supra*, 13 WAYNE L. REV. at 321.
15. *Id.* at 322.
16. Judge Wright refers to Judge Medina's opinion in Merritt-Chapman & Scott Corp. v. Public Util. Dist. No. 2, 319 F.2d 94 (2d Cir. 1963), *cert. denied*, 375 U.S. 968 (1964), which contains 71 citations of

other cases what passes as an attempt at prediction is a mere guess or fiat without any basis in state precedents at all.[17] All such cases are pregnant with the possibility of injustice.[18] Furthermore, the very availability of litigation in a federal court postpones an authoritative decision by the state courts that otherwise would be inevitable.[19] Diversity jurisdiction thus "can badly squander the resources of the federal judiciary" since it uses them in a way which precludes the attainment of one of a judge's most important functions, namely "to establish a precedent and organize a body of law."[20]

New York decisions, many of New York statutes and public documents, 38 to cases from other jurisdictions, and 23 to treatises or law review articles. *See also* Evans v. S. J. Groves & Sons Co., 315 F.2d 335 (2d Cir. 1963), where we had to decide three unsettled questions of New York tort law, one of which had given rise to three separate opinions in the Appellate Division for the First Department and another of which provoked a *dubitante* concurrence by Judge Swan.

The difficulty in determining questions of state law in certain cases has led the Fifth Circuit to abstain in a diversity action where state law on the governing point was particularly unclear. United States Life Ins. Co. v. Delaney, 328 F.2d 483 (5th Cir.) (en banc), *cert. denied*, 377 U.S. 935 (1964). The case was finally decided after the Texas Supreme Court affirmed dismissal of a declaratory judgment action brought by the parties to clarify Texas law. 358 F.2d 714 (5th Cir. 1966). While this approach causes much delay and arguably runs counter to Supreme Court decisions, Note, *Abstention Under* Delaney: *A Current Appraisal*, 49 Texas L. Rev. 247 (1971), it underscores the difficult posture of the federal courts when left to guess on issues of unclear state law.

17. In one such case I began the opinion by saying "[o]ur principal task . . . is to determine what the New York courts would think the California courts would think on an issue about which neither has thought." Nolan v. Transocean Air Lines, 276 F.2d 280, 281 (2d Cir.), *rev'd for consideration of a recent California decision, relevant but not dispositive, which had not been brought to our attention*, 365 U.S. 293 (1961), *adhered to*, 290 F.2d 904 (2d Cir.), *cert. denied*, 368 U.S. 901 (1961). Judge Clark has recently used a rather similar phrase in Allstate Ins. Co. v. Employers Liab. Assurance Corp., 445 F.2d 1278 (5th Cir. 1971). In Holt v. Seversky Electronatom Corp., 452 F.2d 31 (2d Cir. 1971), our court had to predict how the New York Court of Appeals would choose between the conflicting views of Corbin and Williston on a point of contract law.

18. *See* ALI Study 100.

19. *See* J. S. Wright, *supra*, 13 Wayne L. Rev. at 322–23, and cases there cited. *See also* Employers Liab. Assurance Corp. v. Travelers Ins. Co., 411 F.2d 862, 865–66 (2d Cir. 1969).

20. J. S. Wright, *supra*, 13 Wayne L. Rev. at 323. *See also* ALI Study 99.

What, then, are the arguments for retaining diversity jurisdiction for the vast bulk of cases which could have been brought in the state courts? We can dispose of some of them quite speedily. Whatever force there may ever have been in the claim, recently repeated by Professor Moore,[21] that diversity jurisdiction was needed to prevent inferior federal judges from becoming narrow technicians, mired in the intricacies of admiralty, bankruptcy, copyright and patent law, with consequently diminished attractiveness in joining the federal bench, and in my view there never was much,[22] it has been wholly drained by the proliferation of new federal statutes and the birth of the federal common law.[23] The overview I have given of federal jurisdiction in the 1970's or, for that matter, a thumbing of the Federal 2d and Federal Supplement reports, affords conclusive evidence that one ailment from which federal judges are not suffering is lack of breadth which diversity is needed to cure. To the contrary, the dullest cases, at least in the truly civil field, are generally those arising from the diversity jurisdiction. Perhaps Professor Moore would find fascination in construing the opaque language of a fire insurance policy or determining the sufficiency of the evidence that a car was on the wrong side of the road, but most federal judges do not.

Related to this is the contention that diversity is needed to give lawyers an exposure to the federal procedural system and thus enable them to take the pollen back to the states. Today it simply is not true that "for ordinary lawyers without a federal specialty, only under diversity do opportunities for repeated exposure to the federal courts come about."[24] "Ordinary lawyers" appear frequently as assigned

Diversity jurisdiction can also be used to *create* needless conflict between federal and state court proceedings involving the same facts. *See* Ungar v. Mandell, — F.2d —, slip op. p. 819 (2d Cir., Dec. 6, 1972).

21. *See* Moore & Weckstein, *supra*, 43 Texas L. Rev. at 23.
22. Professor Fairman's study of the Supreme Court under the chief justiceship of Chase records the tedium from the diversity cases which constituted the bulk of the Court's business at the time of Chase's appointment and how the new Chief Justice felt at having left great affairs of state for the decision of questions of such small impact and interest. History of the Supreme Court of the United States, vol. VI: Reconstruction and Reunion 1864–88, at 32–35.
23. *See* pp. 110–11 *supra*.
24. J. S. Wright, *supra*, 13 Wayne L. Rev. at 327.

counsel in federal criminal cases and state and federal habeas corpus petitions and, on a retained basis, in all sorts of cases governed by federal law relating to securities, labor, consumer protection, environment, and many other subjects. It is rather diversity that is more nearly the field of the specialist, at least in the metropolitan areas, with nearly two-thirds of the cases being insurance and personal injuries.[25]

We can also dismiss a variation on the lawyers' "interplay" theme, namely, that diversity creates what is called a valuable "partnership of federal and state courts."[26] No explanation is offered as to just what this "partnership" consists of, unless it is a federal court's often unwelcome prediction of state law. Diversity is hardly needed today to make a state court aware of the Federal Rules of Civil Procedure. In any event, the many types of concurrent jurisdiction under federal law afford ample opportunities for partnership—not to speak of the more fruitful organized effort represented by the State-Federal Judicial Councils now existing in almost all the states as a result of the impetus given by Chief Justice Burger.[27]

I find equally unconvincing the argument that federal court justice "like student-lunch programs and free technical advice from the Department of Agriculture, is a socially beneficent service which the federal government should extend when it is constitutional to do so."[28] Apart from the lack of evidence that a federal court, with its

25. A.O. ANN. REP., Table C2 (1972). In almost all personal injury cases the defendant's lawyer is retained by an insurer.
26. *See* Moore & Weckstein, *supra*, 43 TEXAS L. REV. at 27.
27. Burger, *The State of the Judiciary—1970,* 56 A.B.A.J. 929, 933 (1970); *Deferred Maintenance,* 57 A.B.A.J. 425, 426–27 (1971).
28. J. S. Wright, *supra*, 13 WAYNE L. REV. at 327. This is substantially the approach taken in Moore & Weckstein, *supra*, 43 TEXAS L. REV. 1. They would eliminate the provision, dating back to the Judiciary Act of 1789, § 12, that removal cannot be effected by a citizen of the forum state, and any requirement of jurisdictional amount, also prescribed from the beginning, § 11, and would repeal the amendments of 1958 and 1964, whereby a corporation is deemed a resident of the state of its principal place of business as well as of the state of incorporation, and an insurer is deemed a citizen of the same state as the insured. *Id.* at 34–35. The authors say at one point that "[t]he large number of diversity cases filed in and removed to the federal district courts is itself evidence of the desirability and need for the jurisdiction." *Id.* Almost any institution or practice could be justified on such a basis.

built-in inability to make a firm determination of state law, will handle a personal injury or insurance case notably better than a state court having much greater experience, the marginal utility of this service must rank exceedingly low in any scale of priorities of what the Federal Government should do for citizens of the several states.

When all is said and done, the only justification for diversity jurisdiction having the slightest substance is the one so quaintly put by Chief Justice Marshall:[29]

However true the fact may be, that the tribunals of the states will administer justice as impartially as those of the nation, to parties of every description, it is not less true, that the constitution itself either entertains apprehensions on this subject, or views with such indulgence the possible fears and apprehensions of suitors, that it has established national tribunals for the decision of controversies between aliens and a citizen, or between citizens of different states.

On analysis, this concept breaks down into two rather different notions. One, to which I have already adverted, is that the state courts simply are not good enough that a nonresident should have to go there. Evidence reviewed in my 1928 article[30] shows that the state of the state courts in 1789 was indeed such that the Constitution might legitimately entertain such apprehensions or hold indulgent views toward the apprehensions of suitors, and therefore wish to provide a federal forum in cases where the disparate citizenship of the parties afforded a suitable peg. But, at least in most of the states, this surely is not true today. Very likely the federal trial courts, partly because of the method of appointment and the tenure of judges, partly because of their very smallness, are somewhat "better" than most state courts. But there is simply no evidence that "protracted delay, inefficient or untrained personnel, and procedural complexities and restrictions"[31] are characteristic of state trial courts in the 1970's or that such courts are incapable of dispatching ordinary civil litigation not having a federal aspect. On the appellate

29. Bank of the United States v. Deveaux, 9 U.S. (5 Cranch) 61, 87 (1809).

30. *See* Friendly, *supra*, 41 HARV. L. REV. at 497–99.

31. ALI STUDY 101.

level the difference is even less. At all times in the country's history, it has had state appellate judges of a stature altogether comparable to those on the federal bench.[32] If ever there was an American appellate court, even including the Supreme Court, superior to the New York Court of Appeals under the chief judgeships of Hiscock and Cardozo, I have not heard of it.

The other facet of the argument is prejudice properly so called. Obviously, like the point just considered, this does not explain why the in-state citizen should be allowed to invoke federal jurisdiction when he initiates the action, although he cannot do it on removal, and that is the theme of the ALI's proposed reform. But how does the matter stand generally? Looking at the cases of suit or removal by the out-of-stater, the only ones where prejudice could possibly be a factor, we find these categories:

(1) Out-of-state individual plaintiff versus in-state corporate defendant;

(2) Out-of-state corporate plaintiff versus in-state individual defendant;

(3) Out-of-state individual plaintiff versus in-state individual defendant;

(4) Out-of-state corporate plaintiff versus in-state corporate defendant;

(5) In-state individual plaintiff versus out-of-state corporate defendant;

(6) In-state corporate plaintiff versus out-of-state individual defendant;

(7) In-state individual plaintiff versus out-of-state individual defendant;

(8) In-state corporate plaintiff versus out-of-state corporate defendant.

It is hard to believe there is much possibility of prejudice in most suits between corporations, categories (4) and (8).[33] Where an individual and a corporation are adversaries, any prejudice is likely to derive from that fact, not from the corporation's having an out-

32. Until 1891 there were no true federal appellate judges except for the Justices of the Supreme Court.

33. One should except, I suppose, the controversy between the big out-state and the small in-state corporation.

of-state charter.[34] This takes care of categories (1), (2), (5) and (6). We are thus left with items (3) and (7). But the great bulk of the cases in these categories are personal injury actions where the jury knows the real defendant is almost certain to be an insurer, and any prejudice will stem from that and will exist in equal measure in federal court.[35]

Furthermore, the aid a federal court can give in avoiding prejudice against an out-of-stater at least in jury cases is exceedingly limited. Whatever may have been the situation in the past, federal juries are now drawn from the same registration or voting lists as those of the state, although, to be sure, generally from a wider area.[36] One way in which a federal judge, protected by tenure during good behavior, might help the out-of-stater against prejudice by jurors is by greater freedom in directing verdicts or setting them aside. But the power of a federal judge to do the former is surely no greater and in many states may well be less than that of a state judge.[37] The

34. Whether or not Professor Moore is right in thinking that the availability of diversity jurisdiction has been valuable in stimulating out-of-state investment, *supra*, 43 TEXAS L. REV. at 16–17, there is no evidence that this is a significant factor today. See ALI STUDY 105–06 n.10.

35. Efforts at empirical study of the effect of bias, real or fancied, on resort to diversity jurisdiction have yielded disparate results. *Compare* Summers, *Analysis of Factors that Influence Choice of Forum in Diversity Cases*, 47 IOWA L. REV. 933, 937–38 (1962), *with* Note, *The Choice Between State and Federal Court in Diversity Cases in Virginia*, 51 VA. L. REV. 178, 179–84 (1965), and *see* the comment in D. Currie, *The Federal Courts and the American Law Institute*, 36 U. CHI. L. REV. 1, 5 n.19 (1968). Note also the statement by Judge Joseph S. Lord III in *Hearings on S. 1876 Before the Subcomm. on Improvements in Judicial Machinery of the Senate Comm. on the Judiciary*, 92d Cong., 1st Sess. 175 (1972).

36. Jury Selection and Service Act of 1968, § 101, 82 Stat. 54, 28 U.S.C. §§ 1861–63.

37. While the Supreme Court has refrained from deciding whether federal courts are to apply a state or federal standard of sufficiency of evidence in cases dealing with state created rights, Dick v. New York Life Ins. Co., 359 U.S. 437, 444–45 (1959); Mercer v. Theriot, 377 U.S. 152, 156 (1964), the Fourth, Fifth and Ninth Circuits have come out for a federal standard, Wratchford v. S. J. Grover & Sons Co., 405 F.2d 1061, 1064–66 (4th Cir. 1969); Boeing Co. v. Shipman, 411 F.2d 365, 368–70 (5th Cir. 1969) (en banc); Safeway Stores v. Fannan, 308 F.2d 94, 97 (9th Cir. 1962), which severely limits the judge.

standard for the granting of new trials is clearly federal,[38] but I have no basis for believing this to be broader than in most of the states. The argument must therefore be that the federal judge will more freely exercise such powers as he has. This, plus his greater authority to comment on the evidence than is possessed by judges in some states,[39] seem to be the only ways in which he can afford protection against prejudice in jury trials that his opposite number might not—assuming, which is not always the case, that he is less of a xenophobe than his state counterpart. This is an exceedingly scant basis for a jurisdiction that makes up over 25% of the civil docket of the district courts. Whatever may be thought of the proposition that it is better for a thousand guilty to go free rather than have one innocent man suffer, the use of scant federal judge-power cannot be justified simply on the basis that in the small proportion of diversity cases where prejudice against the out-of-stater may exist, a federal court might be of some help in a few. As has been well said, "[T]he security given out-of-state interests by this jurisdiction is not worth the burden of defining and administering it."[40] There need not be concern regarding the added burden that abolition of diversity would cast on the state courts, since their volume of civil litigation is so great that the increment would be unsubstantial.[41]

I would retain two, and only two, pieces of the present diversity jurisdiction. One is for suits between a citizen and foreign states or

---

38. F.R. Civ. P. 59(a).

39. C. Wright, Handbook of the Law of Federal Courts 416 (1970).

40. D. Currie, *supra*, 36 U. Chi. L. Rev. at 49.

   Echoing an observation of Mr. Justice Frankfurter, National Mut. Ins. Co. v. Tidewater Transfer Co., *supra*, 337 U.S. at 651 (dissenting opinion), a commentator has said that "[t]he present utilization of diversity as a head of federal jurisdiction is better explained by the lack of sufficient interest to eliminate it than by any useful purpose it serves." Note, *ALI Proposals to Expand Federal Diversity Jurisdiction: Solution to Multiparty, Multistate Controversies?*, 48 Minn. L. Rev. 1109 (1964).

41. ALI Study 473–74. A study of 30 states by the Senate Judiciary Committee shows that the increase in the civil business of state courts of general jurisdiction from abolition of federal diversity jurisdiction would range from .27 to 1.5%. Burdick, *Diversity Jurisdiction Under American Law Institute Proposals: Its Purpose and Effect on State and Federal Courts*, 48 North Dakota L. Rev. 1, 14–15 (Table 4) (1971).

citizens or subjects thereof.[42] Here, where the burden is exceedingly slight, I join in the conclusion of the *ALI Study* that:[43]

It is important in the relations of this country with other nations that any possible appearance of injustice or tenable ground for resentment be avoided. This objective can best be achieved by giving the foreigner the assurance that he can have his case tried in a court with the best procedures the federal government can supply and with the dignity and prestige of the United States behind it.

I would also retain the Interpleader Act[44] with the addition proposed by the ALI.[45] While the ALI's proposal for a new chapter[46] covering other diversity cases where no state can obtain jurisdiction over all necessary parties is sound in theory, the provisions are, of necessity, exceedingly complicated and its adoption should await demonstration that, with the general enactment of "long-arm" statutes and attendant judicial resourcefulness, there is any real need for them.[47]

It may well be said in criticism that my proposal ignores the realities of political life, and that one should settle for the ALI proposal to eliminate the anomaly of the in-state plaintiff being able to invoke federal jurisdiction against the out-state defendant as the best one can get. I am not convinced that if the forces for judicial reform can overcome the combination of opponents of the ALI proposal—plaintiffs' lawyers who wish the greatest possible freedom of choice of forum, lawyers for corporations doing a nation-wide business who wish to preserve the right of removal, and other disinterested but, in my view, misguided federalophils—they cannot almost as readily perform the complete job. However, if the whole loaf is unattainable, half would be no small blessing.

If the ALI proposals should prove to be the line the solution

42. This is the present 28 U.S.C. § 1332(a)(2) and (3). Since the basis for the jurisdiction would be the possible effect on international relations, I would not be inclined to modify the latter, as Professor Currie suggests, *supra*, 36 U. CHI. L. REV. at 20, to eliminate jurisdiction in the rare case where the foreign plaintiff and defendant are citizens of the same foreign state.
43. ALI STUDY 108.
44. 28 U.S.C. §§ 1335, 2361.
45. ALI STUDY § 2375.
46. *Id.* ch. 160, at 67, 375.
47. *See* D. Currie, *supra*, 36 U. CHI. L. REV. at 29–32; Note, *supra*, 48 MINN. L. REV. 1109.

will take, I would alter them in a few respects. I would eliminate the proposal making an "in-stater" of any individual "who has and for a period of more than two years has had his principal place of business or employment" in the state.[48] This was intended to catch the resident of Greenwich, Connecticut, who commutes every week-day to New York City, or the resident of Camden, New Jersey, who works in Philadelphia, and as to them it is sound enough. But there are only a half-dozen places where this phenomenon occurs on any scale, and the formulation might comprehend other cases, *e.g.*, the commander of an Army base or the teacher on a three-year assignment outside his state, to whom its rationale is only dubiously applicable. The whole game thus is not worth the candle.[49]

On the other hand, I would oppose, for reasons that must be apparent, a number of the ALI proposals for expanding diversity jurisdiction, which, as I stated at the outset, were developed before the explosion of federal court litigation began.[50] The most important of these is allowing one of several defendants to remove whenever he would have been able to do so "if sued alone by any party making a claim against him in the State court action," subject to a right in the federal court to remand all matters that "considered separately would not be within its jurisdiction."[51] One objective of this was to overcome the difficulties arising from the present "separate and independent" claims provision[52] which, with its predecessors, has been deservedly characterized as "one of the most unfortunate provisions

---

48. ALI STUDY § 1302(c).

49. *See* D. Currie, *supra*, 36 U. CHI. L. REV. at 47. On the other hand, I strongly disagree with Professor Currie's rejection of the provision, § 1302(b), relating to the foreign corporation, etc. "that has and for a period of more than two years has maintained a local establishment in a state,"—one of the most valuable of the ALI's proposals. I perceive no justification for allowing a national chain store to remove when a customer has slipped on a banana peel, although the local department store or restaurant could not. *See* Field, *Proposals on Federal Diversity Jurisdiction*, 17 S. CAR. L. REV. 669, 672–73 (1965). Professor Currie's fears of "enormous gray zones that will plague the courts with additional problems of construction" are vastly overdone.

50. *See* p. 4 *supra*.

51. ALI STUDY § 1304(b). I would favor, however, some judicial relaxation on what constitutes fraudulent joinder. See *id.* at 141–42.

52. 28 U.S.C. § 1441(c).

in the entire Judicial Code."[53] I would remove the difficulties more cleanly, without increasing federal jurisdiction, by repealing that clause. The real issue, as Professor David Currie has pointed out,[54] is whether or not we wish to live with Chief Justice Marshall's requirement of complete diversity.[55] I would in the vast run of cases, since it limits the jurisdiction on a rationale at least as satisfactory as any that would broaden it. This is true even though one can conceive of cases where the requirement may produce results not wholly consistent with the traditional justification.[56] Efforts to take care of every variation produce complexity and breed litigation, which is simply not worthwhile when the only consequence of requiring complete diversity is a trial in a state court. Whatever abstract logic these proposals to expand diversity jurisdiction in some respects may have, they are overcome by the greater logic that if the ideal is to abolish the jurisdiction, Congress should not do anything to increase it, even by way of a partial trade-off.

With these qualifications, I endorse the ALI diversity proposal as a significant interim step toward the larger goal of "relieving the federal courts of the overwhelming burden of 'business that intrinsically belongs to the state courts,' in order to keep them free for their distinctive federal business."[57] If even that modest reform cannot be enacted with more than deliberate speed, I see no reason why busy district courts should not promulgate rules that after a certain date all other proceedings shall be preferred for trial over actions where federal jurisdiction is invoked solely on the basis that the parties are citizens of different states, or why circuit councils should not require them to do so.[58]

53. D. Currie, *supra*, 36 U. Chi. L. Rev. at 22.
54. *Id.* at 25.
55. Strawbridge v. Curtiss, 7 U.S. (3 Cranch) 267 (1806).
56. *See* D. Currie, *supra*, 36 U. Chi. L. Rev. at 18–19.
57. Indianapolis v. Chase Nat'l Bank, 314 U.S. 63, 76 (1941).
58. For obvious reasons such a rule could not be applied in cases of removal.

PART VIII

Patents and Taxes

THE REST of these lectures will deal with a quite different set of problems. Here our concern will not be the proper reach of federal jurisdiction; all the topics to be considered clearly fall within even the narrowest view. The concern will be rather with the method by which such cases should be handled. More specifically, the discussion will center on the creation of additional federal courts of specialized jurisdiction, because this will relieve the general courts, or because specialized courts can do a better job, or both. I shall deal with four principal areas—patents, taxes, administrative appeals, and antitrust. In this section I will consider the two former.

Two standard arguments are offered against the creation of specialized courts—the undesirability of specialized judges and, as illustrating this, the unhappy history of the Commerce Court during its brief life between 1910 and 1913.[1] The former can be better considered separately with respect to each area; the substantial objection in my view is not specialization as such, but the fear that a specialized court will be dominated by a particular attitude on its subject-matter. Supposed bias as to the proper regulatory philosophy was, I think, the real cause of the downfall of the Commerce Court. Whether rightly or not, that tribunal came to be regarded as a tool of the railroads against the Interstate Commerce Commission.[2] When we

1. The history, interestingly told in FRANKFURTER & LANDIS 153–74, has aspects of a Greek tragedy.
2. Arguing against this and in defense of the tribunal, Attorney General Wickersham testified before the House Committee on Interstate Commerce that for the period from 1906 to May 1912, the ICC had been reversed in 56% of the cases before the circuit courts, in 45% of the cases before the Supreme Court, and in only 41% of the cases before the Commerce Court. 48 CONG. REC. 6152 (1912); *see* Nathan-

153

take account of the comparative figures of the Court's performance, of the fact that, in Frankfurter's and Landis' words, "[p]robably no court has ever been called upon to adjudicate so large a volume of litigation of as far-reaching import in so brief a time,"[3] and of the lack of any serious criticism of our existing specialized Article III courts, the Court of Claims, the Customs Court and the Court of Customs and Patent Appeals,[4] the débâcle of the Commerce Court sixty years ago ought not to preclude serious consideration of the creation of more specialized courts.

Judicial jurisdiction in patent matters is now divided between specialized and unspecialized tribunals. If the Patent Office denies an application, the applicant may choose between an appeal to the Court of Customs and Patent Appeals and a civil action against the Commissioner in the District Court for the District of Columbia,[5] with an appeal lying to the Court of Appeals for that circuit. A party dissatisfied with a decision of the board of patent interference on a question of priority may appeal to the Court of Customs and Patent Appeals[6] or may sue in any appropriate district court;[7] if the adverse party chooses the latter remedy, the appeal to the Court of Customs and Patent Appeals will be dismissed. No reason appears in either of these situations for allowing a choice between an expert and an inexpert tribunal.[8]

The more familiar types of patent litigation are the action seeking an injunction against infringement of a patent actually issued, and its converse, the action for a declaratory judgment of invalidity or non-infringement. Such actions are brought in the district courts,[9]

son, *The Administrative Court Proposal*, 57 VA. L. REV. 996, 1004–08 (1971).

3. FRANKFURTER & LANDIS 164.

4. *See* 28 U.S.C. §§ 1491–1506, 1541–45.

5. Act of July 19, 1952, ch. 950, § 145, 66 Stat. 803, 35 U.S.C. § 145.

6. Act of July 19, 1952, ch. 950, § 141, 66 Stat. 802, 35 U.S.C. § 141; Act of June 25, 1948, ch. 646, § 1542(1), 62 Stat. 942, 28 U.S.C. § 1542(1).

7. Act of July 19, 1952, ch. 950, § 146, 66 Stat. 803, 35 U.S.C. § 146.

8. Exclusive jurisdiction in the Court of Customs and Patent Appeals with respect to the denial of patents was recommended by a distinguished commission thirty years ago.

9. Act of June 25, 1948, ch. 646, § 1338(a), 62 Stat. 931, *as amended*, 28 U.S.C. § 1338(a). The Court of Claims also hears patent cases

and are subject to the same provisions for appeal as any other case in those courts.

An objection that has long been made to this method of handling patent litigation is the disparity of results. This was put, quite moderately, thirty years ago:[10]

[I]t is widely felt that although the court decisions are a necessary improvement to the prospective and sketchily informed judgment of the Patent Office, they leave much to be desired in consistency and uniformity and consequently in their effect on the confidence of those dealing with meritorious inventions. It is quite possible that in districts where patent litigation is less frequent, a series of cases involving weak or oppressive patents may incline a judge harshly toward meritorious patents; and a converse effect is likewise possible.

The serious problem today is not the differing visceral sensations of district judges, but rather the contrasting attitudes of the various courts of appeals on the issues of invention and novelty[11]—a difference which the Supreme Court's two decisions of 1966,[12] not surprisingly, did not end. This accounts for the mad and undignified races that sometimes occur between a patentee who wishes to sue for infringement in one circuit believed to be benign toward patents, and a user who wants to obtain a declaration of invalidity or non-infringement in one believed to be hostile to them.[13] The stakes have now

where it is alleged that the United States is an infringer. Act of June 25, 1948, ch. 646, 62 Stat. 941, *as amended*, 28 U.S.C. § 1498.

10. Woodward, *A Reconsideration of the Patent System as a Problem of Administrative Law*, 55 HARV. L. REV. 950, 960 (1942) (footnote omitted).

11. Professor Irving Kayton has made an empirical study of the attitude of the circuits toward patents. The extremes range from the Fifth Circuit, which upheld 52% of the patents it considered between February 1966 and September 1970, to the Eighth Circuit, which invalidated every patent it considered during the same period. Kayton, THE CRISIS OF LAW IN PATENTS A-10 (1970).

12. Graham v. John Deere Co., 383 U.S. 1 (1966), with which were decided Calmar, Inc. v. Cook Chem. Co. and Colgate-Palmolive Co. v. Cook Chem. Co.; United States v. Adams, 383 U.S. 39 (1966). These cases represented the first occasion since Great Atlantic & Pacific Tea Co. v. Supermarket Equip. Corp., 340 U.S. 147 (1950), in which the Supreme Court dealt with the issue of patentability.

13. See Kerotest Mfg. Co. v. C-O-Two Fire Equip. Co., 342 U.S. 180 (1952), for a discussion of the relevant considerations when the patentee sues to enforce in one circuit and an alleged infringer brings

become higher than ever. While it was long the rule that a court of appeals should give great respect to the decision of another upholding or denying the validity of a patent,[14] the Supreme Court broke new ground in 1971 by deciding that a declaration of invalidity in a suit for infringement in one circuit would generally work as a collateral estoppel on the patentee from claiming validity in another,[15] although, of course, the converse is not true. If this rule should be extended to actions for declaratory judgments by alleged infringers, as much of the opinion's discussion of judicial economy would suggest, the incentive to anticipate a patentee's suit by instituting such an action in a circuit thought to be tough on patents will be heightened.

Another strong argument for removing patent litigation from the ordinary courts is the increased complexity of their subject-matter. It was not hard for ordinary judges to comprehend a patent like that in one of the leading cases of early years, which substituted porcelain or clay for wood or metal in doorknobs.[16] Indeed, I did not find the subject for what for long was my only patent opinion—women's girdles[17]—to be unduly technical. But the courts must also deal today

a declaratory judgment action in another circuit to find it invalid. An excellent example of this phenomenon is reflected in Mattel, Inc. v. Louis Marx & Co., 353 F.2d 421 (2d Cir. 1965), *petition for cert. dismissed*, 384 U.S. 948 (1966), where less than 24 hours elapsed between the service of process in a declaratory judgment action instituted in the District of New Jersey and the filing of an infringement action in the Southern District of New York.

14. Novadel-Agene Corp. v. Penn, 119 F.2d 764, 766 (5th Cir.), *cert. denied*, 314 U.S. 645 (1941); Cold Metal Process Co. v. Republic Steel Corp., 233 F.2d 828, 837 (6th Cir.), *cert. denied*, 352 U.S. 891 (1956); Georgia-Pacific Corp. v. United States Plywood Corp., 258 F.2d 124, 133 (2d Cir.), *cert. denied*, 358 U.S. 884 (1958).

15. Blonder-Tongue Laboratories, Inc. v. University of Illinois Foundation, 402 U.S. 313 (1971). The Court here accomplished by decision what President Johnson's Commission on the Patent System had recommended should be effected by legislation. *"To Promote the Progress of . . . Useful Arts" in an Age of Exploding Technology*, REPORT OF THE PRESIDENT'S COMMISSION ON THE PATENT SYSTEM 38–39 (1966) [hereinafter cited as JOHNSON COMMISSION REPORT]. The estoppel will not exist if the patentee can establish that he did not have "a full and fair chance to litigate the validity of his patent" in the earlier case. 402 U.S. at 333.

16. Hotchkiss v. Greenwood, 52 U.S. (11 How.) 248 (1851).

17. International Latex Corp. v. Warner Bros. Co., 276 F.2d 557 (2d Cir.), *cert. denied*, 364 U.S. 816 (1960).

with a great number of patents in the higher reaches of electronics, chemistry, biochemistry, pharmacology, optics, harmonics and nuclear physics, which are quite beyond the ability of the usual judge to understand without the expenditure of an inordinate amount of educational effort by counsel and of attempted self-education by the judge, and in many instances, even with it.[18] The judges who hear the case in a suit for infringement on appeal are no better off except for the benefit they can derive from the district court's opinion. Indeed, save in this respect, they are rather worse off since the limited time available for argument prevents their getting as much assistance from counsel as did the district judge and, once the argument is over, it is cumbersome to have further recourse to counsel for help on technical matters that may assume new importance as a result of study.

I am unable to perceive why we should not insist on the same level of scientific understanding on the patent bench that clients demand of the patent bar, or why lack of such understanding by the judge should be deemed a precious asset.[19] As Judge Learned Hand well said, "To judge on our own that this or that new assemblage of old factors was, or was not, 'obvious' is to substitute our ignorance for the acquaintance with the subject of those who were familiar with it."[20] Such superior competence over the experts of the Patent Office as a judge may possess comes "not because of his non-expert personality, nor yet because he hears tax cases, bankruptcy cases, and other private litigation, but because he has the advantage of hind-

18. During an early year on the bench, I was told that a computer patent, then in litigation in the District Court for the Southern District of New York, involved electronics so complex that the subject-matter could be fully understood by only a dozen or so men in the United States. Most of them were in the employ of the parties, and the charmed circle surely did not include the district judge or the judges of the Second Circuit. Fortunately the case was settled.

19. *See* Rifkind, *A Special Court for Patent Litigation? The Danger of a Specialized Judiciary*, 37 A.B.A.J. 425 (1951). One commentator, not fearing specialization, has renewed the proposal, *see* p. 154 *supra,* that denials by the Patent Office be appealable only to the Court of Customs and Patent Appeals. Ditlow, *Judicial Review of Patent Office: A More Rational Review System*, 53 J. PAT. OFF. SOC'Y 205, 221–23 (1971). This proposal would seem to be "half a loaf," or much less, since it would still retain district court jurisdiction for other types of patent litigation.

20. Reiner v. I. Leon Co., 285 F.2d 501, 504 (2d Cir. 1960), *cert. denied,* 366 U.S. 929 (1961).

sight and of the research of industrious counsel who usually spend far more time on searching the art relating to a particular invention than the Patent Office can afford to devote to any one application."[21] It is true that, as a distinguished objector to a specialized patent court has said, "It is hardly to be supposed that the members of a patent court will be so omniscient as to possess specialized skill in chemistry, in electronics, mechanics and in vast fields of discovery yet uncharted."[22] But a Patent Court, following the model of the Court of Claims, would have a number of commissioners to conduct the trials; they could represent a broad spectrum of scientific knowledge and would be assigned cases in accordance with their individual capabilities.[23] The case would thus come before the Patent Court with detailed findings of fact by a disinterested "judge" expert in the subject-matter. Even though no member of the reviewing court could be expert in all the technologies that would be involved, I do not agree that "[t]he expert in organic chemistry brings no special light to guide him in the decision of a problem relating to radioactivity."[24] He is still likely to know a good deal more about radioactivity than someone like the writer, whose college specialty was European history and who avoided science courses because of lack of real comprehension.[25] At the very least, such a judge would contribute a scientific approach and an acquaintance with the lingo not possessed by the common run. Furthermore, such a court could have a staff of experts who would be available both to the commissioners and to the

21. Woodward, *supra*, 55 HARV. L. REV. at 959.
22. Rifkind, *supra*, 37 A.B.A.J. at 426.
23. The commissioners would not sit only in Washington but would conduct trials at places most convenient to the litigants. This proposal seems far superior to that of President Johnson's Commission on the Patent System for a Civil Commissioner to conduct pretrial proceedings in all district courts where justified by the volume of patent litigation. JOHNSON COMMISSION REPORT 39–41. In the rare instance of a suit for damages, unaccompanied by a demand for equitable relief, in which a jury trial was demanded, if the Seventh Amendment were thought to prevent a commissioner from presiding unless the parties agreed (and I do not see why it should), a member of the Patent Court could be assigned.
24. Rifkind, *supra*, 37 A.B.A.J. at 426.
25. Review of applications for prestigious and well-paying scholarships at a leading law school shows that many applicants are making the same mistake even in the computer age.

judges, as law clerks are now. It is true that, as also has been said by way of objection,[26] suits for patent infringement, or for a declaration of invalidity, often involve issues in other branches of the law, notably antitrust.[27] But the judges of a Patent Court would be judges, not laboratory technicians; moreover, experience should make them particularly familiar with the rather esoteric antitrust doctrines relating to patents. If all that is not enough, Supreme Court review with respect to such issues would remain as a safeguard.

This leaves only the fear that a specialized court having exclusive jurisdiction over patent litigation might be overly liberal or unduly strict in its attitude toward patents—more likely the former. I perceive no real basis for this. The patent bar, from whom most of the members of the court should be drawn, is not exclusively engaged in defending patents; the same lawyer will be doing this one month and attacking validity the next. To be sure, the patent bar does have a stake in the existence of a viable patent system. Judge Rich, of the Court of Customs and Patent Appeals, has made this point:[28]

> We should stop thinking in terms of the "strength" of individual patents or the "strength" of the presumption of their validity and concentrate on the strength of the patent *system* . . . . The weakness or strength of individual patents when they get into court is something wholly unrelated to the weakness or strength of the system.

Well-chosen members of a specialized court could not ignore this thought. And here again there would be the safeguard of occasional Supreme Court review.[29]

26. Rifkind, *supra*, 37 A.B.A.J. at 426.
27. *See, e.g.*, Leitch Mfg. Co. v. Barber Co., 302 U.S. 458 (1938); Morton Salt Co. v. G. S. Suppiger Co., 314 U.S. 488 (1942); Mercoid Corp. v. Mid-Continent Inv. Co., 320 U.S. 661 (1944); United States Gypsum Co. v. National Gypsum Co., 352 U.S. 457 (1957).
28. Rich, *The Proposed Patent Legislation: Some Comments*, 35 Geo. Wash. L. Rev. 641, 644 (1967) (emphasis in the original).
29. Arguably Supreme Court review could be restricted to issues other than validity or infringement on the bases that the Patent Court would be better equipped to deal with technical matters and that the Supreme Court should be protected from having to pass on petitions with respect to such matters. However, the importance of maintaining a proper policy with respect to patentability and the impracticability of correcting an improper one by legislation make it best to preserve

Legislation providing for a Patent Court would have to take cognizance of the cases where the validity of a patent arises by way of an affirmative defense, a counterclaim, or an amended complaint, rather than in the complaint itself. Examples would be a suit for royalties where the licensee challenges validity, or an antitrust action for price fixing where the defendant asserts it is acting within the scope of a patent and the plaintiff amends to claim invalidity, whether for patent abuse or on more conventional grounds. If one accepts my thesis of the importance of an expert court for patent litigation, and the desirability of uniform judgments, such cases arising in a federal district court or a state court would be transferable or removable to the Patent Court on motion of either party or on the court's own motion whenever it appeared that a decision might turn on a question of patent law. Refusal to allow transfer or removal would not be a ground for reversal, but any decision on a patent issue would be binding only on the parties[30] and would have no effect as a precedent or as collateral estoppel. While this last provision might slightly impair the effect of *Blonder-Tongue Laboratories*,[31] any adverse consequences of this would be outweighed by the desirability of preserving the Patent Court as the ultimate forum for the resolution of the validity of a patent.

Whether a new Patent Court, in addition to taking over the patent jurisdiction of the present Court of Customs and Patent Appeals, should also take over that court's jurisdiction with respect to the issuance of trademarks,[32] would also require consideration. This would seem desirable if the docket of the court would permit. The Patent Court should not handle the totally unrelated subject of ap-

the Court's certiorari power over issues of validity or infringement, although one would not expect this to be exercised any more frequently than it has been in the recent past. *See* note 12 *supra*.

30. As to them, it should be binding even in subsequent litigation.

31. *Supra*, 402 U.S. at 349–50.

32. Act of June 25, 1948, ch. 646, § 1542(2), 62 Stat. 943, *as amended*, 28 U.S.C. § 1542(2); Act of July 5, 1946, ch. 540, tit. I, § 21, 60 Stat. 435, *as amended*, 15 U.S.C. § 1071(a). Here, as in the case of patent interferences, there is a bifurcated jurisdiction between the Court of Customs and Patent Appeals and the district courts, 15 U.S.C. § 1071(b), with the latter having priority.

peals from the Customs Court;[33] these might be heard by a specialized court devoted solely to that subject, as the Court of Customs and Patent Appeals was from 1909 until 1929,[34] or by the Court of Claims, which I would propose to relieve from concern with tax matters. The present judges of the Court of Customs and Patent Appeals who had or have acquired a patent background presumably would become members of the Patent Court; ample use could be found for the others.

The structure for the judicial determination of disputes over United States taxes incapable of resolution at the administrative level is the result of history rather than logic. Suffice it here to say that a taxpayer disputing his liability for income, gift or estate taxes[35] has a choice among three initial forums: the Tax Court of the United States or, if he is willing and able to pay the tax and sue for a refund,[36] a district court or the Court of Claims. A decision by the Tax Court or a district court is reviewable by the appropriate court of appeals, whose decision, in turn, is subject to review on certiorari by the Supreme Court. A decision by the Court of Claims is subject to review only on certiorari by the Supreme Court. As was said thirty years ago:[37]

If we were seeking to secure a state of complete uncertainty in tax jurisprudence, we could hardly do better than to provide for 87 Courts with original jurisdiction, 11 appellate bodies of coordinate rank, and only a discretionary review of relatively few cases by the Supreme Court.

The worst single feature in this structure is the lack of any point of authoritative determination of questions of statutory interpretation

33. Act of June 25, 1948, ch. 646, § 1541, 62 Stat. 942, *as amended,* 28 U.S.C. § 1541.
34. 36 Stat. 105 (1909); 45 Stat. 1475 (1929).
35. A taxpayer disputing liability for an excise or employment tax must pay the tax and sue for refund in a district court or the Court of Claims. Tax suits by the United States, civil or criminal, may be brought only in the district courts.
36. Flora v. United States, 362 U.S. 145 (1960), *reaff'g* 357 U.S. 63 (1958), established that, when a tax is not "divisible," payment of the entire amount of the assessed deficiency, rather than a lesser token amount, is a prerequisite to a suit for a refund.
37. MAGILL, THE IMPACT OF FEDERAL TAXES 209 (1943).

short of the Supreme Court. The evils were exposed so thoroughly and brilliantly by Professor Roger Traynor, as he then was, in 1938,[38] and by Professor Erwin Griswold, as he then was, in 1944,[39] that the barest summary will suffice: Until 1970, a decision by a court of appeals of one circuit bound no court other than itself and the district courts within the circuit; in that year the Tax Court, reversing a long-standing position,[40] decided that "better judicial administration requires us to follow a Court of Appeals decision which is squarely in point where appeal from our decision lies to that Court of Appeals and to that court alone."[41] If the decision is for the Government, the Supreme Court will rarely grant certiorari on the taxpayer's request in the absence of a conflict; if the decision is against the Government, the Solicitor General normally will not even seek it unless a conflict exists. A study has shown that for the five Supreme Court terms beginning in 1955, the median "conflict-resolving" period, dating from the first court of appeals decision, itself many years after the tax year at issue, ran from a low of three years and one month to a high of eleven years and nine months.[42] However, on a number of

38. Traynor, *Administrative and Judicial Procedure for Federal Income, Estate and Gift Taxes—A Criticism and a Proposal*, 38 COLUM. L. REV. 1393 (1938). Chief Justice Traynor has contributed so greatly to other fields of law—conflicts, criminal procedure, contracts, judgments and torts, to name only a few—that most people have forgotten that he began his career as a tax lawyer. Professor Traynor's original proposal received a great deal of commentary. The principal comments are collected in Ferguson, *Jurisdictional Problems in Federal Tax Controversies*, 48 IOWA L. REV. 312, 371 n.302 (1963).

39. Griswold, *The Need for a Court of Tax Appeals*, 57 HARV. L. REV. 1153 (1944). The study is updated in Del Cotto, *The Need for a Court of Tax Appeals: An Argument and a Study*, 12 BUFFALO L. REV. 5 (1962). The case has again been strongly pressed in *A Report on Complexity and the Income Tax*, 27 TAX L. REV. 327, 354–58 (1972).

40. Arthur L. Lawrence, 27 T.C. 713 (1957), *rev'd on other grounds,* 258 F.2d 562 (9th Cir. 1958).

41. Jack E. Golsen, 54 T.C. 742, 757 (1970) (footnotes omitted). The last phrase points up a serious problem, namely, where the proceeding in the Tax Court involves taxpayers residing in circuits which entertain different views. *See Note, The Old Tax Court Blues: The Need for Uniformity in Tax Litigation*, 46 N.Y.U.L. REV. 970, 981–83 (1971). *Compare* Robert A. Hitt, 55 T.C. 628 (1971), *with* Donald W. Fausner, 55 T.C. 620 (1971).

42. Del Cotto, *supra*, 12 BUFFALO L. REV. at 30.

significant issues, from fifteen to thirty years were required for the resolution of conflicts.[43] When the resolution was against the Government, thousands of taxpayers in Government-deciding circuits had paid taxes they did not owe; when the resolution was in favor of the Government, the revenue had suffered in circuits that had decided otherwise. Thousands of cases had been settled, in light of the uncertainty, on a basis too favorable to one side and too unfavorable to the other. Another evil by-product is that once the Court of Claims has decided a new point in favor of a taxpayer, there may never be a conflict since all similarly situated taxpayers who are in a position to pay the tax can bring their suits there. The obvious solution is a single Court of Tax Appeals to which all appeals from tax decisions of courts of first instance are to be routed.

When the matter was earlier studied, it was clear that the proposed court would encounter no difficulty in handling its work.[44] Happily, although unexpectedly, that is still true. In 1972 there were filed in the courts of appeals 202 appeals from the Tax Court and 260 from tax cases in the district courts where the United States was the defendant—a total of 462.[45] To this figure one should add appeals in cases now decided by the Court of Claims. In 1972, 155 tax cases were filed in that court.[46] Assuming an appeal ratio in present Court of Claims cases as high as 50%, one would have filings of some 500 cases per year. In 1972 no circuit except the First had so

43. *Id.* at 24–31.
44. *See* Griswold, *supra*, 57 HARV. L. REV. at 1179–80; Del Cotto, *supra*, 12 BUFFALO L. REV. at 20–22.
45. A.O. ANN. REP., Tables B3 & B7 (1972). There were also 34 appeals from district courts in tax cases where the United States was the plaintiff. *Id.* Table B7. Dean Griswold would include these in the jurisdiction of the Court of Tax Appeals, *supra*, 57 HARV. L. REV. at 1165. They are a rather mixed bag, including some types of actions, *e.g.*, suits to recover excessive refunds, which one would like to see included, and others, *e.g.*, priority of liens, which may depend primarily on questions of state law that a court of appeals is better qualified to handle. Whether these cases should be included, as Dean Griswold proposed, or left to the ordinary courts of appeals, seems to me to depend on whether the Supreme Court is to retain any tax jurisdiction in other than constitutional cases. If not, I would agree with Dean Griswold. The same applies to the few state cases hinging on a point of federal tax law. *See id.* at 1165–66.
46. REPORT OF THE UNITED STATES COURT OF CLAIMS (1972).

few. Indeed, if one were justified in using the national average case-load per court of appeals judgeship,[47] a court of as few as five judges would suffice for the present, and thus leave ample room for expansion.

That, however, would be a mistaken analogy. The docket of the Court of Tax Appeals would include fewer frivolous or nearly frivolous appeals and more cases of real difficulty than that of any circuit court. Still more important, since a prime purpose of the court would be to secure uniformity on important issues of tax law, the court should place less reliance on the panel system and would have to hear, or rehear, a considerably larger proportion of cases en banc.[48] Furthermore, it seems to be generally accepted that "the Court of Tax Appeals would have to be a circuit court in the true sense" and "to arrange for frequent sittings in a number of cities throughout the country."[49] One may wonder whether this is as self-evident in the jet age as it seemed in 1944; in any event, a half dozen cities should be sufficient for panel sittings. Since it would hardly be feasible for the court to ride circuit to hear cases en banc, procedures should be developed for screening out most cases warranting en banc consideration in advance of argument; when that has not proved possible, the judges not on the panel should be able to participate on the basis of reading the briefs and, desirably, a transcript of the argument. Whether, in light of all this, the court should start off with seven or nine judges, can be fairly debated; I would favor the larger number, coupled with a provision permitting their assignment to sit in other courts.[50]

47. To wit, 132. *See* A.O. ANN. REP. 132 (1971).
48. It might well be desirable for such a court to allow an en banc to be triggered by less than the majority required for the ordinary courts of appeals. Act of June 25, 1948, ch. 646, 62 Stat. 871, *as amended*, 28 U.S.C. § 46(c). Some think that in those courts also there should be something more like the Supreme Court's "rule of four" for the grant of certiorari. Certainly it seems wrong that when a judge is disqualified, he should still be counted in the total, as the present statute demands. *See* Zahn v. International Paper Co., — F.2d —, slip op. p. 141 (2d Cir. Oct. 18, 1972) (denial of en banc).
49. Griswold, *supra*, 57 HARV. L. REV. at 1181.
50. I am less enthusiastic about Dean Griswold's proposal permitting the assignment of other Article III judges into the Court of Tax Appeals. 57 HARV L. REV. at 1181. I would limit this to en banc cases where a judge of the Court of Tax Appeals was disqualified or a vacancy or

The principal objections that have been made to such a court are that it would lack familiarity with local law, which may sometimes figure prominently in tax cases,[51] and that it would be composed of "specialists." With respect to the first objection there is little that can be added to Professor Griswold's analysis;[52] whatever small weight this may have, it is minuscule as compared to the great benefits to be achieved. The second argument is somewhat semantic. Tax lawyers are not narrow specialists; they deal with problems touching every phase of life and, consequently, of law.[53] To such extent as they come to the bench equipped with a knowledge of tax law, which spares them the Herculean efforts at mastering the intricacies of the Internal Revenue Code so vividly described by Judge Learned Hand in his tribute to Judge Swan,[54] that is all to the good. The real fears are two: that the judges will be, or become, unduly government-minded, and that the court would be used to take care of lame ducks rather than for the appointment of men highly qualified for the job. No one could honestly deny that this has sometimes occurred in the four "national" inferior appellate courts—the Court of Claims, the Customs Court, the Court of Customs and Patent Appeals and the Court of Appeals for the District of Columbia Circuit, as, indeed, it has elsewhere. On the other hand, for all the many years I have known it, the Court of Appeals for the District of Columbia Circuit has maintained a level of excellence well above the average for the courts of appeals. There would seem to be an added safeguard with respect to a Court of Tax Appeals; the Treasury would surely not

vacancies had created an even number of judges. Even for these cases, retired judges of the Court of Tax Appeals would provide a better source.

51. Probably the outstanding example is the effect of community property law on questions of estate and gift taxation.

52. 57 HARV. L. REV. at 1188–90.

53. *Id.* at 1183–84.

54. "In my own case the words of such an act as the Income Tax . . . merely dance before my eyes in a meaningless procession: cross-reference to cross-reference, exception upon exception—couched in abstract terms that offer no handle to seize hold of—leave in my mind only a confused sense of some vitally important, but successfully concealed, purport, which it is my duty to extract, but which is within my power, if at all, only after the most inordinate expenditure of time." Hand, *Thomas Walter Swan*, 57 YALE L.J. 167, 169 (1947).

wish to see determinations vitally affecting the revenues in the hands of incompetents. The danger is rather that the Treasury would seek to overload the court with tax lawyers having a background in government. There is some feeling among the bar, whether justified or not, that an unduly large proportion of the members of the Tax Court of the United States has come from these sources and that the court thus is slanted in favor of the Government. Such a belief, along with the occasional desire for a jury trial, undoubtedly is the principal reason for the approximately fifteen hundred cases each year where a taxpayer elects to pay the tax and sue for a refund.[55]

While a statute limiting the proportion of the judges of a Court of Tax Appeals who could come directly from the Bureau of Internal Revenue, other sections of the Treasury, and the Tax Division of the Department of Justice would be of dubious constitutionality, a President would hardly ignore legislative history making Congress' intention clear; if he did, the Senate would always be there to remind him of it. The remaining danger is that the high proportion of tax appeals in which the Government is right might lead the judges of the new court to think it is right in all. But that danger exists today; if anything, it should be mitigated by the expertise properly to be expected in a specialized court.

The remaining issue at the appellate level is the extent of Supreme Court review over the decisions of the Court of Tax Appeals. Everyone would agree there should be such review when the Court of Tax Appeals had decided a substantial constitutional issue; the only question is whether review should be by appeal or certiorari. While the Supreme Court could and would guard against frivolous appeals by requiring a preliminary showing of substantiality,[56] the certiorari device is preferable; in the rare case when there was particular need for a quick settlement by the Supreme Court, certiorari in advance of decision by the Court of Tax Appeals could be sought.[57]

55. *See* Department of Justice Study of the Trial Court System for Federal Civil Tax Disputes, *reprinted in Hearings on S. 2041 Before the Subcomm. on Improvements in Judicial Machinery of the Senate Comm. on the Judiciary*, 90th Cong., 2d Sess. 112 (1968).
56. *See* Griswold, *supra*, 57 HARV. L. REV. at 1167.
57. Act of June 25, 1948, ch. 646, 62 Stat. 928, 28 U.S.C. § 1254(1). If a district court holds a federal tax statute to be unconstitutional, existing legislation would allow the Government to bypass the court

The serious question is whether decisions of the Court of Tax Appeals not presenting constitutional issues should be reviewable by the Supreme Court at all. In my judgment they should not. Allowing such review would not be objectionable from the standpoint of delay if denial of certiorari meant that the point was settled; but the Supreme Court has repeatedly adjured us that this is not at all the case,[58] nor should it be. Allowing Supreme Court review would thus mean that "no point decided by the Court of Tax Appeals would be finally settled and no decision of the Court of Tax Appeals could be relied on with complete safety."[59] The argument that it could be "confidently expected that the Supreme Court would undertake to reexamine very few" decisions of the Court of Tax Appeals, particularly because the possibility of conflict would have been eliminated,[60] is essentially self-defeating. If the Court reviews only one tax case not presenting a constitutional issue in five years, such review is not worth the price in terms of uncertainty.

Several other considerations support the conclusion of no Supreme Court review except for constitutional questions. The interpretation of tax statutes is typically the kind of issue where "it is more important that the applicable rule of law be settled than that it be settled right";[61] indeed, the Government's interest often is only that it not be whipsawed.[62] Furthermore, this is a field which is under constant surveillance by the Treasury and the experienced committees of Congress. A decision by the Court of Tax Appeals seriously damaging to the revenue or grossly unfair to taxpayers can be speedily

of appeals. Act of June 25, 1948, ch. 646, 62 Stat. 928, *as amended*, 28 U.S.C. § 1252. If the Tax Court were given Article III status, as I think it should be, § 1252 presumably would be amended to include it.

58. *See, e.g.*, Maryland v. Baltimore Radio Show, Inc., 338 U.S. 912, 919 (1950) (Frankfurter, J., respecting the denial of the petition for writ of certiorari).
59. Griswold, *supra*, 57 HARV. L. REV. at 1167.
60. *Id.* at 1168.
61. Burnet v. Coronado Oil & Gas Co., 285 U.S. 393, 406 (1932) (Brandeis, J., dissenting).
62. *Cf.* the issue concerning the respective rights of lessor and lessee to percentage depletion presented in United States Steel Corp. v. United States, 445 F.2d 520, 522–28 (2d Cir. 1971), *cert. denied*, 405 U.S. 917 (1972).

corrected for the future; indeed, but for the usually unwarranted fear of prejudicing the result of litigation, clarifying legislation could often have been obtained before the decision was reached. Finally, there is no assurance that a Supreme Court decision in this area will be any sounder than that of a tribunal experienced in tax matters. Rather, it is a considerable understatement to say that "[t]he Supreme Court has not been unduly felicitous in some of its tax decisions."[63] This is no criticism of the Justices, who have more important things to do than saturate themselves in the intricacies of tax law.[64] The final consideration is relieving the Court from the need of considering petitions for certiorari in a field where, by hypothesis, it will grant exceedingly few. Here is a particularly good place to lessen the Court's certiorari load.[65]

With the Court of Tax Appeals thus ensconced and, hopefully, immunized from Supreme Court review except in constitutional cases, we are left with the problem at the trial level. Here, as indicated, there is the anomaly of a trifurcated system of courts of first instance. In the Tax Court, the taxpayer has the advantage of not having to pay the disputed tax, but the disadvantages of a judge not from his locality and the absence of a jury. In the district courts, he can obtain the two latter advantages, but only by paying the tax and suing for a

---

63. Griswold, *supra*, 57 HARV. L. REV. at 1169. Others have gone much further, *e.g.*, Professor Lowndes' well-known statement, "It is time to rescue the Supreme Court from federal taxation; it is time to rescue federal taxation from the Supreme Court" and his supporting analysis. *Federal Taxation and the Supreme Court*, 1960 SUP. CT. REV. 222 *et seq.* (1960). Writing from the standpoint of a political scientist, Professor Martin Shapiro criticizes what he considers the retreat of the Warren Court from tax policy-making, saying that "its present hesitant attitude imparts a confusion and vagueness to the corpus of tax law that appear undesirable in terms of the Court's general institutional interest in the quality of the legal system." LAW AND POLITICS IN THE SUPREME COURT 172 (1964). Professor Lowndes' analysis indicates that greater activism would probably have made things worse.

64. A single ill-chosen phrase in a Supreme Court opinion, very likely not at all critical to the result, can give rise to thousands of tax controversies whose solution will take many years. Recognizing this danger, my mentor, Mr. Justice Brandeis, made it a cardinal principle to keep his tax opinions exceedingly short; although no innocent in tax law, he recognized this to be a field where he was not truly expert. Would that all his successors had shared this modesty!

65. *See* pp. 47–48 *supra*.

refund. Finally, in the Court of Claims, he must pay the tax, and does not obtain a local judge or a jury but, for reasons previously explained, if he wins on an issue of first impression, he will probably win forever, unless some ill-advised or more impecunious taxpayer provokes a conflict elsewhere or Congress changes the law.

Some consistency of decision is achieved within each type of court of first instance. In the Tax Court, consistency among the sixteen judges is sought to be insured by a provision that their reports do not become the decision of the Tax Court for thirty days, during which the Chief Judge may direct that the report be reviewed by the Court,[66] although this is now somewhat marred by the Tax Court's new policy with respect to following the decision of the court of appeals ·to which an appeal will lie.[67] Consistency of district judges within a circuit is enforced, so far as concerns questions of law, by the court of appeals. The Court of Claims has no difficulty maintaining consistency of decision because the full court decides all cases.

Geographic factors within the three forums also differ. The Tax Court has its headquarters in Washington but its judges ride circuit, trying cases in about 50 cities a year as compared to some 300 for the district courts. Court of Claims cases are tried by commissioners who also travel. Although technically a court of first instance, the Court of Claims, which sits only in Washington, operates in practical effect as a court to review the commissioners' proposed decisions.

Finally, the three forums offer different procedures to the litigant. In district court proceedings, discovery, which generally operates in favor of the Government, is governed by the liberal Federal Rules of Civil Procedure. On the other hand, "[t]here is no discovery procedure in the Tax Court and only limited discovery in the Court of Claims."[68]

---

66. INT. REV. CODE OF 1954, § 7460(b).

67. *See* p. 162 *supra*.

68. Department of Justice Study of the Trial Court System for Federal Civil Tax Disputes, *supra* note 55, at 117. Much of the foregoing material comes. from this source. Other useful discussions of multiforum tax problems appear in Ferguson, *supra*, 48 IOWA L. REV. 312; Note, *Forum Reform: Tax Litigation*, 35 U. CIN. L. REV. 644 (1966); Note, *supra*, 46 N.Y.U.L. REV. 970 (1971).

   It goes without saying that, because of the many institutional variations available to a potential tax litigant, the tax bar receives

A 1968 study by the Tax Division of the Department of Justice concluded that "the existing system fails in a number of respects to fulfill the goals of a sound tax court system" and that "the defects are sufficiently important to warrant changes."[69] The report considered various possible changes but took no firm position save the exceedingly trite one that "the exclusive jurisdiction proposal [for any one of the three present trial courts] would be more difficult to implement than the alternative of concurrent jurisdiction."[70]

The one thing most clearly emerging for me is that the tax jurisdiction of the Court of Claims serves no useful purpose now and would be a positive source of harm if a Court of Tax Appeals were established.[71] The rationale for the tax jurisdiction of that court almost completely disappeared in 1954 when Congress removed the $10,000 ceiling for tax refund suits in the district courts.[72] All that remains is the desire to give a taxpayer an option for a national rather than a local forum when he has overpaid or prefers to pay first and sue later,[73] and that could be easily met by corresponding enlargement of the jurisdiction of the Tax Court. The objective of achieving early finality in the determination of non-constitutional tax controversies by a Court of Tax Appeals would be thwarted unless tax decision of the Court of Claims were appealable to it. Yet it would be rather odd to have what really are appellate decisions of a court of seven judges subjected to review by a panel of three or even by an en banc court of more. Whether the Court of Claims would require seven judges after losing its tax jurisdiction would depend on what

continual advice on where to proceed with each type of case. *See, e.g.,* Garbis & Frome, *Selecting the Court for Optimum Disposition of a Tax Controversy,* 27 J. TAXATION 216 (1967); Ash, *Factors Selecting the Forum in Which to Litigate,* N.Y.U. 12TH INST. ON FED. TAX. 935 (1954).

69. Department of Justice Study of the Trial Court System for Federal Civil Tax Disputes, *supra* note 55, at 125.

70. *Id.*

71. *See* 114 CONG. REC. 29,844 (1968) (remarks of Senator Tydings), *and A Report on Complexity and the Income Tax, supra,* 27 TAX L. REV. at 354.

72. Act of July 30, 1954, ch. 648, § 1, 68 Stat. 589, codified at 28 U.S.C. § 1346(a)(1).

73. *E.g.,* to stop the running of interest.

new tasks were given to it.[74] Some of the present judges might wish to be appointed to the Court of Tax Appeals. If others were no longer needed on the Court of Claims, they would constitute a valuable resource for assignment to the hard-pressed courts of appeals.

Going further, I see no really sound reason for preserving a taxpayer's right to resort to a district court rather than requiring him to proceed in the Tax Court, once this was given Article III status[75] and the powers possessed by district courts under the Federal Rules of Civil Procedure. Since the task of preserving decisional consistency would fall to the new Court of Tax Appeals, the Tax Court would not need to have more than a token headquarters in Washington. Rather it could be arranged in regions, each with its own chief judge and clerk's office, and the judges would be spared some of the travel now inflicted upon them. Its jurisdiction would, of course, be enlarged to include refund suits, whether these resulted from overpayment or desire to avoid the running of interest. Removal of tax litigation from the district courts would be a welcome relief to these heavily pressed tribunals. I would also favor abolishing the right to request a jury in a refund action, a special statutory exception to the general rule in suits against the Government[76] and in no way required by the Seventh Amendment.[77]

74. This would surely include the review of determination of excessive profits now vested in the Tax Court by Act of Feb. 25, 1944, ch. 63, § 701(e), 58 Stat. 78, *now* 50 U.S.C. App. § 1191(e), and Act of March 23, 1951, ch. 15, tit. I, § 108, 65 Stat. 21, *as amended,* 50 U.S.C. App. § 1218, and might also include the customs work of the Court of Customs and Patent Appeals.

75. As proposed by Senator Tydings in S. 2041, 90th Cong., 2d Sess. (1968).

    Exclusive Tax Court jurisdiction in civil court tax matters except cases involving liens or collections is favored in *A Report on Complexity and the Income Tax, supra,* 27 Tax L. Rev. at 352–54.

76. Act of July 30, 1954, ch. 648, § 2, 68 Stat. 589, 28 U.S.C. § 2402.

77. Some tax suits by the United States are a different matter. See the discussion in Damsky v. Zavatt, 289 F.2d 46 (2d Cir. 1961).

PART IX

Administrative Review and Antitrust

WITH RESPECT to the proposals in the preceding section about patent and tax litigation, I entertain "no possible probable shadow of doubt, no possible doubt whatever"—although I recognize that others may not share in this certitude.[1] I come now to an area where such clarity concerning the proper judicial organization does not exist even in my own mind—review of administrative action. Here I have definite views about some things that should not be done; with respect to what should be, for the most part I can only suggest some possible lines of development.

Let me begin with some minor reforms well within the frame-work of the present system. Thirty-three years have passed since Chief Justice Stone proposed the transfer of the three-judge district court review of orders of the Interstate Commerce Commission, other than for the payment of money,[2] to the courts of appeals.[3] Although the Commission initially opposed this, its annual reports to Congress since 1963 have consistently recommended it.[4] If there is any justification for the difference in mode of review of orders of the ICC and those of other independent commissions,[5] this has not

---

1. As indicated, I have a shade less assurance about the proposed treatment of tax cases at the trial level except with respect to eliminating the tax jurisdiction of the Court of Claims.
2. 28 U.S.C. § 2321.
3. *Hearings on H.R. 1468, H.R. 1470 and H.R. 2271 Before Subcomm. 3 and 4 of the House Comm. on the Judiciary*, 80th Cong., 2d Sess., and on *H.R. 2915 and H.R. 2916 Before Subcomm. 2 of the House Comm. on the Judiciary*, 81st Cong., 1st Sess. 78 (1949).
4. *E.g.*, 77th ANN. REP. OF THE ICC 16–17 (1963).
5. Review by the courts of appeals of orders of the FCC (except licensing orders exclusively reviewable in the Court of Appeals for the District

been stated. Placing the review of ICC orders in three-judge district courts, one member of which must be a circuit judge, was an expedient hastily devised by Congress in 1913 when it pronounced the death sentence upon the Commerce Court, and no other independent commissions yet existed; the statute is appropriately called the Urgent Deficiencies Act.[6] Creation of such courts disrupts the orderly functioning of the district courts and the courts of appeals, and imposes further unnecessary burdens on the chief judges of the latter. Still worse is the provision for mandatory Supreme Court review of decisions to enjoin ICC orders.[7] While the Court has wisely endeavored to escape these shackles by frequent use of summary affirmance, such action, unlike the denial of certiorari, would seem to have precedential force in theory, however little it may deserve this in fact.

A second desirable step within the present structure would be to adopt the proposal of the Administrative Conference that orders of the National Labor Relations Board should be self-enforcing like those of other agencies, unless a proceeding to review was brought within a reasonably short period.[8] The reasons are amply set forth

of Columbia, 47 U.S.C. § 402(b)), the FMC, the AEC, the Secretary of Agriculture, and the Maritime Administration is provided by 28 U.S.C. § 2341-50. Similar review of orders of the FTC, FPC, SEC, NLRB, CAB, and now many other determinations, *see* pp. 34–35 *supra*, is provided in the governing statutes. A difference, which apparently has impeded a change in the method of review of ICC orders, is that the "general" review statute provides that "[t]he Attorney General is responsible for and has control of the interests of the Government in all court proceedings under this chapter," 28 U.S.C. § 2348, whereas there is no similar provision with respect to orders of many of the other agencies. The Department of Justice wants control over proceedings to review, and the ICC wants the same independence as, *e.g.*, the CAB. Since the agency can intervene under 28 U.S.C. § 2348 and the United States would surely be allowed to do so under the procedure governing most of the independent agencies, does it really matter all that much? I understand that, to the Commission's credit, it has now yielded on this point.

6. Ch. 32, 38 Stat. 219, 220 (1913).

7. 28 U.S.C. § 1253.

8. 1 Recommendations and Reports of the Administrative Conference of the United States 237–67 (1970). The recommendation would give an objecting party thirty days in which to seek review. If no such petition were filed, the Board would file a copy of its order in the appropriate court of appeals and give notice to each respondent.

in the report of the Conference. Presumably this discrimination against the Board must have been a by-product of the hostility to its very creation. After thirty-seven years, it has become sufficiently a part of our national life that it should no longer be treated as a step-child in this respect. This change would eliminate much delay resulting from the necessity for the Board's preparing petitions for enforcement, papers that are rarely read by anyone, and, by my uneducated guess, would effect a reduction of approximately 50% in Labor Board proceedings in the courts of appeals.[9]

Third, I would favor repeal of the statute providing for direct review by the courts of appeals of final orders of deportation,[10] and return this to the district courts. This legislation, sponsored by the long-time chairman of the House Committee on Un-American Activities, the late Representative Walter of Pennsylvania, was enacted in an effort to expedite the deportation of certain highly visible, wealthy aliens who could afford repeated appeals of deportation orders, thereby continually postponing their departure date. While the amendments may have expedited the deportation of some such aliens,[11] it has probably had the opposite effect in the vast majority of cases. Although the matter requires more detailed investigation, such figures as I have seen indicate that prior to this legislation most aliens who failed to obtain a stay of their deportation orders in the district court did not appeal.[12] While a legislative desire to terminate continuous frivolous appeals and habeas corpus petitions of unquestionably deportable aliens is understandable, the chanelling of all such cases

> Unless review was requested within 15 days, the clerk would enter an order of enforcement.

9. At present the respondent has almost nothing to lose by awaiting a petition for enforcement. It often takes the Board as long as a year even to *file* this; the Board then assumes the burden of preparing the appendix, although now, as a result of the Act of July 18, 1966, 80 Stat. 308, *as amended*, 28 U.S.C. § 2412, it can recover costs if it prevails.

10. 8 U.S.C. § 1105a. *See* Note, *Judicial Review of Final Orders of Deportation*, 42 N.Y.U.L. REV. 1155 (1967).

11. Even this is questionable. *See*, *e.g.*, Gambino v. INS, 419 F.2d 1355 (2d Cir.), *cert. denied*, 399 U.S. 905 (1970), where the deportation proceeding was begun in 1957.

12. *See* Foti v. INS, 308 F.2d 779, 785 n.6 (2d Cir. 1962), *rev'd*, 375 U.S. 117 (1963).

directly to the courts of appeals was a mistake. Instead of having to act speedily, the deportee now has six months to file a petition for review and this works as an automatic stay unless the INS moves to vacate it,[13]—which, whether because of the press of business or consideration for the courts of appeals, it does rather infrequently. Also the statute has engendered numerous jurisdictional disputes which have already demanded three Supreme Court decisions and will probably require more.[14] The clear answer to this problem is to place appeals from all final deportation orders back in the district courts, and expect the courts of appeals to give expeditious treatment to those orders of the district courts that are appealed.

A somewhat more debatable change, still within the contours of the existing system, would be to provide that where review of administrative action lies in the district court and that court has affirmed, appeal should be only by leave of the court of appeals.[15] The argument would be that it is enough to grant an aggrieved citizen one judicial look at the action of a disinterested governmental agency, unless a superior judicial body believes the case to present a problem going beyond the particular instance. There would be much to recommend such a procedure, for example, with respect to the many complaints of denial of relief, whether partial or total, by the Social Security Administration, or the review of deportation orders which I would return to the district courts. On the other hand, care would have to be taken not to include in this proposal cases where, due to the anomaly whereby the courts of appeals are the initial judicial forum for review of "orders" but not of "regulations,"[16] initial review

13. 8 U.S.C. § 1105a(a)(1), (3).
14. Foti v. INS, 375 U.S. 217 (1963); Giova v. Rosenberg, 379 U.S. 18 (1964); Cheng Fan Kwok v. INS, 392 U.S. 206 (1968). For an excellent discussion of the continuing jurisdictional uncertainty under the statute, see DAVIS, ADMINISTRATIVE LAW TREATISE § 23.03, at 794–99 (Supp. 1970).
15. The procedure would resemble that of 28 U.S.C. § 1292(b). The question whether the aggrieved party should be allowed to seek certiorari when leave was denied would have to be faced. This should surely be allowed when a substantial constitutional question was raised.
16. *See, e.g.,* Columbia Broadcasting System, Inc. v. United States, 316 U.S. 407 (1942) (chain broadcasting regulations); Abbott Laboratories v. Gardner, 387 U.S. 136 (1967) (regulations requiring printing of

of some of the most important actions of federal agencies takes place in the district courts. A still better solution of that problem is to correct the anomaly so that when the court of appeals has initial review of an agency's "orders," it would also have initial review of that agency's "regulations" in a pre-enforcement challenge for injunctive and declaratory judgment relief.

With this much out of the way, we can approach the broad issue of the desirability of "administrative courts," a subject that has been discussed for nearly forty years.[17] The discussion has been frustrating, in considerable part because while the discussants have used the same words, they have not meant at all the same things. At least three separate threads can be discerned.

The proposal that has attracted most attention over the years found its most influential expression in the separate views of Members McFarland, Stason and Vanderbilt in the Report of the Attorney General's Committee on Administrative Procedure in 1941.[18] The proposal was to strip the agencies, or certain of them, of their "quasi-judicial" functions, or certain of them, and to vest these in separate tribunals, *e.g.*, a Trade Court, a Labor Court, a Transportation Court, a Securities Court, etc. The proposal was somewhat vague on whether the judgments of these "courts" would be subject to review in the ordinary judicial system or by a super-administrative court, presumably having Article III status, which the lower specialized courts would not. After slumbering for fourteen years, the proposal gained new life in 1955 from its endorsement by the Hoover Commission.[19]

established name of prescription drugs); Gardner v. Toilet Goods Ass'n, 387 U.S. 167 (1967) (regulations defining color additives, etc.).

17. For some of the early proposals, see 59 A.B.A. REP. 148–53, 539–64 (1934) (Reports of Special Committee on Administrative Law); 61 A.B.A. REP. 218–27, 232–33, 720–67 (1936) (*id.*); Caldwell, *A Federal Administrative Court*, 84 U. PA. L. REV. 966 (1936).

18. Pp. 203–12 (1941).

19. COMMISSION ON ORGANIZATION OF THE EXECUTIVE BRANCH OF THE GOVERNMENT, REPORT TO THE CONGRESS ON LEGAL SERVICES AND PROCEDURE 84–88 (1955); COMMISSION ON ORGANIZATION OF THE EXECUTIVE BRANCH OF THE GOVERNMENT, TASK FORCE REPORT ON LEGAL SERVICES AND PROCEDURES 1–50 (1955). For discussions of the proposal see Jaffe, *Basic Issues: An Analysis*, 30 N.Y.U.L. REV. 1273, 1283–89 (1955); Nutting, *The Administrative Court*, *id.* at 1384; Schwartz, *Administrative Justice and its Place in the Legal Order*, *id.* at 1390, 1406–10.

An additional spark was furnished the next year by the proposal of
the ABA for the transfer of the adjudicative functions of the Federal Trade Commission and National Labor Relations Board to "one
or more courts of special jurisdiction."[20] Further interest was created
by the memorandum submitted by Louis Hector to the President upon
resigning from the Civil Aeronautics Board.[21] The debate was continued by proposals made by Newton Minow upon his resignation
as Chairman of the Federal Communications Commission.[22] Mr.
Minow agreed with Mr. Hector that the adjudicatory functions of
the principal federal agencies should be transferred to specially created extra-agency courts. In 1965, the former Chairman of the Securities and Exchange Commission, William Cary, strongly disputed
the wisdom of the Hector-Minow proposals.[23] The spark again died,
only to be reignited by a respected and unexpected source, former
Commissioner Elman of the FTC.[24] The general proposal met with

20. *Resolution No. 4, Proceedings of the House of Delegates: Midyear
    Meeting,* 42 A.B.A.J. 371, 374 (1956). This resolution was com-
    mented on by Earl W. Kintner, then General Counsel to the FTC,
    in *The Trade Court Proposal: An Examination of Some Possible
    Defects,* 44 A.B.A.J. 441 (1958).
        A quite different, and highly imaginative, proposal has recently
    been made to create a United States Labor Court with Article III
    status. This court would take over the jurisdiction of the NLRB under
    §§ 8, 208, 209 and 210 of the National Labor Relations Act, and the
    jurisdiction now exercised by district courts under §§ 301, 302 and 303
    of that Act, under the Railway Labor Act and under Title VII of the
    Civil Rights Act. *See* Morris, *The Case for Unitary Enforcement of
    Federal Labor Law,* 26 Sw. L.J. 471, 499 (1972).
21. Hector, *Problems of the CAB and the Independent Regulatory Com-
    missions,* 69 YALE L.J. 931, 939–48 (1960). Mr. Hector's memoran-
    dum caused a flurry of commentary. Kintner, *The Current Ordeal
    of the Administrative Process: In Reply to Mr. Hector,* 69 YALE L.J.
    965 (1960); Berger, *Removal of Judicial Functions from Federal
    Trade Commission to a Trade Court: A Reply to Mr. Kintner,* 59
    MICH. L. REV. 199 (1960); Auerbach, *Some Thoughts on the Hector
    Memorandum,* 1960 WIS. L. REV. 183; MacIntyre, *Administrative
    Court Proposal,* 29 J. OF D.C. BAR ASS'N 316 (1962); Berger, *Reply
    to Commissioner MacIntyre's Attack on the Trade Court Proposal, id.*
    at 337.
22. Minow, *Suggestions for Improvement of the Administrative Process,*
    15 ADMIN. L. REV. 146, 148–53 (1963).
23. Cary, *Why I Oppose The Divorce of the Judicial Function from the
    Federal Regulatory Agencies,* 51 A.B.A.J. 33 (1965).
24. Elman, *A Modest Proposal for Radical Reform,* 56 A.B.A.J. 1045

benign neglect in the latest report of a presidential advisory commission.[25]

The argument for the separation of the "judicial" functions of the agencies takes off from the maxim that no man can properly be judge in his own cause. It continues as follows: The section of the Administrative Procedure Act[26] designed by the majority of the Attorney General's Committee to meet this problem by providing that, with certain exceptions, "[a]n employee or agent engaged in the performance of investigative or prosecuting functions for an agency in a case may not, in that or a factually related case, participate or advise in the decision, recommended decision, or agency review . . . except as witness or counsel in public proceedings," does not effect adequate insulation between the prosecutor and the judge. In the first place, and with this I agree, there is great doubt whether it is really followed. Moreover, the agency will often have participated to the extent of issuing a complaint.[27] Beyond this, the case for keeping adjudicative functions in the agency is not so strong as once appeared. As the broad terms of the regulatory statute are given explicit content by administrative decision and court review, the need for commingling of functions diminishes. Moreover, due to the high turnover of agency members, the supposedly expert agencies are not really

(1970). Mr. Elman was earlier on record as opposing the removal of adjudication from the agencies. Elman, *A Note on Administrative Adjudication*, 74 YALE L.J. 652, 655 (1965).

25. PRESIDENT'S ADVISORY COUNCIL ON EXECUTIVE ORGANIZATION, A NEW REGULATORY FRAMEWORK, REPORT ON SELECTED INDEPENDENT REGULATORY AGENCIES 51–56 (1971). The Council's own proposals with respect to judicial review do not merit serious consideration, for reasons I have stated elsewhere. 23 ADMIN. L. REV. 345, 352–53 (1971). See, to the same effect, Nathanson, *The Administrative Court Proposal*, 57 VA. L. REV. 996 (1971); Views of the Administrative Conference of the United States on the "Report on Selected Independent Agencies of the President's Advisory Council on Executive Organization" 5–6 (1971).

26. Administrative Procedure Act, § 5(d), 5 U.S.C. § 554(d). The section does not apply to ratemaking. American Tel. & Tel. Co. v. FCC, 449 F.2d 439 (2d Cir. 1971); *see* DAVIS, ADMINISTRATIVE LAW TREATISE § 13.02, at 458 (Supp. 1970).

27. If this is a serious objection, I do not understand why more attention has not been given to the possibility of meeting it, as the Taft-Hartley Act did, by creating an independent general counsel for the NLRB who alone has power to file complaints. 29 U.S.C. § 153(d).

very expert; such expertise as exists lies rather in the staff. Yet it is exactly there that the separation of functions provisions of the APA is least effective; the trial attorney who would not think of venturing into a member's office to talk about a case might not exhibit the same restraint with a section head or even a member's assistant after a Saturday night poker game.[28] While I do not deny that these arguments have some force,[29] the removal of adjudicatory functions from the agencies would be, on balance, undesirable.

The first consideration in an argument for retention of agency adjudicatory power is that the agency is by no means invariably a prosecutor. While the FTC generally is cast in that role, the NLRB usually is,[30] and the SEC is in disciplinary cases, many of the agencies normally are not. Examples are a decision by the CAB whether the public convenience and necessity requires a new air route and, if so, who should operate it, and a choice by the FCC among rival applicants for a television license. With respect to all such agency endeavors, the basic premise of the argument for relieving the agencies of their "judicial" functions, namely, that no man should be judge in his own cause, thus disappears. It also does so in rate-making if the proceeding is initiated by a complaint of a user or a competitor or a petition by the regulated utility, rather than on the complaint of the agency itself. No one could defend a system whereby rate proceedings of the former sort were "adjudicated" by the agency

28. See Friendly, *A Look at the Federal Administrative Agencies,* 60 COLUM. L. REV. 429, 438 (1960), *reprinted in* BENCHMARKS 65, 76 (1967).

29. Another frequently encountered argument in favor of the removal of adjudicatory responsibilities from the agencies is the point that agency members do not have sufficient time to consider carefully each case before them. *See, e.g.,* Minow, *supra,* 15 ADMIN. L. REV. at 149. The argument continues that, since agency members are forced to rely on staff reports, and often issue decisions written by their staff, the quality of decision-making would be raised by the creation of administrative courts. While this argument stems from former members and thus is not easily dismissable, I do not believe the point begins to tip the scales. Some screening of the cases to be heard by all members, as well as a reduction in the size of the record, would alleviate this problem and, for reasons pointed out above, a fairly high level of staff participation will always be necessary due to the rapid turnover in agency membership.

30. Not always, however—*e.g.,* in representation determinations.

and rate complaints initiated by the agency fell under the jurisdiction of a transportation or public utility "court." Moreover, apart from such niceties, the fixing of rates, no matter at whose instance and whether for the past or for the future, involves elements of policy that must be determined by the agency responsible for regulating the particular utility. This is particularly clear in minimum rate regulation, where decision will dictate not only what a shipper must pay but the future of competing forms of transportation.[31] Indeed, even in the activities of an agency that are primarily "prosecutorial," such as the NLRB's unfair labor practice jurisdiction, policy-making intrudes so far, and so properly, into the decisional process that separating out the "judicial" function would be fraught with danger. Would the public interest really have been furthered if an NLRB willing to give a broad reading to the employee organization provision of the Wagner Act had been regularly frustrated by a "Labor Court"? Was it not better that, save for the normal functioning of judicial review, the Board should have its way until it reached a point where Congress decided to give further instructions? Furthermore, as Professor Jaffe has well said, the proponents of administrative courts manifest "a disregard for discretion as a *continuing* function of government";[32] he might have added a disposition to ignore how many new problems can arise in fields thought to have been well-tilled. Once an agency has been given responsibility for regulating an area or a phase of the economy, it must have all the tools needed to do the job, not just some.[33] Although much more could be said,

31. *See* FRIENDLY, THE FEDERAL ADMINISTRATIVE AGENCIES, ch. VI, The Minimum Rate Power of the Interstate Commerce Commission 106–40 (1962).

32. Jaffe, *Basic Issues: An Analysis, supra*, 30 N.Y.U.L. REV. at 1285. Speaking of the report of the Hoover Task Force, he continues, "[d]iscretion for a day is, as it were, the theme. Discretion will yield its harvest of rules and regulations and can then be put back in the box." *Id.*

33. Another illustration of the evils of separation is furnished by the lengthy proceedings before the FPC for determining the prices at which independent producers could sell natural gas in interstate commerce for resale, resulting from Phillips Petroleum Co. v. Wisconsin, 347 U.S. 672 (1954). There is now much criticism, whether justified or not, that poorly planned "area rates" set by the Commission in these cases, are responsible for insufficient supplies of, and "excessive de-

perhaps I have already lingered too long on what is really a problem of administrative law rather than federal jurisdiction. My excuse, apart from my long-standing interest in the subject, is to dispel any illusion that the path of reform with respect to judicial review of administrative action lies in this direction.

Another and quite different thread in the "administrative court" proposals would be to scrap our system of review of administrative action by the ordinary courts and substitute an entirely separate set of tribunals modeled on the French system of administrative courts culminating in the Conseil d'Etat. Study has surely proved how seriously erroneous were the adverse views of French administrative law which, in an excess of parochialism, were entertained a half century ago. Many scholars now believe the French system affords the citizen greater protection against arbitrary governmental action than do those of this country or England.[34] The French courts will annul administrative action not only for "error of law" either in failing to recognize the terms of a statute or in giving it "an improper significance or meaning"; they will also review "mixed questions of law and fact."[35] Evidently they enjoy the full confidence of the public; indeed, my own impression is that they are more highly regarded than the general courts. Yet, at the same time, they seem to have avoided the hostility of the executive. Procedures that have had such success are surely entitled to respectful consideration.

A system based on the French model would have all the review and enforcement powers now possessed by the courts of appeals and three-judge and sometimes one-judge district courts, and a great deal more. It would take in the Tax Court, the Customs Court, the Court of Claims, the Court of Customs and Patent Appeals, and suits against

---

mand" for, natural gas. *See, e.g.*, MacAvoy, *The Regulation-Induced Shortage of Natural Gas,* 14 J. LAW & ECON. 167, 169–71 (1971). How convenient, and how detrimental, it would be if the FPC were able to shrug off such criticisms on the basis that the rates had been fixed by a Natural Gas Court!

34. Professor Robson, before the English Committee on Ministers' Powers, proposed the creation of an administrative appeal court and the abolition of the jurisdiction of the High Court of Justice in administrative matters. *See* B. SCHWARTZ, FRENCH ADMINISTRATIVE LAW AND THE COMMON-LAW WORLD 20–21 (1954); R. ROBSON, JUSTICE AND ADMINISTRATIVE LAW 618 (3d ed. 1951).

35. B. SCHWARTZ, *supra* note 34, at 239–42.

the Government in the district courts under the Tucker Act, the Federal Tort Claims Act, the Suits in Admiralty Act, and the Public Vessels Act. Moreover, it would include actions for prohibitory or mandatory injunctions against federal officers, including the mandamus jurisdiction under 28 U.S.C. section 1361. Such a system might even encompass actions by the Government or its agencies to enforce regulatory statutes in the absence of an administrative proceeding, for example, civil antitrust suits by the Department of Justice, enforcement actions by the SEC, and suits for the collection of taxes or those under the Fair Labor Standards Act. Such a system would take over the whole gamut of controversies between the federal government and the citizen save those covered by the criminal law.

In theory I can see much merit in such a system. It would create a corps of judges truly experienced in administrative matters, yet with a jurisdiction so broad as to guard against any evils of overspecialization and a hierarchy of courts that should attract men of great talent. It would also provide uniformity in the application of procedural rules. I surely would not reject it on the ground stressed in Professor Bernard Schwartz' interesting book, *French Administrative Law and the Common-Law World*, namely, the danger that a litigant might find, after many months of struggle, that he had picked the wrong court system.[36] This problem could be satisfactorily met by combining the ALI's proposal for foreclosure of jurisdictional issues that are not early raised[37] with ready provision for transfer of cases found to have been brought in the wrong system; once the case was transferred, it should remain even if the jurisdictional holding were wrong. My negative view would rest rather on the ground that so radical a change from centuries of tradition could be justified only by proof that our system has not worked in the past or that it cannot be expected to work in the future. I do not believe either proposition can be established.

The third thread in the administrative court proposals is different still. It would leave the agencies and the scope of review as they are. I will assume, for simplicity, it would also leave district court review of administrative actions and appeals from such review to the courts

36. *Id.* at 315.
37. ALI STUDY § 1386.

of appeals as they are, although it would doubtless be more logical to take all such review out of the general court system. But it would remove petitions to review administrative action from the courts of appeals and vest these[38] in a Court of Administrative Appeals.

The first thing to do in analyzing this proposal is to see how much business the court would have. In 1972 the courts of appeals had 1,307 appeals from administrative boards and commissions, a 20% increase from the previous year.[39] From this one would have to deduct, as a result of proposals previously made, say half of the 740 NLRB cases and all of the 175 INS cases. To the resulting figure one would have to add 52 three-judge court reviews of ICC orders.[40] The Court of Administrative Appeals would thus have an initial annual caseload of approximately more than 800 filings, which, however, for reasons indicated earlier, could be expected to increase rather rapidly. In view of the much greater than average difficulty of these cases, the load would soon outrun the court's capabilities.

One argument for the creation of a Court of Administrative Appeals is to alleviate the burdens on the courts of appeals. If the reforms here advocated with respect to tax appeals[41] and Labor Board and deportation orders were to be made, the further alleviation, some 800 cases out of a 1972 total of 12,379, would not be very great, based on the present volume—less than half of what could be accomplished by the abolition of diversity jurisdiction.[42] Furthermore, many of these cases, particularly Labor Board cases which, even after the 50% reduction I would anticipate from making the Board's orders self-enforcing, would still constitute the largest single group, involve issues of such small pecuniary amount that attendance at Washington, or any other single city, would be an undue burden.

38. Including, of course, the three-judge district court review of ICC orders, *see* pp. 173–74 *supra*.

39. A.O. Ann. Rep., Table B3 (1972).

40. A.O. Ann. Rep., Table 47b (1972).

41. This would include not only the 202 appeals from the Tax Court, but at least 260 appeals from tax refund judgments of the district courts. A.O. Ann. Rep., Tables B3 & B7 (1972).

42. *Id.*, Table B7. The alleviation, and the caseload of the Court of Administrative Appeals, would be much increased if review proceedings now conducted by the district courts were also to be transferred. *See* pp. 182–83 *supra*.

Like the Court of Tax Appeals, the Court of Administrative Appeals would have to ride circuit—not only an inconvenience to the judges but a likely source of delay.[43] This is a factor often of great importance in this area; my experience is that there is no category of appeals which courts of appeals more frequently feel required to hear on an expedited basis.

A second advantage asserted for a Court of Administrative Appeals is that it will assure greater expertise both on procedural and on substantive questions. The argument as to the former is unimpressive. A judge who finds enormous difficulties in wending his way through the Internal Revenue Code need experience no such frustration with respect to the Administrative Procedure Act, many of whose provisions simply embody conceptions of elementary fairness that are the very warp and woof of procedural law. The possibility of acquiring greater expertise on substantive matters is considerably better. It is often urged that the variety of matters coming before such a court (atomic energy, electricity and gas, air, rail, motor and water transportation, communication by telephone, telegraph, radio and television, securities regulation,[44] unfair labor practices, and many others) would prevent the acquisition of real expertise in any particular area, such as the Court of Appeals for the District of Columbia Circuit has undoubtedly acquired over the years by virtue of its exclusive jurisdiction over appeals from the FCC's licensing decisions.[45] Granting force to this argument, I still think that *some* gain

43. Calendaring is considerably slowed when an argument must await a sitting at a convenient place.
44. Superficial viewers of the subject rarely recognize that the SEC makes a contribution to the load of administrative appeals, roughly 20 per year, which is nowhere near its relative importance in the regulatory area. A.O. ANN. REP., Table B3, at 247 (1971).
45. 47 U.S.C. § 402(b). Compare the comment with reference to the District of Columbia Circuit by Caldwell, *The Proposed Federal Administrative Court, supra*, 36 A.B.A.J. at 82:
Its members are familiar with the radio technical jargon and, in arguing a case before it, it is unnecessary to take most of your time explaining frequencies, channels, kilocycles, millivolts-per-meter and the many other words that must be understood before a court can pass on the claims made by the parties, and before it can even determine who the necessary parties are. It is able also, as it must be in radio, to see a particular case in its proper setting in regard to radio communications as a whole.

in substantive expertise would be both possible and highly beneficial. A judge who has gone through even one minimum rate case is better equipped for a second than when he was as a virgin; the third time he will be better still. A proper use of the panel system would allow for further development of expertise; and the court could have a modest size staff of technical experts in the principal areas subject to its jurisdiction. There would thus be a significant gain in expertise on the substantive side.

A third argument for a Court of Administrative Appeals is that it would avoid conflicting decisions and thus reduce the load, but also the role, of the Supreme Court in this area. Here again, we must distinguish between procedural and substantive questions. There would hardly be uniformity concerning the former if the courts of appeals retained jurisdiction over district court review of administrative action. On the substantive side there would be a noticeable increase in uniformity. No one can deny this would be an advantage in cases where decision turns on the sufficiency of the evidence, including the validity of inferences drawn from undisputed facts. It is a bad thing when one circuit acquires a reputation as "labor" oriented and another as "company" oriented, to the extent that this causes the kind of race we observed with respect to patents.[46] It is also a bad thing if a party to a transportation dispute can obtain a more favorable decision in its "home" court than in that of its adversary.[47] As against this, so long as the regulatory statutes are less than pellucid and the Supreme Court is to play a part in these matters, there may be value in the expression of different points of view on legal issues that are subject to fair differences of opinion. An example would be the dispute among the circuits over the use of union organization cards that

46. *See* p. 155 *supra.* The story of the most notorious of these cases —General Electric Company's race to the Seventh Circuit, and the International Union of Electrical Workers to the District of Columbia Circuit, with the case ending up in the Second, where the unfair labor practice occurred, is interestingly told in Carrington, *Crowded Dockets and the Courts of Appeals: The Threat to the Function of Review and the National Law, supra,* 82 HARV. L. REV. at 598–601. *See also* Comment, *Forum Shopping in the Review of NLRB Orders,* 28 U. CHI. L. REV. 552 (1961); Note, *Forum-Shopping Appellate Review of FTC Cease and Desist Orders,* 1968 UTAH L. REV. 316.

47. *See* FRIENDLY, BENCHMARKS 141 & n.33 (1967).

was ultimately decided in *NLRB v. Gissel Packing Co.*[48] Another example would be the dispute, decided by *NLRB v. Exchange Parts Co.*,[49] whether a company which confers economic benefits shortly before a representation election with the purpose of influencing the vote has committed an unfair labor practice. And there are methods for at least reducing the invidious kind of forum shopping encouraged by the "first instituted" rule[50] without suppressing the differences of opinions on substantive matters among the circuits that may be useful in provoking a Supreme Court ruling. Unlike issues of the interpretation of the Internal Revenue Code, the interpretation of regulatory statutes cannot generally be described as falling into the category where "it is more important that the applicable rule of law be settled than that it be settled right . . . even where the error is a matter of serious concern, provided correction can be had by legislation."[51] In contrast to the Internal Revenue Code, such statutes are not kept under continuous legislative scrutiny. Major revisions come only rarely, and an interpretation by a Court of Administrative Appeals would be likely to stand for a long time unless it truly outraged Congress or the Supreme Court, which would necessarily regard its certiorari jurisdiction (if it were given any in other than constitutional cases) as something to be exercised quite restrictively.

This leads to the counterargument that such a court would be *too* expert. Here, as with patents and taxes, the real force of the objection is not that the judges would know too much about the Administrative Procedure Act, on the one hand, or the Interstate

48. 395 U.S. 575 (1969). While the Fourth Circuit stood alone in its total rejection of such cards, *see* 395 U.S. at 590 & n.6, there was much variation in the degree to which the circuits would allow cards unambiguous on their face to be challenged on the basis of misrepresentation or coercion by union organizers. *See* 395 U.S. at 604–05.
49. 375 U.S. 405 (1964).
50. 28 U.S.C. § 2112(a). *See* Comment, *A Proposal to End the Race to the Court House in Appeals from Federal Administrative Orders*, 68 COLUM. L. REV. 166 (1968). This proposal, to center such review in the Court of Appeals for the District of Columbia Circuit when there was no sufficient reason for having it elsewhere, might have particular appeal now that the role of that court as Supreme Court of the District has been partially eliminated, Act of July 29, 1970, 84 Stat. 473.
51. Burnet v. Coronado Oil & Gas Co., 285 U.S. 393, 406 (1932) (Brandeis, J., dissenting) (footnote omitted). See the discussion at p. 167 *supra*.

Commerce Act, the National Labor Relations Act, the Federal Communications Act, etc., on the other, qualities that in and of themselves are surely desirable, but that they would have too one-sided a point of view. Here is where the spectre of the Commerce Court[52] would truly become Banquo's ghost. One important difference is that we are envisioning a court not confined to one agency but encompassing a large number, so that there is less danger of its coming to believe itself more expert than the agencies under review. Although I would favor using panels of members who were expert in certain subjects, their decisions would be subject to review by the court en banc, and here, as in the case of the Court of Tax Appeals,[53] I would allow less than a majority to invoke an in banc court. The real fear, as in the case of the Court of Tax Appeals, is that the court would be overloaded with lame ducks and former agency members;[54] the answer is generally the same.[55]

The arguments for and against a Court of Administrative Appeals thus are in fair balance. What will ultimately be decisive are two things: One is whether the reforms advocated up to this point will permit the courts of appeals to carry their loads; if not, a Court of Administrative Appeals would give significant help. Another is whether the need for reducing the Supreme Court's load of certiorari petitions will require elimination of those in administrative appeals not involving constitutional issues. If this modification becomes necessary, there would be a good case for a Court of Administrative Appeals having final jurisdiction in such cases.[56] In order to insure uniformity, the new court would have to be given original or appellate jurisdiction over administrative review of cases now heard in the district courts, with attendant problems of volume.

My conclusion thus is that the proposal for a general Court of Administrative Appeals should neither be adopted immediately nor dismissed out of hand, but rather should be kept under consideration

---

52. *See* pp. 153–54 *supra*.
53. *See* p. 164 & n.48 *supra*.
54. In this instance the same person might well qualify under both rubrics.
55. *See* p. 166 *supra*.
56. *See* Friendly, *A Federal Court of Administrative Appeals?*, CASE AND COMMENT 23, 26 (March–April 1969).

both by the Administrative Conference and by the Judicial Conference of the United States.

Some recent developments have raised the question whether there is need for a specialized administrative review court of much more limited scope. A good deal of the malaise about administrative decisions affecting the environment arises from the fact that the agency is not considered to be truly disinterested. The Federal Power Commission is more concerned with averting another blackout than with the Hudson River fishery; the Federal Highway Administration wants to build highways; the Atomic Energy Commission is interested in the development of atomic power. Hence, even though such an agency has complied with the procedural requirements of the National Environmental Policy Act and has produced a reasoned impact statement, its decision to go ahead is naturally suspect, and there is clamor for judicial review on the merits even in cases where there is no administrative record and no explicit statutory provision for review.[57]

Better solutions should be found. The best would be for Congress to give clearer directions with respect to the ordering of priorities; if it did, judicial review on the issue of compliance with these directions would be appropriate. But experience teaches the unlikelihood of this solution; Congress generally prefers to indulge in platitudes which leave actual decision elsewhere.[58] Short of that, one might envision a Board of Review, with members of the highest competence and standing, which, on the basis of the agency's factual findings, would make the ultimate value judgment, at least in cases of truly great importance. Such a Board should assure reasonable uniformity of policy, and, if it were placed in the White House,[59] the

57. Dissenting from the denial of certiorari in Scenic Hudson Preservation Conference v. FPC, 407 U.S. 926 (1972), where there was a record and judicial review was provided by the controlling statute, Mr. Justice Douglas urged that courts should ignore the statutory direction that agency findings supported by substantial evidence shall be deemed conclusive since this should be limited to matters within the agency's expertise. While I see no adequate legal basis for this, I appreciate the feeling behind it.

58. Some of the reasons for this are analyzed in Friendly, *supra* note 31, at 166–68.

59. This would not conflict with the views expressed in *id.* at 147–59,

line of responsibility would be clear. Some of the problems are obvious—further delay, in some instances a second-guessing of a "quasi-judicial" agency, the difficulty in disentangling environmental from other considerations, the dangers of pressure and of poor appointments—but these are not beyond reasonable cure if the will exists and we can hardly expect perfection in so controversial a field. Certainly it is better that value judgments of the sort here at issue should be made by appointees of the President, having the aid of an expert staff, than by random panels of federal judges, each with his own biases on such matters and none having access to disinterested sources of information.[60]

However, if the enthusiasm for the federal judiciary's taking over the running of the country should thrust this task also on the courts, it might be better to have a Court of Environmental Appeals than to leave such decisions to the general courts. This would avoid the evils of random choice of judges, with consequent lack of decisional uniformity, and would give the court the assistance of an expert staff. In short, if instead of a Board of Review such as I have outlined, we must have substantive judicial review, perhaps it should be by a specialized court.[61]

If Mars had antitrust laws, a visitor from that planet would surely regard the variety of methods we use for enforcing ours as beyond rational comprehension. For some violations[62] the United States may bring a criminal prosecution in a district court. If it does this and obtains a conviction, appeal by the defendant lies to the court of appeals and thence, by either side, to the Supreme Court on application for certiorari. Alternatively, the Government can, and

since the Board of Review would not impinge on the area of the agency's expertise.

60. Professor Morris R. Cohen once said that "the judicial system . . . is intellectually the weakest part of our government. It has the least opportunity to get adequate information on the issues which it has to decide." AMERICAN THOUGHT: A CRITICAL SKETCH 164 (1954).

61. The recent Federal Water Pollution Control Act, § 9, 86 Stat. 816 (1972), directs the President, through the Attorney General, to prepare a study of the feasibility of such an Environmental Court.

62. Namely, violation of §§ 1 or 2 of the Sherman Act, 15 U.S.C. §§ 1, 2, and, amazingly, § 3 of the Robinson-Patman Act, 15 U.S.C. § 13a.

much more frequently does, proceed by civil suit. In that event, it may file a certificate that the case is of such general public importance as to require expedition. Curiously, expedition is to be accomplished by having the evidence heard by three judges rather than one,[63] a process which may take weeks or months for a single judge and, because of their differing calendar problems, would take much longer for three. Mercifully, this procedure has not been invoked since the 1940's.[64] The final decision of the district judge in a civil case is appealable directly to the Supreme Court as of right;[65] his grant or denial of a preliminary injunction is not appealable anywhere,[66] although the grant of such an injunction in a merger or acquisition case may have the same practical effect as that of a final one.[67] Whenever the Government could bring a civil action, so may "[a]ny person who shall be injured in his business or property";[68] a private plaintiff may obtain, in addition to an injunction, "threefold the damages by him sustained, and the cost of suit, including a reasonable attorney's fee."[69] Particularly as a result of the expanded notion of class actions under the 1966 revision of Rule 23 of Federal Civil Procedure, the number of plaintiffs and the potential recoveries in such actions may be astronomical.[70]

63. 15 U.S.C. § 28.
64. AREEDA, ANTITRUST ANALYSIS 46 n.118 (1967).
65. 15 U.S.C. § 29. The Court takes a relatively broad scope of review in these cases, United States v. E.I. DuPont de Nemours & Co., 353 U.S. 586, 610 (1957) (Burton, J., dissenting), especially when the issue is the proper form of relief, United States v. E.I. DuPont de Nemours & Co., 366 U.S. 316, 322–23 (1961).
66. *See* Tidewater Oil Co. v. United States, — U.S. —, 41 U.S.L.W. 4053 (Dec. 6, 1972).
67. *See, e.g.,* United States v. Chrysler Corp., 232 F. Supp. 651 (D.N.J. 1964). Upon the issuance of a temporary injunction, Chrysler abandoned its proposed merger with Mack Trucks, Inc., B.N.A. ANTITRUST & TRADE REG. REP. 180, at B-2 (1964).
68. 15 U.S.C. § 15.
69. *Id.*
70. *See* Handler, *The Shift from Substantive to Procedural Innovations in Antitrust Suits—The Twenty-Third Annual Antitrust Review,* 71 COLUM. L. REV. 1, 5–12 (1971). As noted above, at p. 21 n.34, a further avenue of potentially enormous and duplicating recoveries has recently been blocked by Hawaii v. Standard Oil Co., 405 U.S. 251 (1972), where the Court held that a state may not recover, on a *parens patriae* theory, for damages to its "general economy," and is a

Although the legal issues in such cases may be quite as difficult and important as in actions by the United States, review is by the courts of appeals, subject only to the Supreme Court's general certiorari powers.

Not satisfied with the above patchwork, Congress created an additional antitrust enforcement agency, the Federal Trade Commission, in 1914. Like some children, this one reflected antithetical aspirations of two parents. Those hostile to big business thought it would be a more effective enforcer of the antitrust laws than the Department of Justice working through the courts; big business expected it to lay down ground rules more definite than the "rule of reason."[71] Again, like many children, it has satisfied neither parent. Its mandate is even broader than that of the Department of Justice under the Sherman and Clayton Acts, since it can also condemn any anticompetitive practice that it finds "unfair."[72] As noted above, proceedings before the FTC have been regarded as a particularly striking instance of the evils of an agency that has made a complaint acting as the judge. Except for its ample investigative powers, it seems to have done little in the antitrust field that the Department of Justice could not have done equally well.[73] Although FTC cases presumably are every bit as important as Government civil suits in the district courts, appeal follows the usual administrative pattern of initial review by a court of appeals followed by application for certiorari to the Supreme Court. The process has been condemned on the ground that "courts have been known to pretend that the Commission has merely drawn an ordinary inference from the evidence . . . when the case actually required a definition of the governing legal standard . . . ."[74] If ever there were a crazy-quilt, this is it.

proper plaintiff in a private antitrust suit only to the extent of damages suffered in its proprietary capacity.

71. Standard Oil Co. v. United States, 221 U.S. 1 (1911); *see* AREEDA, *supra* note 64, at 24–26; R. CUSHMAN, THE INDEPENDENT REGULATORY COMMISSIONS 177–213 (1941); G. HENDERSON, THE FEDERAL TRADE COMMISSION, ch. 1 (1924).

72. Federal Trade Commission Act § 5, 15 U.S.C. § 45(a)(6). *See, e.g.,* FTC v. Brown Shoe Co., 384 U.S. 316 (1966); FTC v. Sperry & Hutchinson Co., 405 U.S. 233 (1972).

73. One of its specialties has been the Robinson-Patman Act, which the Department of Justice seems quite willing to leave to it.

74. AREEDA, *supra* note 64, at 34, citing FTC v. Consolidated Foods Co.,

Presumably no one would devise such a system—or lack of one—if he were starting fresh.

At least three reforms would seem to be clearly demanded. After three decades of desuetude, it is time to remove the three-judge provision from the statute book. Congress should grant the Supreme Court's request that it be relieved of mandatory review of district court decisions in Government civil antitrust cases and that these should be routed through the courts of appeals,[75] which already have jurisdiction over appeals from criminal convictions and judgments in private suits. Such action would automatically render orders granting or denying temporary injunctions in Government civil suits appealable to the courts of appeals. If we assume that the relatively few criminal antitrust prosecutions must be left as they now are, what remains for consideration is the important question whether some better method can be found for handling civil antitrust litigation at the trial stage.

The objections to trial of civil antitrust cases in the district courts are most vividly illustrated by "the big case." The point was effectively made by Judge Wyzanski:[76]

[I]n recent years antitrust litigation . . . [has] involved an enormous, nearly cancerous, growth of exhibits, depositions, and *ore tenus* testimony. Few judges who have sat in such cases have attempted to digest the plethora of evidence, or indeed could do so and at the same time do justice to other litigation in their courts.

Even when the judge has thus failed in his duty,[77] his calendar of

380 U.S. 592 (1965). *See also id.* ¶ 566, at 509, discussing the *Brown Shoe* decision, *supra*, 384 U.S. 316.
75. *See* p. 33 & n.100 *supra*.
76. United States v. Grinnell Corp., 236 F. Supp. 244, 247 (D.R.I. 1964), *aff'd except as to decree*, 384 U.S. 563 (1966). Figures for some famous cases will be found in the *Report to the Judicial Conference of the Committee on Procedure in Anti-trust and other Protracted Cases*, chaired by Judge Prettyman, 13 F.R.D. 62, 63–64 (1951). The pretrial procedures recommended by the Committee can reduce the length of trial but still will usually not prevent this from spreading over weeks or even months.
77. Perhaps the failure to examine all the proffered "evidence" is not really a breach of duty, since my impression is that much of the records in "big" cases, as in many administrative proceedings, could be eliminated without much loss. Surely there is a duty on counsel to

other business will be seriously disrupted by a trial of this length, particularly in districts with relatively few judges or even in larger ones utilizing the individual calendar plan.[78] In contrast to equally protracted multi-defendant criminal cases, the judge is unlikely to have had previous experience or be able to profit from the new expertise so painfully achieved. Finally, as economics has become increasingly mathematical,[79] the testimony in antitrust cases, especially those brought by the Government, may become almost impossible for the ordinary judge to comprehend.[80] Why then should not such cases be tried to an expert tribunal of some sort? Here we might take a leaf out of the English book. The Restrictive Trade Practices Court contains judges, lay members with knowledge of industry, commerce or public affairs appointed for a term of years, and other temporary lay members chosen for their experience in the particular field. A case is usually heard by one judge and several lay members.[81] If we had such an expert court, properly staffed, there would seem to be little need for continuing the antitrust functions of the Federal Trade Commission.[82]

screen the evidence before submission. *See* United States v. United Shoe Mach. Corp., 93 F. Supp. 190 (D. Mass. 1950).

78. One solution might be to assign such cases to senior judges—if they are willing to take them and have a reasonable chance of survival!

79. *See, e.g.,* Peltzman, *Entry in Commercial Banking,* 8 J. LAW & ECON. 11 (1965); Stigler, *The Economic Effects of the Antitrust Laws,* 9 J. LAW & ECON. 225 (1966); Telser, *Cut-throat Competition and the Long Purse, id.* at 259.

80. The problem is not altogether new, as witness Judge Wyzanski's employing an economist, Carl Kaysen, as his law clerk when he was trying United States v. United Shoe Mach. Corp., 110 F. Supp. 295 (D. Mass. 1953), *aff'd,* 347 U.S. 521 (1954). *See* Kaysen, *An Economist as the Judge's Law Clerk in Sherman Act Cases,* 12 ABA ANTITRUST SECTION 43 (1958). And, of course, it is not confined to the trial level. Economists have long been critical of Supreme Court antitrust decisions for lack of sound economic analysis. *See, e.g.,* Bork & Bowman, *The Crisis in Antitrust,* 65 COLUM. L. REV. 363 (1965); Ferguson, *Tying Arrangements and Reciprocity: An Economic Analysis,* 30 LAW & CONTEMP. PROB. 552 (1965).

81. *See* Diplock, *Antitrust and the Judicial Process,* 7 J. LAW & ECON. 27, 39–40 (1964).

82. For reasons already limned, I am not altogeher clear whether need exists without one. *The Attorney General's National Committee*

If antitrust enforcement were exclusively in the hands of the Government, I think much could be said for moving this way. The "if," however, runs contrary to fact. Apart from the political unfeasibility of eliminating the private suit, I would not regard this as desirable, since many restraints are too localized to invite the time and attention of the staff of the national agencies but can have serious anticompetitive effects.[83] Yet I do not see the private antitrust suit fitting comfortably into the framework of an Antitrust Court. The inconvenience to suitors—often the defendant as well as the plaintiff—in having to come to one central location would require the court to "ride circuit," with the difficulties noted in other instances. A further problem arises from the fact that, in contrast to patent litigation, where a jury is generally waived even when one could be demanded, such waiver in private antitrust suits is far less common.[84] If a jury is required, much of the benefit of an expert

to Study the Antitrust Laws 375 (1955), rejected "two suggestions equally drastic—on the one hand, to abolish the Commission's antitrust function—or, on the other, to transfer from the Department to the Commission all antitrust matters,"—without saying why. The latter suggestion is indeed impracticable, at least as long as criminal sanctions remain. I question whether there would be much sentiment for creating an antitrust administrative agency today, particularly in view of the flourishing of the private antitrust suit. About the only argument for the dual scheme of enforcement I can see is that an independent agency, the terms of whose members expire at different times, affords some assurance against laxness by an administration not truly devoted to the vigorous application of antitrust laws. This scarcely seems sufficient.

83. *See* AREEDA, *supra* note 64, at 35–36. Whether there should not be modifications in the remedy, *e.g.*, against the mandatory award of treble damages, is another matter. *The Attorney General's National Committee to Study the Antitrust Laws, supra* note 82, at 379, favored vesting in the trial judge discretion as to whether to impose double or treble damages.

84. I here assumed, as I did in the discussion of patent litigation, that, despite NLRB v. Jones & Laughlin Steel Corp., 301 U.S. 1, 48–49 (1937), Congress could not constitutionally deny jury trial when the plaintiffs seeks a "legal" remedy. *See* 5 MOORE, FEDERAL PRACTICE ¶ 38.16, especially ¶ 38.16[4], & ¶ 38.17 (1971). The validity of the assumption seems even greater with respect to private antitrust litigation, since the common law recognized tort actions in at least a part of the area now included in the private antitrust action. *See*

tribunal is lost. For these reasons I do not see a sufficient case for an Antitrust Court at the moment. As with the proposal for the Court of Administrative Appeals, and with considerably more conviction, I would put this on the back burner.

RESTATEMENT OF TORTS §§ 764–65; 1 HARPER & JAMES, TORTS § 6.13, at 522 (1956); Letwin, *The English Common Law Concerning Monopolies*, 21 U. CHI. L. REV. 355 (1954).

PART X

Conclusion

I SHOULD ADD a word by way of summary. Under the proposals here made, we would have two new courts, both of Article III status. There would be a Patent Court, exercising trial jurisdiction mainly through commissioners and devoting its time almost exclusively to appellate activities, with a certiorari jurisdiction in the Supreme Court, probably very rarely exercised on such issues as validity and infringement. There would be a Court of Tax Appeals, subject to certiorari only in cases where substantial constitutional issues were raised. Creation of these courts would call for changes in the Court of Customs and Patent Appeals and the Court of Claims. The Tax Court of the United States would become an Article III court, and its jurisdiction would be expanded to include refund suits. We would have thirteen circuits rather than eleven. There would be a few other minor structural changes, chiefly in the review of Government civil antitrust actions and administrative orders. In the main, however, the structure of the federal court system would continue to be substantially what it now is. We would not have any such disruption of settled practices as would attend upon the creation of a new National Court of Appeals intermediate between the state courts and the courts of appeals on the one hand, and the Supreme Court on the other.

We would expect the district courts and the courts of appeals to devote themselves to the great work for which they are uniquely equipped—assuring protection of rights guaranteed by the Constitution, enforcing civil rights legislation, dealing with controversies between the citizen and the federal government, applying the federal criminal law, interpreting and applying acts of Congress that furnish protection, both old and new, to consumers, investors and the environment, dealing with federal labor and antitrust legislation as well

197

as such traditional federal specialties as admiralty, bankruptcy and copyright, and controlling the states so that congressional policy will not be impeded either by too niggardly or too expansive local requirements. When I have sometimes spoken of these tasks as burdens, I have used the word in its primary sense of a care or responsibility, not with the secondary connotation of grieveousness. The discharge of these tasks in a growing and ever more litigiously minded society will demand the elimination of cases that should not be in any courts —FELA actions, some seamen's actions in addition to the suits by shore-based harbor workers removed by recent legislation, and motor vehicle accident litigation. It will require almost total elimination or, if this is not attainable, drastic curtailment of diversity jurisdiction. We do not have to determine whether federal jurisdiction in that area is actually harmful as some think, or moderately beneficial as others do. Even on the latter view, its rank is simply too low to warrant retention on any reasonable scale of priorities. If one weighs retention of diversity jurisdiction against the changes in the jurisdiction and practices of the courts of appeals and the Supreme Court, admittedly undesirable in themselves but possibly necessary to prevent the ships from sinking, which have been discussed in Part II, can any reasonable mind favor the former?

Do I expect these changes to occur? I am not so naive as to suppose that much of it will happen in 1973 or that all of it will happen in my time or perhaps even in yours. While judiciary legislation might not seem highly controversial, that very fact may make it more difficult to secure. As Professor Hurst has said:[1]

It is easier to accept situational pressures toward drift or inertia than to labor to formulate issues and muster support of interested parties to get a bill drawn and pressed to passage.

Since the proponents have not much to gain politically, even a small amount of opposition can create a roadblock. After demonstrating the need for a Court of Tax Appeals, Professor Griswold recognized it might be threatened by "the essential over-conservatism of the bar."[2]

1. HURST, LEGAL ELEMENTS IN UNITED STATES HISTORY 1, 30, *in* 5 PERSPECTIVES IN AMERICAN HISTORY (1971).
2. Senator Root recognized that change is rather regularly opposed by "lawyers who had succeeded and were content with things as they

His recognition of the obstacle proved more accurate than his prophecy that in the particular instance it might be readily overcome. Nearly thirty years later, the goal is still unattained. In the apt phrase coined by one professor at this law school and recently unveiled by another,[3] the bar is all too prone to the position:

Come weil, come woe, my status is quo.

The task will be to convince the Judiciary Committees of the Congress that, while indeed few votes will be gained in an election by a great new Judiciary Act, it is also true that, despite fulminations by interested groups or even by bar associations succumbing too quickly to their influence, few such votes will be lost.

Against the negative factors, there are signs giving hope for constructive change. As I indicated at the outset, the explosive growth of federal judicial business is itself a powerful agent against donothingism. The American Law Institute's Study has been a valuable catalyst. We have one institution, the Administrative Office of the Courts, which regularly produces reliable and illuminating figures of the workloads of the federal courts, and another, the Federal Judicial Center, which is actively concerned with reform. The Judicial Conference of the United States and also, in certain areas, the Administrative Conference can play important roles. Congress has authorized a Commission to study circuit realignment and some other matters relating to the courts of appeals; there are other stirrings in the Judiciary Committees of both houses; and we have a Chief Justice with greater concern for the proper functioning of the federal courts than any since William Howard Taft.

Out of such concern and interest some good must come. If these lectures should contribute to the ferment even in a small degree, they will have served the purpose of one for whom the federal courts have been a lifelong interest and, more recently, a career. I am grateful to the Columbia Law School for giving me this opportunity.

were; who did not want practice and proceedings changed from that with which they were familiar . . . ." Root, *The Layman's Criticism of the Lawyer*, 39 A.B.A. REP. 386, 391 (1914). He had himself given proof of this by his own opposition to the abolition of the Circuit Courts, 46 CONG. REC. 2136 (1911).

3. Professor Gellhorn, quoted by Professor Cary in 23 ADMIN. L. REV. at 395 (1971).